Refactoring for Software Design Smells

Refactoring for Software Design Smells
Managing Technical Debt

Girish Suryanarayana

Ganesh Samarthyam

Tushar Sharma

AMSTERDAM • BOSTON • HEIDELBERG • LONDON
NEW YORK • OXFORD • PARIS • SAN DIEGO
SAN FRANCISCO • SINGAPORE • SYDNEY • TOKYO

Morgan Kaufmann is an imprint of Elsevier

Acquiring Editor: Todd Green
Editorial Project Manager: Lindsay Lawrence
Project Manager: Punithavathy Govindaradjane
Designer: Mark Rogers

Morgan Kaufmann is an imprint of Elsevier
225 Wyman Street, Waltham, MA, 02451, USA

Library of Congress Cataloging-in-Publication Data
Suryanarayana, Girish
  Refactoring for software design smells: managing technical debt/Girish Suryanarayana, Ganesh
Samarthyam, Tushar Sharma.
      pages cm
Includes bibliographical references and index.
ISBN: 978-0-12-801397-7 (paperback)
1. Software refactoring. 2. Software failures. I. Samarthyam, Ganesh. II. Sharma, Tushar. III. Title.

QA76.76.R42S86 2015
005.1′6–dc23

                    2014029955

British Library Cataloguing-in-Publication Data
A catalogue record for this book is available from the British Library.

ISBN: 978-0-12-801397-7

For information on all MK publications
visit our website at www.mkp.com

Working together
to grow libraries in
developing countries

www.elsevier.com • www.bookaid.org

To Amma, Anna, Vibha, and Sai Saadhvi
-Girish

To my little princess Tanmaye
-Ganesh

To Papa, Mummy, Pratibha, and Agastya
-Tushar

Contents

Foreword by Grady Booch

There is a wonderful book by Anique Hommels called *Unbuilding Cities: Obduracy in Urban Sociotechnical Change* that speaks of the technical, social, economic, and political issues of urban renewal. Cities grow, cities evolve, cities have parts that simply die while other parts flourish; each city has to be renewed in order to meet the needs of its populace. From time to time cities are intentionally refactored (many cities in Europe were devastated in World War II and so had to be rebuilt); most times cities are refactored in bits (the Canary Warf renewal in London comes to mind), but sometimes the literal and figurative debt is so great a once great city falls into despair (present day Detroit, for example).

Software-intensive systems are like that. They grow, they evolve, sometimes they wither away, and sometimes they flourish. The concept of technical debt is central to understanding the forces that weigh upon systems, for it often explains where, how, and why a system is stressed. In cities, repairs on infrastructure are often delayed and incremental changes are made rather than bold ones. So it is again in software-intensive systems. Users suffer the consequences of capricious complexity, delayed improvements, and insufficient incremental change; the developers who evolve such systems suffer the slings and arrows of never being able to write quality code because they are always trying to catch up.

What delights me about this present book is its focus on technical debt and refactoring as the actionable means to attend to it.

When you have got a nagging tiny gas leak on a city block, a literal smell will lead you to the underlying cause. Software-intensive systems are like that as well, although the smells one may observe therein are far more subtle and invisible to all the senses save to the clever cognitive ones. As you read on in this book, I think you will find one of the more interesting and complex expositions of software smells you will ever find. Indeed, you have in your hand a veritable field guide of smells, sort of like the very real *Birds of the West Indies*, except about software, not sparrows.

Abstraction, encapsulation, modularization, and hierarchy: these are all elements fundamental to software engineering best practices, and you will see these highlights explained as well. In all, I think you will find this a delightful, engaging, actionable read.

Grady Booch
IBM Fellow and Chief Scientist for
Software Engineering, IBM Research

Foreword by Dr. Stéphane Ducasse

Working with real and large object-oriented applications made me and my coauthors (O. Nierstrasz and S. Demeyer) think about object-oriented reengineering patterns. Our idea was to record good approaches to handle these systems at the design level but also with a bit of process. This is how Object-Oriented Reengineering Patterns (http://scg.unibe.ch/download/oorp/) came to life after 3 years of intensive work. In the same period I reviewed the book "Refactoring: Improving the Design of Existing Code" by Martin Fowler because we were working on language-independent refactorings. To me, books like these are milestones. They create a foundation for our engineering science.

When as JOT associate editor, I saw the authors' article describing the work presented in this book, I became an immediate supporter. I immediately asked if they would write a book and if I could be a reviewer. Why? Because a good book on Smells was still missing. And we daily face code smells. "Refactoring for Software Design Smells" is an excellent book. It is another milestone that professionals will use. It captures the deep knowledge experts have when facing real code. It puts in shape and word the complex knowledge that experts acquire after years of experience. I daily program either Pharo runtime and libraries or the Moose software and data analysis platform, and there is not a single day where I'm not challenged by design. Why? Because design, real design, is not simple. Even with a lot of practice and experience design is challenging. This is why having good abstractions to play with is important. Patterns and smells are really effective ways to capture such experience and reflection about the field.

I like the idea that I have access to excellent books that I can suggest to my students, colleagues, and friends. I like books that fill you up and make you think about your own practices. There are few of such ones and they are like gems. And "Refactoring for Software Design Smells" is one of those.

It is the book I would have loved to write (but I probably would not have been able to) as a complement to the Fowler's refactoring book, and my Object-Oriented Reengineering Patterns book. I'm sure that you will learn a lot from it and that you will enjoy it. I want to thank Girish, Ganesh, and Tushar (the authors of this book) to have spent their time to write it. I know that the process is long and tedious but this is an important part of our culture and knowledge that they capture and offer to you. I also want to thank them for their invitation to write this foreword.

Stéphane Ducasse

(Dr. Stéphane Ducasse is an expert in and fond of object design, language design, and reflective programming. He has contributed to Traits which got introduced in Pharo, Perl-6, PHP 5.4, and Squeak and influenced Fortress and Scala. He is one of the lead developers of Pharo (http://www.pharo.project.org/), an open-source live programming language, IDE and platform. He is an expert in software analysis and reengineering. He is one of the developers of the Moose analysis platform http://www.moosetechnology.org and he recently cocreated http://www.synectique.eu, a company delivering advanced tools adapted to client problems.)

Foreword by Dr. Stephane Ducasse

Preface

As a program is evolved its complexity increases unless work is done to maintain or reduce it.

Lehman's law of Increasing Complexity [1]

WHAT IS THIS BOOK ABOUT?

Change is inevitable and difficult! This is true not only about life but also about software. Software is expected to evolve continuously to meet the ever-increasing demands of its users. At the same time, the intangible nature of software makes it difficult to manage this continuous change. What typically results is poor software quality[1] and a huge technical debt.

This book tells you how to improve software quality and reduce technical debt by discovering and addressing smells in your design. Borrowing a phrase from the health care domain "a good doctor is one who knows the medicines but a great doctor is one who knows the disease," our approach is grounded on the philosophy that "a good designer is one who knows about design solutions but a great designer is one who understands the problems (or smells) in the design, how they are caused, and how they can be addressed by applying proven and sound design principles." The goal of this book is, therefore, to guide you into becoming a better designer—one who can recognize and understand the "disease" in his design, and can treat it properly, thereby, improving the quality of the software and keeping technical debt under control.

WHAT DOES THIS BOOK COVER?

This book presents a catalog of 25 structural design smells and their corresponding refactoring towards managing technical debt. We believe that applying software design principles is the key to developing high-quality software. We have, therefore, organized our smell catalog around four basic design principles. Smells are named after the specific principle they violate. The description of each smell reveals the design principle that the smell violates, discusses some factors that can cause that smell to occur, and lists the key quality attributes that are impacted by the smell. This allows the reader to get an idea of the technical debt incurred by the design.

---

[1] Capers Jones [3] finds that poor software quality costs more than US $150 billion per year in the United States and greater than US $500 billion per year worldwide.

Each smell description also includes real-world examples as well as anecdotes based on experience with industrial projects. Accompanying each example are potential refactoring solutions that help address the particular instance of the smell. We believe that the impact of a smell can only be judged based on the design context in which it occurs. Therefore, we also explicitly consider situations wherein a smell may be purposely introduced either due to constraints (such as language or platform limitations) or to realize an overarching purpose in the design.

Smells can be found at different levels of granularity, including architecture and code. Similarly, smells can be either structural or behavioral in nature. Rather than surveying a wide range of smells pertaining to different levels of granularity and nature, we focus only on "structural" and "design-level" smells in this book. Further, the book discusses only those smells that are commonly found in real-world projects and have been documented in literature.

WHO SHOULD READ THIS BOOK?

Software Architects and Designers—If you are a practicing software architect or a designer, you will get the most out of this book. This book will benefit you in multiple ways. As an architect and designer, your primary responsibility is the software design and its quality, and you (more than anyone else) are striving to realize quality requirements in your software. The knowledge of design smells and the suggested refactorings covered in this book will certainly help you in this regard; *they offer you immediately usable ideas for improving the quality of your design.* Since this book explicitly describes the impact of smells on key quality attributes, you will gain a deeper appreciation of how even the smallest design decision has the potential to significantly impact the quality of your software. Through the real-world anecdotes and case studies, you will become aware of what factors you should be careful about and plan for in order to avoid smells.

Software Developers—We have observed in practice that often developers take shortcuts that seemingly get the work done but compromise on the design quality. We have also observed that sometimes when the design does not explicitly address certain aspects, it is the developer who ends up making key design decisions while coding. In such a case, if design principles are incorrectly applied or not applied at all, smells will arise. We believe that reading this book will help developers realize how their seemingly insignificant design decisions or shortcuts can have an immense impact on software quality. This realization will help them transform themselves into better developers who can detect and address problems in the design and code.

Project Managers—Project managers constantly worry about the possible schedule slippages and cost overruns of their projects. There is an increased awareness today that often the primary reason for this is technical debt, and many project managers are, therefore, always on the look out for solutions to reduce technical debt. Such project managers will benefit from reading this book; they will gain a better understanding of the kinds of problems that manifest in the design and have an increased appreciation for refactoring.

Students—This book is very relevant to courses in computer science or software engineering that discuss software design. A central focus of any software design course is the fundamental principles that guide the modeling and design of high-quality software. One effective way to learn about these principles is to first study the effects (i.e., smells) of wrong application or misapplication of design principles and then learn about how to apply them properly (i.e., refactoring). We, therefore, believe that reading this book will help students appreciate the value of following good design principles and practices and prepare them to realize high-quality design in real-world projects post completion of their studies.

WHAT ARE THE PREREQUISITES FOR READING THIS BOOK?

We expect you to have basic knowledge of object-oriented programming and design and be familiar with at least one object-oriented language (such as C++, Java, or C#). We also expect you to have knowledge of object-oriented concepts such as class, abstract class, and interface (which can all be embraced under the umbrella terms "abstraction" or "type"), inheritance, delegation, composition, and polymorphism.

HOW TO READ THIS BOOK?

This book is logically structured into the following three parts:

- **Chapters 1 and 2** set the context for this book. Chapter 1 introduces the concept of technical debt, the factors that contribute to it, and its impact on software projects. Chapter 2 introduces design smells and describes the principle-based classification scheme that we have used to categorize and name design smells in this book.
- **Chapters 3–6** present the catalog of 25 design smells. The catalog is divided into four chapters that correspond to the four fundamental principles (abstraction, encapsulation, modularization, and hierarchy) that are violated by the smells. For each design smell, we provide illustrative examples, describe the impact of the smells on key quality attributes, and discuss the possible refactoring for that smell in the context of the given examples.
- **Chapters 7 and 8** present a reflection of our work and give you an idea about how to repay technical debt in your projects. Chapter 7 revisits the catalog to pick up examples and highlight the interplay between smells and the rest of the design in which the smells occur. Chapter 8 offers practical guidance and tips on how to approach refactoring of smells to manage technical debt in real-world projects.

The appendices contain a listing of design principles referenced in this book, a list of tools that can help detect and address design smells, a brief summary of the UML-like notations that we have used in this book, and a suggested reading list to help augment your knowledge of software design.

Given the fact that Java is the most widely used object-oriented language in the world today, we have provided coding examples in Java. However, the key take-away is in the context of design principles, and is therefore applicable to other object-oriented languages such as C++ and C# as well. Further, we have used simple UML-like class diagrams in this book which are explained in Appendix C.

Many of the examples discussed in this book are from JDK version 7.0. We have interpreted the smells in JDK based on the limited information we could glean by analyzing the source code and the comments. It is therefore possible that there may be perfectly acceptable reasons for the presence of these smells in JDK.

We have shared numerous anecdotes and case studies throughout this book, which have been collected from the following different sources:

- Experiences reported by participants of the online *Smells Forum*, which we established to collect smell stories from the community.
- Incidents and stories that have been shared with us by fellow attendees at conferences, participants during guest lectures and trainings, and via community forums.
- Books, journals, magazines, and other online publications.
- Experiences of one of the authors who works as an independent consultant in the area of design assessment and refactoring.

We want to emphasize that our goal is *not* to point out at any particular software organization and the smells in their design through our anecdotes, case studies, or examples. Rather, our sole goal is to educate software engineers about the potential problems in software design. Therefore, it should be noted that the details in the anecdotes and case studies reported in this book have been modified suitably so that confidential details such as the name of the organization, project, or product are not revealed.

This is a kind of book where you do not have to read from first page to last page—take a look at the table of contents and jump to the chapters that interest you.

WHERE CAN I FIND MORE INFORMATION?

You can get more details about the book on the Elsevier Store at http://www.store.elsevier.com./product.jsp?isbn=9780128013977. You can find more information, supplementary material, and resources at http://www.designsmells.com. For any suggestions and feedback, please contact us at designsmells@gmail.com.

WHY DID WE WRITE THIS BOOK?

Software design is an inherently complex activity and requires software engineers to have a thorough knowledge of design principles backed with years of experience and loads of skill. It requires careful thought and analysis and a deep understanding of the requirements. However, today, software engineers are expected to build really complex software within a short time frame in an environment where requirements are continuously changing. Needless to say, it is a huge challenge to maintain the quality of the design and overall software in such a context.

We, therefore, set out on a task to help software engineers improve the quality of their design and software. Our initial efforts were geared toward creating a method for assessing the design quality of industrial software (published as a paper [4]). We surveyed a number of software engineers and tried to understand the challenges they faced during design in their projects. We realized that while many of them possessed a decent theoretical overview of the key design principles, they lacked the knowledge of how to apply those principles in practice. This led to smells in their design.

Our survey also revealed a key insight—design smells could be leveraged to understand the mistakes that software engineers make while applying design principles. So, we embarked on a long journey to study and understand different kinds of smells that manifest in a piece of design. During this journey, we came across smells scattered across numerous sources including books, papers, theses, and tools and started documenting them. At the end of our journey, we had a huge collection of 530 smells!

We had hoped that our study would help us understand design smells better. It did, but now we were faced with the humongous task of making sense of this huge collection of smells. We, therefore, decided to focus only on structural design smells. We also decided to limit our focus to smells that are commonly found in real-world projects. Next, we set out on a mission to meaningfully classify this reduced collection of smells. We experimented with several classification schemes but were dissatisfied with all of them. In the midst of this struggle, it became clear to us that if we wanted to organize this collection so that we could share it in a beneficial manner with fellow architects, designers, and developers, our classification scheme should be linked to something fundamental, i.e., design principles. From this emerged the following insight:

> *When we view every smell as a violation of one or more underlying design principle(s), we get a deeper understanding of that smell; but perhaps more importantly, it also naturally directs us toward a potential refactoring approach for that smell.*

We built upon this illuminating insight and adopted Booch's fundamental design principles (abstraction, encapsulation, modularization, and hierarchy) as the basis for our classification framework. We categorized and aggregated the smells based on which of the four design principles they primarily violated, and created an initial catalog of 27 design smells. We published this initial work as a paper [5] and were encouraged when some of the reviewers of our paper suggested that it would be a good idea to expand this work into a book. We also started delivering corporate training on the topic of design smells and observed that software practitioners found our smell catalog really useful. Buoyed by the positive feedback from both the reviewers of the paper and software practitioners, we decided to develop our initial work into this book.

Our objective, through this book, is to provide a framework for understanding how smells occur as a violation of design principles and how they can be refactored to manage technical debt. In our experience, the key to transforming into a better designer is to *use smells as the basis to understand how to apply design principles effectively in practice*. We hope that this core message reaches you through this book.

We have thoroughly enjoyed researching design smells and writing this book and hope you enjoy reading it!

Acknowledgments

There are a number of people who have been instrumental in making this book see the light of day. We take this opportunity to sincerely acknowledge their help and support.

First, we want to thank those who inspired us to write this book. These include pioneers in the area of software design and refactoring, including Grady Booch, David Parnas, Martin Fowler, Bob Martin, Stéphane Ducasse, Erich Gamma, Ward Cunningham, and Kent Beck. Reading their books, articles, and blogs helped us better understand the concepts of software design.

Next, we want to thank all those who helped us write this book. In this context, we want to deeply appreciate the people who shared their experiences and war stories that made their way into the book. These include the attendees of our training sessions, participants of the online Smells Forum that we had set up, and the numerous people that we talked to at various conferences and events.

We would also like to thank the technical reviewers of this book: Grady Booch, Stéphane Ducasse, and Michael Feathers. Their critical analyses and careful reviews played a key role in improving the quality of this book. We are also thankful to Venkat Subramaniam for providing valuable review comments and suggestions. In addition, we would like to thank our friends Vishal Biyani, Nandini Rajagopalan, and Sricharan Pamudurthi for sparing their time and providing thoughtful feedback.

We are deeply indebted to Grady Booch and Stéphane Duccase for believing in our work and writing the forewords for our book.

This book would not have been possible without the overwhelming help and support we received from the whole team at Morgan Kaufmann/Elsevier. A special thanks to Todd Green who believed in our idea and provided excellent support from the time of inception of the project to its realization as a book that you hold in your hands. We also would like to convey our sincere thanks to Lindsay Lawrence for supporting us throughout the book publishing process. Further, we thank Punithavathy Govindaradjane and her team for their help during the production process Finally, our thanks to Mark Rogers for his invaluable contribution as the designer.

Finally, we want to express our gratitude toward those who supported us during the writing process. Our special thanks to K Ravikanth and PVR Murthy for their insightful discussions which helped improve the book. Girish and Tushar would like to thank Leny Thangiah, Rohit Karanth, Mukul Saxena, and Ramesh Vishwanathan (from Siemens Research and Technology Center, India) and Raghu Nambiar and Gerd Hoefner (from Siemens Technologies and Services Pvt. Ltd., India) for their constant support and encouragement. Ganesh would like to thank Ajith Narayan and Hari Krishnan (from ZineMind Technologies Pvt. Ltd., India) for their support.

We spent countless weekends and holidays working on the book instead of playing with our kids or going out for shopping. We thank our families for their constant love, patience, and support despite the myriad long conferencing sessions that we had during the course of this book project.

Technical Debt

The first and most fundamental question to ask before commencing on this journey of refactoring for design smells is: What are design smells and why is it important to refactor the design to remove the smells?

Fred Brooks, in his book *The Mythical Man Month*, [6] describes how the inherent properties of software (i.e., complexity, conformity, changeability, and invisibility) make its design an "essential" difficulty. Good design practices are fundamental requisites to address this difficulty. One such practice is that a software designer should be aware of and address *design smells* that can manifest as a result of design decisions. This is the topic we cover in this book.

So, what are design smells?

Design smells are certain structures in the design that indicate violation of fundamental design principles and negatively impact design quality.

In other words, a design smell indicates a potential problem in the design structure. The medical domain provides a good analogy for our work on smells. The symptoms of a patient can be likened to a "smell," and the underlying disease can be likened to the concrete "design problem."

This analogy can be extended to the process of diagnosis as well. For instance, a physician analyzes the symptoms, determines the disease at the root of the symptoms, and then suggests a treatment. Similarly, a designer has to analyze the smells found in a design, determine the problem(s) underlying the smells, and then identify the required refactoring to address the problem(s).

Having introduced design smells, let us ask why it is important to refactor[1] the design to remove the smells.

The answer to this question lies in *technical debt*—a term that has been receiving considerable attention from the software development community for the past few years. It is important to acquire an overview of technical debt so that software developers can understand the far-reaching implications of the design decisions that they make on a daily basis in their projects. Therefore, we devote the discussion in the rest of this chapter to technical debt.

---

[1] In this book, we use the term *refactoring* to mean "behavior preserving program transformations" [13].

1.1 WHAT IS TECHNICAL DEBT?

Technical debt is the debt that accrues when you knowingly or unknowingly make wrong or non-optimal design decisions.

Technical debt is a metaphor coined by Ward Cunningham in a 1992 report [44]. Technical debt is analogous to financial debt. When a person takes a loan (or uses his credit card), he incurs debt. If he regularly pays the installments (or the credit card bill) then the created debt is repaid and does not create further problems. However, if the person does not pay his installment (or bill), a penalty in the form of interest is applicable and it mounts every time he misses the payment. In case the person is not able to pay the installments (or bill) for a long time, the accrued interest can make the total debt so ominously large that the person may have to declare bankruptcy.

Along the same lines, when a software developer opts for a quick fix rather than a proper well-designed solution, he introduces technical debt. It is okay if the developer pays back the debt on time. However, if the developer chooses not to pay or forgets about the debt created, the accrued interest on the technical debt piles up, just like financial debt, increasing the overall technical debt. The debt keeps increasing over time with each change to the software; thus, the later the developer pays off the debt, the more expensive it is to pay off. If the debt is not paid at all, then eventually the pile-up becomes so huge that it becomes immensely difficult to change the software. In extreme cases, the accumulated technical debt is so huge that it cannot be paid off anymore and the product has to be abandoned. Such a situation is called *technical bankruptcy*.

1.2 WHAT CONSTITUTES TECHNICAL DEBT?

There are multiple sources of technical debt (Figure 1.1). Some of the well-known dimensions of technical debt include (with examples):

- **Code debt:** Static analysis tool violations and inconsistent coding style.

- **Design debt:** Design smells and violations of design rules.

- **Test debt:** Lack of tests, inadequate test coverage, and improper test design.

- **Documentation debt:** No documentation for important concerns, poor documentation, and outdated documentation.

In this book, we are primarily concerned with the design aspects of technical debt, i.e., design debt. In other words, when we refer to technical debt in this book, we imply design debt.

To better understand design debt, let us take the case of a medium-sized organization that develops software products. To be able to compete with other organizations

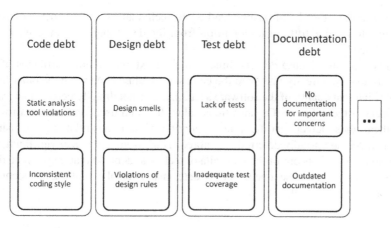

FIGURE 1.1

Dimensions of technical debt.

in the market, this organization obviously wants to get newer products on the market faster and at reduced costs. But how does this impact its software development process? As one can imagine, its software developers are expected to implement features faster. In such a case, the developers may not have the opportunity or time to properly assess the impact of their design decisions. As a result, over time, such a collection of individual localized design decisions starts to degrade the structural quality of the software products, thereby contributing to the accumulation of design debt.

If such a product were to be developed just once and then no longer maintained, the structural quality would not matter. However, most products are in the market for a long time period and therefore have an extended development and maintenance life cycle. In such a case, the poor structural quality of the software will significantly increase the effort and time required to understand and maintain the software. This will eventually hurt the organization's interests. Thus, it is extremely important for organizations to monitor and address the structural quality of the software. The work that needs to be invested in the future to address the current structural quality issues in the software is design debt.

An interesting question in the context of what constitutes technical debt is whether defects/bugs are a part of this debt. Some argue that defects (at least some of them) originate due to technical debt, thus are part of technical debt. There are others who support this viewpoint and argue that if managers decide to release a software version despite it having many known yet-to-be-fixed defects, these defects are a part of technical debt that has been incurred.

However, there are others in the community who argue that defects do not constitute technical debt. They argue that the main difference between defects and technical debt is that defects are visible to the users while technical debt is largely invisible. We support this stance. In our experience, defects are rarely ignored by the organization and receive much attention from the development teams. On the other hand, issues leading to technical debt are mostly invisible and tend to receive little or no attention from the development teams. Why does this happen?

This happens because defects directly impact external quality attributes of the software that are directly visible to the end users. Technical debt, on the other hand, impacts internal quality of the software system, and is not directly perceivable by the end users of the software. Organizations value their end users and cannot afford to lose them; thus, defects get the utmost attention while issues related to "invisible" technical debt are usually deferred or ignored. Thus, from a practical viewpoint, it is better to leave defects out of the umbrella of technical debt, so that they can be dealt with separately; otherwise, one would fix defects and mistakenly think that technical debt has been addressed.

1.3 WHAT IS THE IMPACT OF TECHNICAL DEBT?

Why is it important for a software practitioner to be aware of technical debt and keep it under control? To understand this, let us first understand the components of technical debt. Technical debt is a result of the principal (the original hack or shortcut), and the accumulated interest incurred when the principal is not fixed. The interest component is compounding in nature; the more you ignore it or postpone it, the bigger the debt becomes over time. Thus, it is the interest component that makes technical debt a significant problem.

Why is the interest compounding in nature for technical debt? One major reason is that often new changes introduced in the software become interwoven with the debt-ridden design structure, further increasing the debt. Further, when the original debt remains unpaid, it encourages or even forces developers to use "hacks" while making changes, which further compounds the debt.

Jim Highsmith [45] describes how Cost of Change (CoC) varies with technical debt. A well-maintained software system's actual CoC is near to the optimal CoC; however, with the increase in technical debt, the actual CoC also increases. As previously mentioned, in extreme cases, the CoC can become prohibitively high leading to "technical bankruptcy."

Apart from technical challenges, technical debt also impacts the morale and motivation of the development team. As technical debt mounts, it becomes difficult to introduce changes and the team involved with development starts to feel frustrated and annoyed. Their frustration is further compounded because the alternative—i.e., repaying the whole technical debt—is not a trivial task that can be accomplished overnight.

It is purported that technical debt is the reason behind software faults in a number of applications across domains, including financing. In fact, a BBC report clearly mentions technical debt as the main reason behind the computer-controlled trading error at U.S. market-maker Knight Capital that decimated its balance sheet [46].

CASE STUDY

To understand the impact that technical debt has on an organization, we present the case of a medium-sized organization and its flagship product. This product has been on the market for about 12 years and has a niche set of loyal customers who have been using the same product for a number of years.

Due to market pressures, the organization that owns the product decides to develop an upgraded version of the product. To be on par with its competitors, the organization wants to launch this product at the earliest. The organization marks this project as extremely important to the organization's growth, and a team of experienced software architects from outside the organization are called in to help in the design of the upgraded software.

As the team of architects starts to study the existing architecture and design to understand the product, they realize pretty soon that there are major problems plaguing the software. First and foremost, there is a huge technical debt that the software has incurred during its long maintenance phase. Specifically, the software has a monolithic design. Although the software consists of two logical components—client and server—there is just a single code base that is being modified (using appropriate parameters) to either work as a client or as a server. This lack of separation of client and server concerns makes it extremely difficult for the architects to understand the working of the software. When understanding is so difficult, it is not hard to imagine the uncertainty and risk involved in trying to change this software.

The architects realize that the technical debt needs to be repaid before extending the software to support new features. So they execute a number of code analyzers, generate relevant metrics, formulate a plan to refactor the existing software based on those metrics, and present this to the management. However, there is resistance against the idea of refactoring. The managers are very concerned about the impact of change. They are worried that the refactoring will not only break the existing code but also introduce delays in the eventual release of the software. They refer the matter to the development team. The development team seems to be aware of the difficulty in extending the existing code base. However, surprisingly, they seem to accept the quality problems as something natural to a long-lived project. When the architects probe this issue further, they realize that the development team is in fact unaware of the concept of technical debt and the impact that it can have on the software. In fact, some developers are even questioning what refactoring will bring to the project. If the developers had been aware of technical debt and its impact, they could have taken measures to monitor and address the technical debt at regular intervals.

The managers have another concern with the suggestion for refactoring. It turns out that more than 60% of the original developers have left the project, and new people are being hired to replace them. Hence, the managers are understandably extremely reluctant to let the new hires touch the 12-year old code base. Since the existing code base has been successfully running for the last decade, the managers are fearful of allowing the existing code to be restructured.

So, the architects begin to communicate to the development team the adverse impacts of technical debt. Soon, many team members become aware of the cause behind the problems plaguing the software and become convinced that there is a vital need for refactoring before the software can be extended. Slowly, the team starts dividing into pro-refactoring and anti-refactoring groups. The anti-refactoring group is not against refactoring per se, but does not want the focus of the current release to be on refactoring. The pro-refactoring group argues that further development would be difficult and error-prone unless some amount of refactoring and restructuring is first carried out.

Eventually, it is decided to stagger the refactoring effort across releases. So, for the current release, it is decided to refactor only one critical portion of the system. Developers are also encouraged to restructure bits of code that they touch during new feature development. On paper, it seems like a good strategy and appears likely to succeed.

However, the extent of the incurred technical debt has been highly underestimated. The design is very tightly coupled. Interfaces for components have not been defined. Multiple responsibilities

Continued

> **CASE STUDY—cont'd**
>
> have been assigned to components and concerns have not been separated out. At many places, the code lacks encapsulation. As one can easily imagine, each and every refactoring is difficult, error-prone, and frustrating. In short, it seems like a nightmare. The team starts to feel that it would be better to rewrite the entire software from scratch.
>
> In the end, in spite of the well laid-out strategy, there is considerable delay in the release of the product. In fact, to reduce further delays in the release, the number of new features in the release is significantly reduced. So, when the product is eventually released in the market, it is 6 months later than originally planned and with a very small set of new features! Although the product customers are not happy, they are promised a newer version with an extended set of features in a few months' time. This is possible because the refactoring performed in the current release positions the design for easier extension in the future. In other words, since part of the debt has been paid (which otherwise could have led the project into technical bankruptcy), it has paved the way for further extension of the product!

1.4 WHAT CAUSES TECHNICAL DEBT?

The previous section discussed the impact of technical debt in a software system. To pay off the technical debt or to prevent a software system from accruing technical debt, it is important to first think about why technical debt happens in the first place.

Ultimately, the decisions made by a manager, architect, or developer introduce technical debt in a software system. For instance, when a manager creates or modifies a project plan, he can decide whether to squeeze in more features in a given time span or to allocate time for tasks such as design reviews and refactoring that can ensure high design quality. Similarly, an architect and a developer have to make numerous technical decisions when designing or implementing the system. These design or code-level decisions may introduce technical debt.

Now, the question is: Why do managers or architects or developers make such decisions that introduce technical debt in the software system? In addition to lack of awareness of technical debt, the software engineering community has identified several common causes that lead to technical debt, such as:

- **Schedule pressure**: Often, while working under deadline pressures to get-the-work-done as soon as possible, programmers resort to hasty changes. For example, they embrace "copy-paste programming" which helps get the work done. They think that as long as there is nothing wrong syntactically and the solution implements the desired functionality, it is an acceptable approach. However, when such code duplication accumulates, the design becomes incomprehensible and brittle. Thus, a tight schedule for release of a product with new features can result in a product that has all the desired features but has incurred huge technical debt.

- **Lack of good/skilled designers**: Fred Brooks, in his classic book *The Mythical Man Month* [6], stressed the importance of good designers for a successful project. If designers lack understanding of the fundamentals of software design and principles, their designs will lack quality. They will also do a poor job while reviewing their team's designs and end up mentoring their teams into following the wrong practices.

- **Lack of application of design principles**: Developers without the awareness or experience of actually applying sound design principles often end up writing code that is difficult to extend or modify.

- **Lack of awareness of design smells and refactoring**: Many developers are unaware of design smells that may creep into the design over time. These design smells are indicative of poor structural quality and contribute to technical debt. Design smells can be addressed by timely refactoring. However, when developers lack awareness of refactoring and do not perform refactoring, the technical debt accumulates over time.

Often, given the different cost and schedule constraints of a project, it may be acceptable to temporarily incur some technical debt. However, it is critical to pay off the debt as early as possible.

1.5 HOW TO MANAGE TECHNICAL DEBT?

It is impossible to avoid technical debt in a software system; however, it is possible to manage it. This section provides a brief overview of high-level steps required to manage technical debt.

Increasing awareness of technical debt: Awareness is the first step toward managing technical debt. This includes awareness of the concept of technical debt, its different forms, the impact of technical debt, and the factors that contribute to technical debt. Awareness of these concepts will help your organization take well-informed decisions to achieve both project goals and quality goals.

Detecting and repaying technical debt: The next step is to determine the extent of technical debt in the software product. Identifying specific instances of debt and their impact helps prepare a systematic plan to recover from the debt. These two practical aspects of managing technical debt are addressed in detail in Chapter 8.

Prevent accumulation of technical debt: Once technical debt is under control, all concerned stakeholders must take steps to ensure that the technical debt does not increase and remains manageable in the future. To achieve this, the stakeholders must collectively track and monitor the debt and periodically repay it to keep it under control.

Design Smells

Do you smell it?

That smell.

A kind of smelly smell.

The smelly smell that smells…smelly
Mr. Krabs[1]

The previous chapter introduced technical debt and its impact on a software organization. We also looked at the various factors that contribute to technical debt. One such factor is inadequate awareness of design smells and refactoring. We have repeatedly observed in software development projects that designers are aware of the fundamental design principles, but sorely lack knowledge about the correct application of those principles. As a result, their design becomes brittle and rigid and the project suffers due to accumulation of technical debt.

Psychologists have observed that mistakes are conducive to learning, and have suggested that the reason lies in the element of surprise upon finding out that we are wrong. There is also a well-known cliché that we learn more from our mistakes than our successes.

This book, therefore, adopts an approach different from the traditional approaches towards software design. Instead of focusing on design principles and applying them to examples, we take examples of design *smells*, and discuss why they occurred and what can be done to address them. In the process, we reveal the design principles that were violated or not applied properly. We believe that such an approach towards design that focuses on smells will help the readers gain a better understanding of software design principles and help them create more effective designs in practice.

Before we delve into the catalog of smells, we first discuss why we need to care about smells and various factors that lead to the occurrence of smells. We then present a simple, yet powerful classification framework that helps categorize smells based on the design principles that the smells violate.

---

[1] "SpongeBob SquarePants", episode "Help Wanted", season one, aired on May 1, 1999.

2.1 WHY CARE ABOUT SMELLS?

One of the key indicators of technical debt is poor software quality. Consider some of the common challenges that developers face while working in software projects that are accumulating technical debt:

- The software appears to be getting insanely complex and hard to comprehend. Why is the "understandability" of software getting worse?

- The software continues to change with requests for defect fixes and enhancements and takes increasingly more time for the same. Why is the software's "changeability" and "extensibility" getting worse?

- Logically, there seem to be many aspects or parts of the software that can be reused. However, why is it becoming increasingly difficult to reuse parts of the software (i.e., why is its "reusability" getting worse)?

- Customers are becoming increasingly unhappy about the software and want a more reliable and stable product. The quality assurance team is finding it more difficult to write tests. Why is the software's "reliability" and "testability" getting worse?

Since software design is known to have a major impact on software quality, and the focus of this book is on software design, we summarize these above qualities[2] in the context of software design in Table 2.1. Note that we use the term *design fragment* in this table to denote a part of the design such as an abstraction (e.g., a class,

Table 2.1 Important Quality Attributes and Their Definitions

Quality Attribute	Definition
Understandability	The ease with which the design fragment can be comprehended.
Changeability	The ease with which a design fragment can be modified (without causing ripple effects) when an existing functionality is changed.
Extensibility	The ease with which a design fragment can be enhanced or extended (without ripple effects) for supporting new functionality.
Reusability	The ease with which a design fragment can be used in a problem context other than the one for which the design fragment was originally developed.
Testability	The ease with which a design fragment supports the detection of defects within it via testing.
Reliability	The extent to which the design fragment supports the correct realization of the functionality and helps guard against the introduction of runtime problems.

---

[2] Please note that there are numerous other important quality attributes (such as performance and security) that are impacted by structural design smells. However, we believe an in-depth discussion of these qualities and their relationship to design smells is an entire book in itself, and hence omitted it from this book.

interface, abstract class) or a collection of abstractions and their relationships (e.g., inheritance hierarchies, dependency graphs).

We need to care about smells because smells negatively impact software quality, and poor software quality in turn indicates technical debt. To give a specific example, consider a class that has multiple responsibilities assigned to it in a clear violation of the Single Responsibility Principle (see Appendix A). Note that this smell is named Multifaceted Abstraction in this book (see Section 3.4). Table 2.2 provides an

Table 2.2 Impact of Multifaceted Abstraction on Key Quality Attributes

Quality Attribute	Impact of Multifaceted Abstraction on the Quality Attribute
Understandability	A class with the Multifaceted Abstraction smell has multiple aspects realized into the abstraction, increasing the cognitive load on the user. When a class has multiple responsibilities, it takes more time and effort to understand each responsibility, how they relate to each other in the abstraction, etc. This adversely affects its understandability.
Changeability & extensibility	When a class has multiple responsibilities, it is difficult to determine which members should be modified to support a change or enhancement. Further, a modification to a member may impact unrelated responsibilities within the same class; this in turn can have a ripple effect across the entire design. For this reason, the amount of time and effort required to change or extend the class while still ensuring that the resulting ripple effect has no adverse impact on the correctness of the software is considerably greater. These factors negatively impact changeability and extensibility.
Reusability	Ideally, a well-formed abstraction that supports a single responsibility has the potential to be reused as a unit in a different context. When an abstraction has multiple responsibilities, the entire abstraction must be used even if only one of the responsibilities needs to be reused. In such a case, the presence of unnecessary responsibilities may become a costly overhead that must be addressed. Thus the abstraction's reusability is compromised. Further, in an abstraction with multiple responsibilities, sometimes the responsibilities may be intertwined. In such a case, even if only a single responsibility needs to be reused, the overall behavior of the abstraction may be unpredictable, again affecting its reusability.
Testability	Often, when a class has multiple responsibilities, these responsibilities may be tightly coupled to each other, making it difficult to test each responsibility separately. This can negatively impact the testability of the class.
Reliability	The effects of modification to a class with intertwined responsibilities may be unpredictable and lead to runtime problems. For instance, consider the case in which each responsibility operates on a separate set of variables. When these variables are put together in a single abstraction, it is easy to mistakenly access the wrong variable, resulting in a runtime problem.

overview of how this smell impacts the design quality in terms of the quality attributes defined in Table 2.1. Note that the specific impact of each smell on key quality attributes is described in Chapters 3 to 6.

The impact of design smells is not limited to just software quality. In some cases, it can even severely impact the reputation of the organization. For instance, the presence of design smells in a framework or a library (i.e., software that exposes an Application Programming Interface(API)) that is going to be used by clients can adversely impact how the organization is perceived by the community. This is because it is hard to fix design smells in the API/framework once the clients start using the API.

2.2 WHAT CAUSES SMELLS?

Since smells have an impact on design quality, it is important to understand smells and how they are introduced into software design. We want to point out that since design smells contribute to technical debt, there is some overlap in the causes of design smells and technical debt. Thus, some of the causes of technical debt that were discussed in the previous chapter are relevant here, for example, lack of good designers and lack of refactoring; to avoid repetition, we did not include them here. Figure 2.1 shows a pictorial summary of the causes of smells discussed in this section.

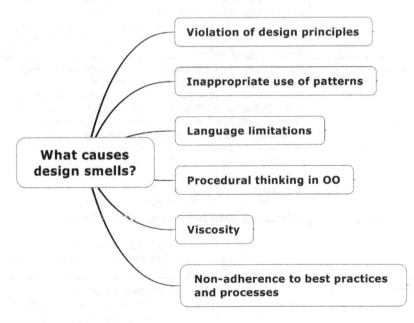

FIGURE 2.1

Common causes of design smells.

2.2.1 VIOLATION OF DESIGN PRINCIPLES

Design principles provide guidance to designers in creating effective and high-quality software solutions. When designers violate design principles in their design, the violations manifest as smells.

Consider the `Calendar` class that is part of the `java.util` package. A class abstracting real-world calendar functionality is expected to support date-related functionality (which it does), but the `java.util.Calendar` class supports time-related functionality as well. An abstraction should be assigned with a unique responsibility. Since `java.util.Calendar` class is overloaded with multiple responsibilities, it indicates the violation of the principle of abstraction (in particular, violation of the Single Responsibility Principle). We name this the Multifaceted Abstraction (see Section 3.4) smell because the class supports multiple responsibilities.

Similarly, consider the class `java.util.Stack` which extends `java.util.Vector`. `Stack` and `Vector` conceptually do not share an IS-A relationship because we cannot substitute a `Stack` object where an instance of `Vector` is expected. Hence this design indicates a violation of the principle of hierarchy (specifically, the violation of the principle of substitutability - see Appendix A). We name this smell Broken Hierarchy (Section 6.8) since substitutability is broken.

2.2.2 INAPPROPRIATE USE OF PATTERNS

Sometimes, architects and designers apply well-known solutions to a problem context without fully understanding the effects of those solutions. Often, these solutions are in the form of design patterns, and architects/designers feel pressured to apply these patterns to their problem context without fully understanding various forces that need to be balanced properly. This creates designs that suffer from symptoms such as too many classes or highly coupled classes with very few responsibilities [81].

Applying design patterns must be a very methodical and thought-out process. A design pattern, as captured by its class and sequence diagram notations, is only a reference solution; thus, there can be hundreds of variants of the design pattern, each with a particular consequence. An architect/designer who does not fully understand the finer aspects and implications of using a particular variation can end up severely impacting the design quality.

There is an interesting interplay between design smells and design patterns. Often, the most suitable way to address a design smell is to use a particular design pattern. However, it is also the case that the (wrong, unnecessary, or mis-)application of a design pattern can often lead to a design smell (also called an *antipattern*)!

2.2.3 LANGUAGE LIMITATIONS

Deficiencies in programming languages can lead to design smells. For example, Java did not support enumerations in its initial versions, hence programmers were forced to use classes or interfaces to hold constants. This resulted in the introduction of Unnecessary Abstraction smell (Section 3.5) in their designs. As another example, consider the classes `AbstractQueuedSynchronizer` and `AbstractQueuedLongSynchronizer` from JDK. Both classes derive directly from `AbstractOwnableSynchronizer` and the methods differ in the primitive types they support (`int` and `long`). This resulted in an Unfactored Hierarchy smell (see Section 6.3). Since the generics feature in Java does not support primitive types, it is not possible to eliminate such code duplication when programming in Java.

2.2.4 PROCEDURAL THINKING IN OO

Often, when programmers with procedural programming background transition to object-oriented paradigm, they mistakenly think of classes as "doing" things instead of "being" things. This mindset manifests in the form of using imperative names for classes, functional decomposition, missing polymorphism with explicit type checks, etc., which result in design smells in an object-oriented context (for example, see Section 3.2).

2.2.5 VISCOSITY

One of the reasons that developers may resort to hacks and thus introduce design smells instead of adopting a systematic process to achieve a particular requirement is *viscosity* [79]. Viscosity is of two types: software viscosity and environment viscosity. Software viscosity refers to the "resistance" (i.e., increased effort and time) that must be encountered when the correct solution is being applied to a problem. If, on the other hand, a hack requires less time and effort (i.e., it offers "low resistance"), it is likely that developers will resort to that hack, giving rise to design smells.

Environment viscosity refers to the "resistance" offered by the software development environment that must be overcome to follow good practices. Often, if the development environment is slow and inefficient and requires more time and effort to follow good practices than bad practices, developers will resort to bad practices. Factors that contribute to the environment viscosity include the development process, reuse process, organizational requirements, and legal constraints.

2.2.6 NONADHERENCE TO BEST PRACTICES AND PROCESSES

Industrial software development is a complex affair that involves building of large scale software by a number of people over several years. One of the ways such complexity can be better managed is through adherence to processes and best practices. Often, when a process or practice is not followed correctly or completely, it can result in design smells. For instance, a best practice for refactoring is that a "composite refactoring" (i.e., a refactoring that consists of multiple steps [13]) should be performed atomically. In other words, either all or no steps in the refactoring should be executed. If this best practice is not adhered to and a composite refactoring is left half-way through, it can lead to a design smell (see anecdote in Section 6.9 for an example).

2.3 HOW TO ADDRESS SMELLS?

Clearly, smells significantly impact the design quality of a piece of software. It is therefore important to find, analyze, and address these design smells. Performing refactoring is the primary means of repaying technical debt. Note that the refactoring suggestions for each specific smell are described as part of the smell descriptions in Chapters 3 to 6. Further, Chapter 8 provides a systematic approach for repaying technical debt via refactoring.

2.4 WHAT SMELLS ARE COVERED IN THIS BOOK?

Smells can be classified as architectural, design (i.e., microarchitectural), or implementation level smells. It is also possible to view smells as structural or behavioral smells. We limit our focus in this book to structural design smells (see Figure 2.2).

	Structural	Behavioral
Architecture		
Design	✓	
Implementation		

FIGURE 2.2

Scope of smells covered in this book.

The discussion on smells in this book is focused on popular object-orientation languages such as Java, C#, and C++. We also limit ourselves to language features supported in all three languages. For example, we do not cover multiple-inheritance in detail and limit as much as possible to single inheritance since multiple class inheritance is not supported in Java and C#.

Note that none of the design smells covered in this book are invented by us. All the design smells covered in this book have been presented or discussed earlier in research papers, books, or documentation of design analysis tools.

2.5 A CLASSIFICATION OF DESIGN SMELLS

When we set out to study structural design smells, we found 283 references to structural design smells in the existing literature. We realized that it is difficult to make sense of these smells unless we have a proper classification framework in place. In general, classification of entities improves human cognition by introducing hierarchical abstraction levels. Classification not only makes us mentally visualize the entities, but also helps us differentiate them and understand them. Therefore, we wanted to create a classification framework for structural design smells.

2.5.1 DESIGN PRINCIPLES BASED CLASSIFICATION OF SMELLS

While we were exploring possible classification schemes for design smells, we realized that it would be very useful to developers if they were aware of the design principle that was violated in the context of a smell. Thus, we sought to classify design smells as a violation of one or more design principles. Another factor that influenced our use of this classification scheme is that if we can easily trace the cause of smells to violated design principles, we can get a better idea of how to address them.

For design principles, we use the *object model* (which is a conceptual framework of object orientation) of Booch et al. [47]. The four "major elements" of his object model are abstraction, encapsulation, modularization,[3] and hierarchy. These are shown in Table 2.3. These principles are described in further detail in the introduction to Chapters 3, 4, 5, and 6.

We treat the four major elements of Booch's object model as "design principles" and refer to them collectively as PHAME (Principles of Hierarchy, Abstraction, Modularization, and Encapsulation). These principles form the foundation of the smell classification scheme used in this book. Thus, each design smell is mapped to that particular design principle that the smell most negatively affects.

Table 2.3 High-level Principles Used in Our Classification

Design Principle	Description
Abstraction	The principle of abstraction advocates the simplification of entities through reduction and generalization: reduction is by elimination of unnecessary details and generalization is by identification and specification of common and important characteristics [48].
Encapsulation	The principle of encapsulation advocates separation of concerns and information hiding [41] through techniques such as hiding implementation details of abstractions and hiding variations.
Modularization	The principle of modularization advocates the creation of cohesive and loosely coupled abstractions through techniques such as localization and decomposition.
Hierarchy	The principle of hierarchy advocates the creation of a hierarchical organization of abstractions using techniques such as classification, generalization, substitutability, and ordering.

2.5.2 NAMING SCHEME FOR SMELLS

We realized that in order to be useful to practitioners, our naming scheme for smells should be carefully designed. Our objectives here were four-fold:

---

[3] For the ease of naming smells, we have used the term *modularization* instead of the original term *modularity* used by Booch et al. [47].

- The naming scheme should be uniform so that a standard way is used to name all the smells

- The naming scheme should be concise so that it is easy for practitioners to recall

- Smells should be named such that it helps the practitioner understand what design principle was mainly violated due to which the smell occurred

- The name of a smell should qualify the violated design principle so that it gives an indication of how the smell primarily manifests

To achieve these objectives, we developed a novel naming scheme for design smells. In this naming scheme, each smell name consists of two words: an adjective (the first word) that qualifies the name of the violated design principle (the second word). Since the name of a smell consists of only two words, it is easy to remember. Further, specifying the violated design principle in the smell name allows a designer to trace back the cause of a smell to that design principle. This helps guide him towards adopting a suitable solution to address that specific smell. Figure 2.3

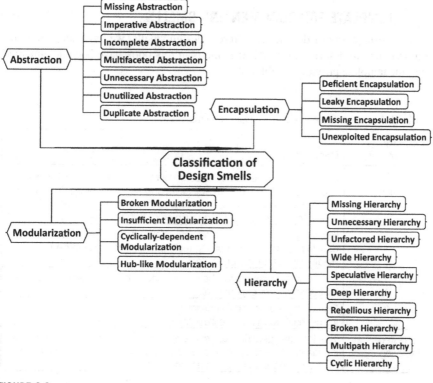

FIGURE 2.3

Classification of design smells.

illustrates our classification scheme (based on PHAME) and the naming scheme for smells covered in this book.

Note that these four design principles are not mutually exclusive. Therefore, the cause of some of the smells can be traced back to the violation of more than one design principle. In such situations, we leverage the enabling techniques for each principle, i.e., depending on the enabling technique it violates, we classify the smell under the corresponding principle. Let us discuss this using an example.

Consider the smell where data and/or methods that ideally should have been localized into a single abstraction are separated and spread across multiple abstractions. We could argue that this smell arises due to wrong assignment of responsibilities across abstractions, therefore this smell should be classified under abstraction. We could also argue that since there is tight coupling between abstractions across which the data and/or methods are spread, this smell should be classified under modularization. To resolve this situation, we look at the enabling technique that this smell violates. In this case, this smell directly violates the enabling technique for modularization, "localize related data and methods," hence we classify this smell under modularization.

2.5.3 TEMPLATE FOR DOCUMENTING SMELLS

For a consistent way of describing different design smells, we have adopted a uniform template to describe them. All the smells in this book have been documented using the template provided in Table 2.4.

Table 2.4 Design Smell Template Used in This Book

Template Element	Description
Name & description	A concise, intuitive name based on our naming scheme (comprises two words: first word is an adjective, and second word is the primarily violated design principle). The name is followed by a concise description of the design smell (along with its possible forms).
Rationale	Reason/justification for the design smell in the context of well-known design principles and enabling techniques. (See Appendix A for a detailed list of design principles)
Potential causes	List of typical reasons for the occurrence of the smell (a nonexhaustive list based on our experience).
Example(s)	One or more examples highlighting the smell. If a smell has multiple forms, each form may be illustrated using a specific example.
Suggested refactoring	This includes generic high-level suggestions and steps to refactor the design smell, and a possible refactoring suggestion for each example discussed in the Examples section.

Table 2.4 Design Smell Template Used in This Book—cont'd

Template Element	Description
Impacted quality attributes	The design quality attributes that are *negatively* impacted because of this smell. The set of design quality attributes that are included for this discussion in the context of smells includes understandability, change-ability, extensibility, reusability, testability, and reliability (see Table 2.1).
Aliases	Alternative names documented in literature that are used to describe the design smell. This includes variants, i.e., design smells documented in literature that are fundamentally identical to, but exhibit a slight variation from, the smell. The variation may include a special form, or a more general form of the design smell.
Practical considerations	Sometimes, in a real-world context, a particular design decision that introduces a smell may be purposely made either due to constraints (such as language or platform limitations) or to address a larger problem in the overall design. This section provides a non-exhaustive list of such considerations.

Chapters 3 to 6, respectively, cover smells that violate the principles of abstraction, encapsulation, modularization, and hierarchy.

Abstraction Smells

The principle of abstraction advocates the simplification of entities through reduction and generalization: reduction is by elimination of unnecessary details and generalization is by identification and specification of common and important characteristics.

Let us start with a trivial question: What is this figure? (Figure 3.1)

FIGURE 3.1

Human smiley face.

Of course it is a human smiley face, but how do we decide on that answer? We arrive at it through abstraction! There are hundreds of millions of human faces and each and every face is unique (there are some exceptions). How are we able to cope with this complexity? We eliminated non-essential details such as hair styles and color. We also arrived at the answer by generalizing commonalities such as every face has two eyes and when we smile our lips curve upwards at the ends.

Abstraction is a powerful principle that provides a means for effective yet simple communication and problem solving. Company logos and traffic signs are examples of abstractions for communication. Mathematical symbols and programming languages are examples of abstraction as a tool for problem solving.

21

Modern software is so complex that it often spans millions of lines of code. To tame the complexity of such systems, we need to apply powerful principles such as abstraction in the most effective way possible. How do we apply the principle of abstraction in software design?

We list below some key enabling techniques that we have gleaned from our experience that allow us to apply the principle of abstraction in software design (Figure 3.2):

- **Provide a crisp conceptual boundary and an identity**. Each abstraction should have a crisp and clear conceptual boundary and an identity. For instance, instead of "passing around" a group of data values representing a date, coordinates of a rectangle, or attributes of an image, they can be created as separate abstractions in the code.

- **Map domain entities**. There should be a mapping of vocabulary from the problem domain to the solution domain, i.e., objects recognized by the problem domain should be also represented in the solution domain. For instance, if there is a clip art that you can insert in a word processor application, it is easier to comprehend the design when it also has a corresponding abstraction named ClipArt.

- **Ensure coherence and completeness**. An abstraction should completely support a responsibility. For instance, consider a class representing a combo box. If the class supports disabling or hiding certain elements, it should provide an option for enabling or showing those elements as well; providing some of the methods and leaving a few would leave an abstraction incoherent and incomplete.

- **Assign single and meaningful responsibility**. Ensure that each abstraction has a unique non-trivial responsibility assigned to it. For instance, a class representing an

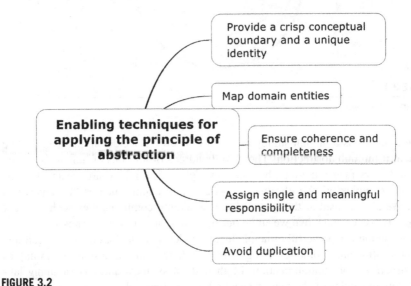

FIGURE 3.2

Enabling techniques for applying abstraction.

image should not be overloaded with methods for converting one kind of image representation format to another format. Furthermore, it does not make sense to create a class named PI that serves as a placeholder for holding the value of the constant π.

- **Avoid duplication**. Ensure that each abstraction—the name as well as its implementation—appears only once in design. For instance, you may require creating a class named List when designing a list control in Graphical User Interfaces, a linked-list data structure, or for maintaining a TO-DO list; however, naming all these abstractions as List will confuse the users of your design. Similarly, implementation duplication (copying the code for priority queue data structure for implementing a scheduler) will introduce additional effort in maintaining two pieces of the same code.

Interestingly, each smell described in this chapter maps to a violation of an enabling technique. Figure 3.3 gives an overview of the smells that violate the

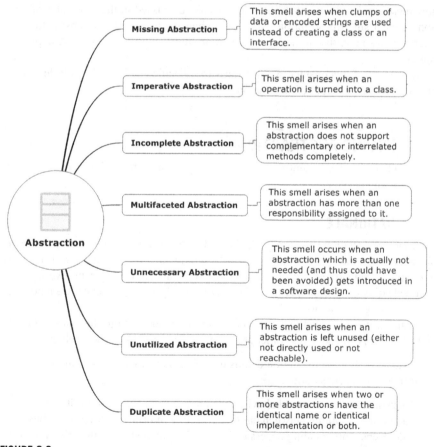

FIGURE 3.3

Smells resulting due to the violation of the principle of abstraction.

Table 3.1 Design Smells and the Abstraction Enabling Techniques They Violate

Design Smell (s)	Violated Enabling Technique
Missing Abstraction (see Section 3.1)	Provide a crisp conceptual boundary and a unique identity
Imperative Abstraction (see Section 3.2)	Map domain entities
Incomplete Abstraction (see Section 3.3)	Ensure coherence and completeness
Multifaceted Abstraction, Unnecessary Abstraction, Unutilized Abstraction (see Sections 3.4, 3.5, 3.6)	Assign single and meaningful responsibility
Duplicate Abstraction (see Section 3.7)	Avoid duplication

principle of abstraction, and Table 3.1 provides an overview of mapping between these smells and the enabling technique(s) they violate. A detailed explanation of how these smells violate enabling techniques is discussed in the Rationale subsection of each smell description. Note that when we use the term "abstraction" to refer to a design entity, it means a class or an interface unless otherwise explicitly stated.

In the rest of this chapter, we'll discuss the specific smells that result due to the violation of the principle of abstraction.

3.1 MISSING ABSTRACTION

This smell arises when clumps of data or encoded strings are used instead of creating a class or an interface.

3.1.1 RATIONALE

An enabling technique for applying the principle of abstraction is to *create entities with crisp conceptual boundaries and a unique identity*. Since the abstraction is not explicitly identified and rather represented as raw data using primitive types or encoded strings, the principle of abstraction is clearly violated; hence, we name this smell Missing Abstraction.

Usually, it is observed that due to the lack of an abstraction, the associated data and behavior is spread across other abstractions. This results in two problems:

- It can expose implementation details to different abstractions, violating the principle of encapsulation.

- When data and associated behavior are spread across abstractions, it can lead to tight coupling between entities, resulting in brittle and non-reusable code. Hence, not creating necessary abstractions also violates the principle of modularization.

3.1.2 POTENTIAL CAUSES

Inadequate design analysis

When careful thought is not applied during design, it is easy to overlook creating abstractions and use primitive type values or strings to "get the work done." In our experience, this often occurs when software is developed under tight deadlines or resource constraints.

Lack of refactoring

As requirements change, software evolves and entities that were earlier represented using strings or primitive types may need to be refactored into classes or interfaces. When the existing clumps of data or encoded strings are retained as they are without refactoring them, it can lead to a Missing Abstraction smell.

Misguided focus on minor performance gains

This smell often results when designers compromise design quality for minor performance gains. For instance, we have observed developers using arrays directly in the code instead of creating appropriate abstractions since they feel that indexing arrays is faster than accessing members in objects. In most contexts, the performance gains due to such "optimizations" are minimal, and do not justify the resultant trade-off in design quality.

3.1.3 EXAMPLES

Example 1

Consider a library information management application. Storing and processing ISBNs (International Standard Book Numbers) is very important in such an application. It is possible to encode/store an ISBN as a primitive type value (long integer/decimal type) or as a string. However, it is a poor choice in this application. Why? To understand that, let's take a quick look at ISBNs.

ISBN can be represented in two forms—10-digit form and 13-digit form—and it is possible to convert between these two forms. The digits in an ISBN have meaning; for example, an ISBN-13 number consists of these elements: *Prefix Element, Registration Group Element, Registrant Element, Publication Element*, and *Checksum*. The last digit of an ISBN number is a checksum digit, which is calculated as follows: starting from the first digit, the values of the odd digits are kept the same, and the values of even numbered digits are multiplied by three; the sum of all the values modulo 10 is the value of the last digit. So, given a 10 or 13 digit number, you can validate whether the given number is a valid ISBN number. ISBN numbers can be converted to barcodes, and a barcode processor can recognize an ISBN number.

Implementation of a library information management application involves logic that accepts, validates, processes, or converts between ISBN numbers. It is possible to encode ISBN numbers as strings or as a primitive type value in such an application. However, in such a case, the logic that processes the numbers will be spread as well as duplicated in many places. In the context of a library information system that has considerable logic involving ISBN numbers, not encapsulating ISBN numbers as class(es) indicates a Missing Abstraction smell.

Example 2

Applications are often characterized by clumps of primitive type data values that are always used together. In many cases, these data clumps indicate a Missing Abstraction. Consider a drawing application that allows a user to select and manipulate a rectangular region of an image. One (naïve) way to represent this rectangular region is to either use two pairs of values—say variables of double type (x1, y1) and (x2, y2)—or variables of double type (x1, y1) and (height, width). These values will always be used together and passed along to multiple methods. Such "data clumps" [7] indicate a Missing Abstraction.

Example 3

Strings are often used to encode information. In the case of APIs (Application Programming Interface), the problem with encoding data in strings is that once the API is released, it is very difficult to change the encoding format since clients that depend on the API will be affected. Let us take a look at a detailed example from Java Development Kit (JDK).

From 1.0 version of Java, the stack trace was printed to the standard error stream as a string with `printStackTrace()` method:

```
public class Throwable {
  public void printStackTrace();
  // other methods elided.
}
```

Client programs that needed programmatic access to the stack trace elements had to write code to process the stack trace to get, for example, the line numbers or find if the bug is a duplicate of another already-filed bug. Due to this dependence of client programs on the format of the string, the designers of JDK were forced to retain the string encoding format in future versions of JDK.

3.1.4 SUGGESTED REFACTORING

The refactoring for this smell is to create abstraction(s) that can internally make use of primitive type values or strings. For example, if a primitive type value is used as a "type-code," then apply "replace type-code with class"; furthermore, create or move operations related to the data such as constructors, validation methods, and copying methods within the new class. For a detailed discussion of refactoring for this smell, see Kerievsky's book [50].

Suggested refactoring for Example 1

The example discussed the need to handle different kinds of ISBN numbers such as ISBN-10 and ISBN-13. A potential refactoring would be to abstract ISBN as an abstract class or interface with common operations in it. `ISBN-10` and `ISBN-13` can be subclasses that extend the `ISBN` supertype (see Figure 3.4).

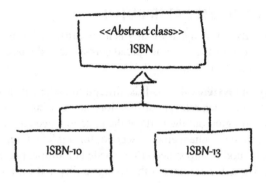

FIGURE 3.4

Suggested refactoring for ISBN example (Example 1).

Suggested refactoring for Example 2

Revisiting the example of the drawing application, a refactoring suggestion would be to abstract the required fields into a new class—say Rectangle class or SelectedRegion class—and move methods operating on these fields to the new class.

Suggested refactoring for Example 3

In the context of the stack trace example, a refactoring suggestion is that instead of first encoding stack trace elements as strings and then exposing them to clients, these stack trace elements should be exposed programmatically. The Java API was improved in version 1.4 to have programmatic access to the stack trace through the introduction of StackTraceElement class. Note that even though a new method is added, the method printStackTrace() and the format of the stack trace has been retained to support the existing clients.

```
public class Throwable {
  public void printStackTrace();
  public StackTraceElement[] getStackTrace(); // Since 1.4
  // other methods elided.
}
```

The StackTraceElement is the "Missing Abstraction" in the original design. It was introduced in Java 1.4 as follows:

```
public final class StackTraceElement {
  public String getFileName();
  public int getLineNumber();
  public String getClassName();
  public String getMethodName();
  public boolean isNativeMethod();
}
```

3.1.5 IMPACTED QUALITY ATTRIBUTES

- **Understandability**—When a key entity is not represented as an abstraction and the logic that processes the entity is spread across the code base, it becomes difficult to understand the design.

- **Changeability** and **Extensibility**—It is difficult to make enhancements or changes to the code when relevant abstractions are missing in design. First, it is difficult even to figure out the parts of the code that need to be modified to implement a change or enhancement. Second, for implementing a single change or enhancement, modifications need to be made at multiple places spread over the code base. These factors impact the changeability and extensibility of the design.

- **Reusability** and **Testability**—Since some abstractions that correspond to domain or conceptual entities are missing, and the logic corresponding to the entities is spread in the code base, both reusability and testability of the design are impacted.

- **Reliability**—An abstraction helps provide the infrastructure to ensure the correctness and integrity of its data and behavior. In the absence of an abstraction, the data and behavior is spread across the code base; hence, integrity of the data can be easily compromised. This impacts reliability.

3.1.6 ALIASES

This smell is also known in literature as:

- "Primitive obsession" [7]—This smell occurs when primitive types are used for encoding dates, currency, etc. instead of creating classes.

- "Data clumps" [7]—This smell occurs when there are clumps of data items that occur together in lots of places instead of creating a class.

3.1.7 PRACTICAL CONSIDERATIONS

Avoiding over-engineering
Sometimes, entities are merely data elements and don't have any behavior associated with them. In such cases, it may be over-engineering to represent them as classes or interfaces. Hence, a designer must carefully examine the application context before deciding to create an explicit abstraction. For example, check if the following are needed (a non-exhaustive list) to determine if creating an abstraction is warranted:

- default initialization of data values using constructors

- validation of the data values

- support for pretty printing the data values

- acquired resources (if any) are to be released

3.2 **IMPERATIVE ABSTRACTION**

This smell arises when an operation is turned into a class. This smell manifests as a class that has only one method defined within the class. At times, the class name itself may be identical to the one method defined within it. For instance, if you see class with name Read that contains only one method named read() with no data members, then the Read class has Imperative Abstraction smell. Often, it is also seen in the case of this smell that the data on which the method operates is located within a different class.

It should be noted that it is sometimes desirable to turn an operation into a class. Section 3.2.7 covers this aspect in greater detail.

3.2.1 **RATIONALE**

The founding principle of object-orientation is to capture real world objects and represent them as abstractions. By following the enabling technique *map domain entities*, objects recognized in the problem domain need to be represented in the solution domain, too. Furthermore, each class representing an abstraction should encapsulate data and the associated methods. Defining functions or procedures explicitly as classes (when the data is located somewhere else) is a glorified form of structured programming rather than object-oriented programming. One-operation classes cannot be representative of an "abstraction," especially when the associated data is placed somewhere else. Clearly, this is a violation of the principle of abstraction. Since these classes are 'doing' things instead of 'being' things, this smell is named Imperative Abstraction.

If operations are turned into classes, the design will suffer from an explosion of one-method classes and increase the complexity of the design. Furthermore, many of these methods that act on the same data would be separated into different classes and thus reduce the cohesiveness of the design. For these reasons, this smell also violates the principles of encapsulation and modularization.

3.2.2 **POTENTIAL CAUSES**

Procedural thinking

A common cause for this smell is procedural thinking in an object-oriented setup. One of the authors was once involved in a project where a programmer from C background had designed a system in Java. In the resultant design, data that would have been encapsulated within "structs" in C was mapped to Java classes containing only public data members. The operations on the data were encapsulated in *separate* Java classes! The procedural thinking of his C experience resulted in the design of a procedural program that was, however, implemented in an object-oriented language.

3.2.3 EXAMPLES

Example 1

Consider the case of a large-sized financial application. This application employs classes named CreateReport, CopyReport, DisplayReport, etc. to deal with its report generation functionality. Each class has exactly one method definition named create, copy, display, etc., respectively, and suffers from Imperative Abstraction smell. The data items relating to a report such as name of the report, data elements that need to be displayed in the report, kind of report, etc. are housed in a "data class" named Report.

The smell not only increases the number of classes (in this case there are at least four classes when ideally one could have been used), but also increases the complexity involved in development and maintenance because of the unnecessary separation of cohesive methods (Figure 3.5).

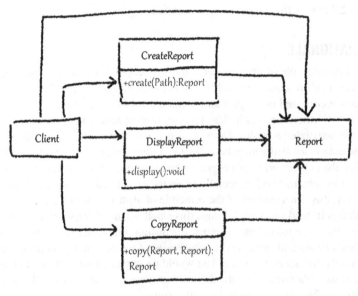

FIGURE 3.5

Class diagram for the report generation functionality (Example 1).

Example 2

Figure 3.6 shows a small fragment of the design of an image processing application. The objective behind the classes shown in the figure is to compare two images and store the differences in the images. The Application class uses the calculateOff-set() method in OffsetCalculator class to calculate the offset between two given images. The calculated offset is returned to the Application, which then invokes the saveOffset() method in SaveHandler class to store it.

A deeper look at the OffsetCalculator and SaveHandler classes shows that they *only* contain one method each, namely calculateOffset() and saveOffset(), respectively. Thus, the `OffsetCalculator` and `SaveHandler` classes suffer from the Imperative Abstraction smell.

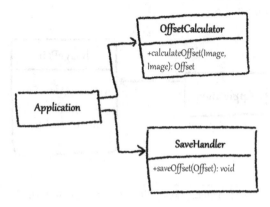

FIGURE 3.6

Class diagrams for the image processing application (Example 2).

3.2.4 SUGGESTED REFACTORING

To refactor the Imperative Abstraction design smell, you have to either find or create an appropriate abstraction to house the method existing within the Imperative Abstraction. You also have to encapsulate the data needed by the method within the same abstraction to improve cohesion and reduce coupling.

Suggested refactoring for Example 1

For the report generation part of the financial application, a suggested refactoring is to move the methods in each of the classes suffering from Imperative Abstraction to the `Report` class itself (see Figure 3.7). Moving all the report-related operations to the `Report` class makes the `Report` class a proper "abstraction" and also removes the Imperative Abstraction smell. The design becomes cleaner and less complex.

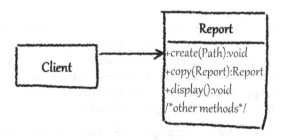

FIGURE 3.7

Suggested refactoring for the report generation functionality (Example 1).

Suggested refactoring for Example 2

For the image processing application, a potential refactoring solution is to use an ImagePair class that encapsulates the offset calculation and offset saving operations. This is shown in Figure 3.8.

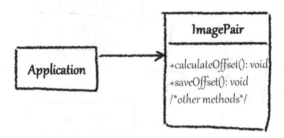

FIGURE 3.8

Suggested refactoring for the image processing application (Example 2).

A question that may arise here is, "Are we not mixing up the responsibilities of calculating the offset and saving it, within a single class? Are we not violating Single Responsibility Principle?" To address this, one way to think about this design is that the actual opening of a file or setting up a connection to a database to save the offset is going to be encapsulated in a different class (not shown here). So the saveOffset() method is going to invoke that other class. In other words, the responsibility of "saving the offset" is not really getting mixed in the ImagePair class.

3.2.5 IMPACTED QUALITY ATTRIBUTES

- **Understandability**—An abstraction with this smell does not have a direct mapping to the problem domain; it only represents a part of the behavior of a domain entity but does not represent the entity itself. Thus understandability of the abstraction is poor. Having numerous single-method classes leads to "class explosion" and complicates the design, and thus impacts the understandability of the overall design.

- **Changeability and Extensibility**—The presence of an Imperative Abstraction smell does not impact the changeability and extensibility of the abstraction itself. However, if a modification or enhancement is required to a domain or conceptual entity (which is realized by multiple abstractions), it will require changes to multiple abstractions throughout the design. Thus, the changeability and extensibility of the overall design are impacted.

- **Reusability**—Consider the report generation functionality that was discussed in Example 1. If we want to reuse this functionality in a different context, we would have to take the CreateReport, CopyReport, and DisplayReport classes along with the class that serves to hold the report data, and adapt them to the new context. Clearly, this would require much more effort than if we were to reuse the Report class (discussed in Suggested refactoring for Example 1).

- **Testability**—If an abstraction with Imperative Abstraction smell is self-sufficient, it is easy to test it. However, typically, in designs that have this smell, multiple abstractions with single operations need to be collectively tested. This impacts testability of the overall design.

ANECDOTE

One of the anecdotes we came across in the Smells Forum concerned a toolkit development project written in Java. Just before the release of the product, experts external to the team performed a systematic design review to evaluate the design quality of the software.

During the review, it was observed that the name of a class was Diff and it had only one method named findDiff()! The findDiff() method would take two versions of a csv (comma separated values) file and report the difference between the files. It was obvious that the class had Imperative Abstraction smell.

A deeper look at the design revealed that most classes had names starting with a verb such as "generate," "report," "process," and "parse." These classes mostly had one public method with other methods serving as private helper methods. There was almost no use of class inheritance (interface inheritance was used, but mainly for implementing standard interfaces such as Comparable and Cloneable). This was a bigger finding—the design followed "functional decomposition" and not "object-oriented decomposition"!

Reflecting on the toolkit design revealed that object-oriented decomposition could have been more beneficial for the project, since such an approach would have helped making adaptations to variations as well as implementing new features easier. Since the toolkit consisted of tools that "do" things, developers unconsciously designed and evolved the software using a "functional decomposition" approach.

The design review results surprised the development team! They had never anticipated that the cause for one of the key structural problems in their project was a "procedural programming" mindset. Even though the team consisted of experienced designers, a major problem like this was overlooked.

However, changing the toolkit to follow an object-oriented decomposition approach would require rearchitecting the whole toolkit. Since there were already a large number of customers using the toolkit, it was a risky endeavor to take-up this reengineering activity. Hence, the management decided to live with the existing design.

Reflecting on this anecdote highlights the following key insights:
- Even when a person is part of and is familiar with a project, it is easy for him to overlook obvious design problems. Our experience shows that systematic and periodic design reviews by experts (external to the project) help identify opportunities for improving the design quality of the software [4].
- The presence of certain smells often indicates a much deeper problem in design. In this case, unraveling the cause behind the Imperative Abstraction smell revealed "functional decomposition" to be the deeper problem.
- It is ironic that the most critical problems are often found just before a release. It is very risky to "fix" the design so late in such cases. So, learning about smells and avoiding them throughout the development cycle is important in maintaining the quality of the design and avoiding technical debt.

3.2.6 ALIASES

This smell is also known in literature as:

- "Operation class" [51,52]—This smell occurs when an operation that should have been a method within a class has been turned into a class itself.

3.2.7 PRACTICAL CONSIDERATIONS

Reification

"Reification" is the promotion or elevation of something that is not an object into an object. When we reify behavior, it is possible to store it, pass it, or transform it. Reification improves flexibility of the system at the cost of introducing some complexity [52].

Many design patterns [54] employ reification. Examples:

- State pattern: Encoding a state-machine.

- Command pattern: Encoding requests as command objects. A permitted exception for this smell is when a Command pattern has been used to objectify method requests.

- Strategy pattern: Parameterizing a procedure in terms of an operation it uses.

In other words, when we consciously design in such a way to elevate non-objects to objects for better reusability, flexibility, and extensibility (i.e., for improving design quality), it is not a smell.

3.3 INCOMPLETE ABSTRACTION

This smell arises when an abstraction does not support complementary or interrelated methods completely. For instance, the public interface of an abstraction may provide an `initialize()` method to allocate resources. However, a `dispose()` method that will allow clean-up of the resources before it is deleted or re-collected[1] may be missing in the abstraction. In such a case, the abstraction suffers from Incomplete Abstraction smell because complementary or interrelated methods are not provided completely in its public interface.

3.3.1 RATIONALE

One of the key enabling techniques for abstraction is to "*create coherent and complete abstractions.*" One of the ways in which coherence and completeness of an abstraction may be affected is when interrelated methods are not supported by the abstraction. For example, if we need to be able to add or remove elements in a data structure, the type abstracting that data structure should support both `add()` and

---

[1] In languages that support garbage collection.

`remove()` methods. Supporting only one of them makes the abstraction incomplete and incoherent in the context of those interrelated methods.

If an abstraction supports such interrelated methods only partially, it may force the users of the abstraction to implement the rest of the functionality. Sometimes, to overcome the problem of such an incomplete interface exposed by an abstraction, clients attempt to access the internal implementation details of the abstraction directly; in this way, encapsulation may be violated as a side-effect of not applying the principle of abstraction properly. Further, since one of the interrelated methods is implemented somewhere else, cohesion is compromised and the *Single Responsibility Principle* (*SRP*) (which per definition requires a responsibility to be *completely* encapsulated by a class) is violated. Since complementary or interrelated methods are not provided completely in the abstraction, this smell is named Incomplete Abstraction.

3.3.2 POTENTIAL CAUSES

Missing overall perspective
When designers or developers create abstractions to add new features, their focus is usually limited to the actual specific requirements that need to be supported. In this process, they overlook if the abstraction supports all the interrelated methods completely or not.

Not adhering to language or library conventions
Consider the container `java.util.HashMap` in JDK. For retrieving an element based on the given input key, the `get()` method first compares the hash code of the input key (using the `hashCode()` method) with the mapped key found in the hash map; next, it invokes `equals()` method on the input key to check if it equals the mapped key. Now, if a class does not override `hashCode()` and `equals()` methods together and the objects of that class are used in `HashMap`, it is possible that the retrieval mechanism will not work correctly. Hence, one of the conventions required by the Java library is that these two methods should be overridden together in a class when the objects of that class are used with hash-based containers.

Such conventions also exist in other languages such as C# and C++. For instance, in C++, it is better to define either all of default constructor, copy constructor, assignment operator, and destructor (virtual destructor if the class would be used polymorphically) or none. If there are any missing definitions (e.g., virtual destructor), the abstraction is incomplete and could result in runtime problems.

Sometimes developers overlook such language or library conventions, and provide only partial set of methods. In such cases, it leads to Incomplete Abstraction smell.

3.3.3 EXAMPLES

Example 1
An interesting instance of "Incomplete Abstraction" is observed in JDK's `javax.swing.ButtonModel` interface. It provides `setGroup()` method, which according to

its documentation, "identifies the group the button belongs to—needed for radio buttons, which are mutually exclusive within their group." The `ButtonModel` interface does not provide the symmetric `getGroup()` method and hence suffers from Incomplete Abstraction smell.

Example 2

The *Abstract Factory* pattern [54] is a creational pattern that allows families of objects to be created. Figure 3.9 shows the solution structure of the pattern. Interestingly, the abstract factory as defined by the pattern does not specifically include the responsibility to delete the objects they have created. While this may not be needed in languages that support garbage collection, we have encountered several cases in real-world projects where an Abstract Factory pattern has been used correctly but object deletion has been overlooked by designers since it is not explicitly addressed in the pattern. Thus, if the factory classes shown in Figure 3.9 were to be used as they are, the resulting design would exhibit Incomplete Abstraction smell.

ANECDOTE

An attendee at one of the design forums shared an interesting anecdote that is relevant here. He was working on the development of a software tool that facilitated the configuration of smart devices. A week before the tool's release, it was observed that the tool was characterized by a number of memory leaks. To quickly identify and address the cause of these runtime memory leaks, an expert on memory leaks was called in as a consultant.

Based on past experience, the consultant could guess that the reason for memory leaks was that there were some objects that were not getting cleaned up properly. So, he started examining how and when objects were getting deleted at runtime. He found out that while there was a systematic procedure to create objects, there was little or no attention paid to how those created objects were eventually deleted. Most developers had seemingly completely ignored the deletion of created objects!

To understand the reason, the consultant decided to dig deeper. He found out that the source of the problem was that the project architect had only listed "creation" methods in the design document that he had handed to the developers. When queried, the project architect said that he expected the software developers to "understand" that a method marked for object creation in his design was actually a placeholder for both "creation and deletion" methods. He stated that it is obvious that objects that are created need to be cleaned up and, therefore, the software developers writing the code should have taken care of object deletion as well.

When the consultant asked the software developers responsible for code construction about this, they said that they are told to "strictly follow the design drafted by the architect" so that there is no architecture erosion or over-engineering on their part. Therefore, they tended to overlook or seldom care about concerns not explicitly captured in the design.

There are two insights that emerge from this anecdote:
- Architects should be extremely careful and diligent about what is communicated in the design document. A stringent review of design is needed to expose issues such as the ones mentioned above.
- A healthy environment needs to exist in the project team that allows developers to give feedback to the architect(s) about the prescribed design. In fact, new age development methodologies such as those based on Agile promote the idea of "collective ownership" of the design and architecture. This means making all the team members responsible for the design and involving all of them in the design decisions that are made so that everyone's understanding is enhanced and a high-quality design emerges.

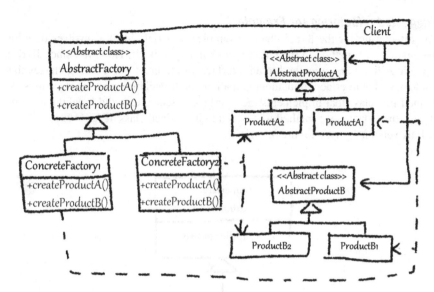

FIGURE 3.9

Class diagram for the Abstract Factory pattern [54].

3.3.4 SUGGESTED REFACTORING

If you find interfaces or classes that are missing "complementary and symmetric" methods, it possibly indicates an Incomplete Abstraction. Table 3.2 lists some of the common pairs of operations. Note that these merely serve as exemplars of common usage and the actual names will vary depending on the context. For example, the names of operations in the context of a Stack would be push and pop, whereas in the context of data streams, it would be source and sink. The refactoring strategy for this smell is to preferably introduce the missing complementary operation(s) in the interface or class itself.

Also, if there are any language or library conventions that require providing inter-related methods together, the refactoring is to add any such missing methods in the abstraction.

Table 3.2 Some Common Symmetric Method Pairs

Min/max	Open/close	Create/destroy	Get/set
Read/write	Print/scan	First/last	Begin/end
Start/stop	Lock/unlock	Show/hide	Up/down
Source/target	Insert/delete	First/last	Push/pull
Enable/disable	Acquire/release	Left/right	On/off

Suggested refactoring for Example 1

The refactoring for the ButtonModel example from JDK ideally involves defining the getGroup() method in the ButtonModel interface itself. However, since JDK is a public API, adding a method to an interface would break the existing classes that implement that interface (remember that all methods declared in an interface must be defined in a class that implements the interface). Hence, to avoid breaking existing clients, the getGroup() method was added in its derived class DefaultButtonModel in JDK version 1.3 (see Figure 3.10).

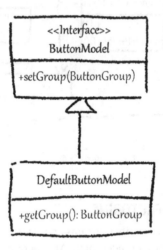

FIGURE 3.10

Refactoring for ButtonModel interface in JDK 1.3 (Example 1).

So, the lesson that we learn from this example is that it is difficult to evolve interfaces, and hence it is important to be aware of and avoid smells such as Incomplete Abstraction when designing APIs.

Suggested refactoring for Example 2

The suggested refactoring for the Abstract Factory example would be to ensure that, when the context requires, the responsibility of object deletion is also explicitly included within the AbstractFactory class [19]. This will allow creation and deletion of objects to be handled within a single class. This decreases the complexity arising from addressing object creation and deletion mechanisms in separate classes, and improves the maintainability of the system.

It should be noted, in the same way, a Factory Disposal Method pattern [19] can be used to help delete created objects in the context of Factory Method pattern [54].

3.3.5 IMPACTED QUALITY ATTRIBUTES

- **Understandability**—Understandability of the abstraction is adversely impacted because it is difficult to comprehend why certain relevant method(s) are missing in the abstraction.

- **Changeability** and **Extensibility**—Changeability and extensibility of the abstraction are not impacted. However, when complementary methods are separated across abstractions, changes or enhancements to one method in an abstraction may impact the other related abstractions.

- **Reusability**—If some of the operations are not supported in an abstraction, it is harder to reuse the abstraction in a new context because the unsupported operations will need to be provided explicitly.

- **Reliability**—An Incomplete Abstraction may not implement the required functionality, resulting in defects. Furthermore, when methods are missing, the clients may have to work around to provide the required functionality, which can be error-prone and lead to runtime problems. For instance, when a method for locking is provided in an abstraction without the related unlock method, the clients will not be able to release the lock. When clients try to implement the unlock functionality in their code, they may try to directly access the internal data structures of the abstraction; such direct access can lead to runtime errors.

3.3.6 ALIASES

This smell is also known in literature as:

- "Class supports incomplete behavior" [18]—This smell occurs when the public interface of a class is incomplete and does not support all the behavior needed by objects of that class.

- "Half-hearted operations" [63]—This smell occurs when interrelated methods provided in an incomplete or in an inconsistent way; this smell could lead to runtime problems.

3.3.7 PRACTICAL CONSIDERATIONS

Disallowing certain behavior

Sometimes, a designer may make a conscious design decision to not provide symmetric or matching methods. For example, in a read-only collection, only `add()` method may be provided without the corresponding `remove()` method. In such a case, the abstraction may appear incomplete, but is not a smell.

Using a single method instead of a method pair

Sometimes, APIs choose to replace symmetrical methods with a method that takes a boolean argument (for instance, to enforce a particular naming convention such as

JavaBeans naming convention that requires accessors to have prefixes "get," "is," or "set"). For example, classes such as `java.awt.MenuItem` and `java.awt.Component` originally supported `disable()` and `enable()` methods. These methods were deprecated and are now replaced with `setEnabled(boolean)` method. Similarly, `java.awt.Component` has the method `setVisible(boolean)` that deprecates the methods `show()` and `hide()`. One would be tempted to mark these classes as Incomplete Abstractions since they lack symmetric methods, i.e., `getEnabled()` and `getVisible()` respectively. However, since there is no need for corresponding getter methods (as these methods take a boolean argument), these classes do not have Incomplete Abstraction smell.

3.4 MULTIFACETED ABSTRACTION

This smell arises when an abstraction has *more than one* responsibility assigned to it.

3.4.1 RATIONALE

An important enabling technique to effectively apply the principle of abstraction is to *assign single and meaningful responsibility* for each abstraction. In particular, the Single Responsibility Principle says that an abstraction should have a single well-defined responsibility and that responsibility should be entirely encapsulated within that abstraction. An abstraction that is suffering from Multifaced Abstraction has more than one responsibility assigned to it, and hence violates the principle of abstraction.

The realization of multiple responsibilities within a single abstraction leads to a low degree of cohesion among the methods of the abstraction. Ideally, these responsibilities should have been separated out into well-defined, distinct, and cohesive abstractions. Thus, the low degree of cohesion within a Multifaceted Abstraction also leads to the violation of the principle of modularization.

Furthermore, when an abstraction includes multiple responsibilities, it implies that the abstraction will be affected and needs to be changed for multiple reasons. Our experience shows that there is often a strong correlation between the frequency of change in elements of a design and the number of defects in that element. This means that a Multifaceted Abstraction may likely suffer from a greater number of defects. A Multifaceted Abstraction lowers the quality of the design and should be refactored to avoid building up the technical debt. Since the abstraction has multiple "faces" or "responsibilities", it is named Multifaceted Abstraction.

3.4.2 POTENTIAL CAUSES

General-purpose abstractions

When designers introduce an abstraction with a generic name (examples: `Node`, `Component`, `Element`, and `Item`), it often becomes a "placeholder" for providing all the functionality *related* (but not necessarily belonging) to that abstraction. Hence, general purpose abstractions often exhibit this smell.

Evolution without periodic refactoring
When a class undergoes extensive changes over a long period of time without refactoring, other responsibilities start getting introduced in these classes and design decay starts. In this way, negligence toward refactoring leads to the creation of monolithic blobs that exhibit multiple responsibilities.

The burden of processes
Sometimes the viscosity of the software and environment (discussed earlier in Section 2.2.5) serves to discourage the adoption of good practices. As discussed in the case of Insufficient Modularization smell (Section 5.2), to circumvent the long process that must be followed when a new class is added to the design, developers may choose to integrate new unrelated features within existing classes leading to Multifaceted Abstraction smell.

Mixing up concerns
When designers don't give sufficient attention to the separation of different concerns (e.g., not separating domain logic from presentation logic), the resulting abstraction will have Multifaceted Abstraction smell.

3.4.3 EXAMPLE
In his book, Neal Ford mentions `java.util.Calendar` class as an example of a class having multiple responsibilities [64]. A class abstracting real-world calendar functionality is expected to support dates, but the `java.util.Calendar` class supports time related functionality as well, and hence this class suffers from Multifaceted Abstraction smell.

Since methods supporting date and time are combined together, the interface of `Calendar` class is large and difficult to comprehend. This difficulty in using this class has prompted the creation of alternatives. One such alternative is Joda,[2] which is a replacement of standard Java date and time API. In fact, due to the difficulties with the existing `Calendar` class and other classes related to date and time processing, a new date and time API has been introduced in JDK version 8.

Note: Classes exhibiting Multifaceted Abstraction are usually large and complex. For example, `java.util.Calendar` class (in JDK 7) spans 2825 lines of code and has 67 methods and 71 fields! However, large or complex implementation is not an essential characteristic of classes having Multifaceted Abstraction smell; see the discussion on Insufficient Modularization smell (Section 5.2).

---

[2] http://www.joda.org/joda-time/.

ANECDOTE

While working as an independent consultant, one of the authors was asked by a start-up company to help them identify refactoring candidates in a project that involved graphical displays in hand-held devices. The author ran many tools including object-oriented metrics, design smells detection, and clone detector tools on the code-base to identify refactoring candidates. One of the classes identified for refactoring was a class named Image. The class had 120 public methods realizing multiple responsibilities in more than 50,000 lines of code. When running a design smell detection tool, the tool showed Image class to have "Schizophrenic class" smell (the tool defined "Schizophrenic class" smell as a class having a large public interface with clients using disjoint group of methods from the class interface).

When the author proposed refactoring of the Image class, the team objected, saying that the Image class followed the SRP and hence there was no need to refactor it. Specifically, they argued that the class had a comprehensive set of methods that related to loading, rendering, manipulating, and storing the image, and all these methods were logically related to images.

In their argument, the project team completely missed the notion of "granularity" of responsibilities. If you take a look at an image processing application, almost everything is related to images: does it mean we should put everything in a single class named Image? Absolutely not. Each abstraction has a concrete, specific, and precise responsibility (instead of a coarse-grain high-level responsibility).

Coming back to the case under discussion, upon further probing, the team lead admitted that the class was one of the most frequently modified classes during defect fixes and feature enhancements. He also added that they changed the Image class for different reasons. The author and the team lead then had several discussions on how this problem could be avoided. Finally, the team lead accepted that there was an urgent need to refactor the Image class. As a result, four modules (or namespaces)—named ImageLoader, ImageRenderer, Image-Processor, and ImageWriter (relating to loading, rendering, manipulating, and persisting functionality, respectively)—were extracted from the original Image class. With this refactoring, the main benefit was that the changes became localized. For example, if any change that related to image rendering was required, only the code in ImageRenderer module would need to be changed.

The main take-away that can be identified from this experience is that "responsibility" (as in Single "Responsibility" Principle) does not mean logical grouping of all functionality related to a concept. Rather "responsibility" refers to a concrete, specific, and precise responsibility that has one reason to change!

3.4.4 SUGGESTED REFACTORING

When a class has multiple responsibilities, it will be non-cohesive. However, it is likely that you will find methods and fields that form logical clusters. These logical clusters are candidates for applying "extract class" refactoring. In particular, new class(es) can be created out of existing classes having Multifaceted Abstraction smell and the relevant methods and fields can be moved to the new class(es).

Note that, depending on the context, the extracted class may either be used directly only by the original class, or may be used by the clients of the original class (Figure 3.11).

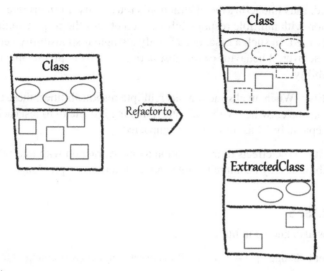

FIGURE 3.11

'Extract class' refactoring for Multifaceted Abstraction.

Suggested refactoring for the Example

For the Calendar class, a possible refactoring is to extract time-related functionality from the Calendar class into a new Time class and move the relevant methods and fields into the newly extracted class. Java 8 has introduced new classes supporting date and time (and other classes such as clocks, duration, etc.) in a package named java.time so that future clients can use this new package instead.

3.4.5 IMPACTED QUALITY ATTRIBUTES

- **Understandability**—A Multifaceted Abstraction increases the cognitive load due to multiple aspects realized into the abstraction. This impacts the understandability of the abstraction.

- **Changeability** and **Extensibility**—When an abstraction has multiple responsibilities, it is often difficult to figure out what all members within the abstraction need to be modified to address a change or an enhancement. Furthermore, a modification to a responsibility may impact unrelated responsibilities provided within the same abstraction, which may lead to ripple effects across the entire design.

- **Reusability**—Ideally, a well-formed abstraction that performs a single responsibility has the potential to be reused as a unit. When an abstraction has multiple responsibilities, the entire abstraction must be used even if only one of the responsibilities needs to be reused. In such a case, the presence of unnecessary responsibilities may become a costly overhead that must be addressed, thus impacting the abstraction's reusability. Furthermore, in an abstraction with multiple responsibilities, sometimes the responsibilities may be intertwined. In such a case, even if only a single responsibility needs to be reused, the overall behavior of the abstraction may be unpredictable affecting its reusability.

- **Testability**—When an abstraction has multiple responsibilities, these responsibilities may be entwined with each other, making it difficult to test each responsibility separately. Thus, testability is impacted.

- **Reliability**—The effects of modification to an abstraction with intertwined responsibilities may be unpredictable and lead to runtime problems.

3.4.6 ALIASES
This smell is also known in literature as:

- "Divergent change" [7]—This smell occurs when a class is changed for different reasons.

- "Conceptualization abuse" [30]—This smell occurs when two or more non-cohesive concepts have been packed into a single class of the system.

- "Large class" [7,24,57,58]—This smell occurs when a class has "too many" responsibilities.

- "Lack of cohesion" [59]—This smell occurs when there is a large type in a design with low cohesion, i.e., a "kitchen sink" type that represents many abstractions.

3.4.7 PRACTICAL CONSIDERATIONS
None.

3.5 UNNECESSARY ABSTRACTION
This smell occurs when an abstraction that is actually not needed (and thus could have been avoided) gets introduced in a software design.

3.5.1 RATIONALE
A key enabling technique to apply the principle of abstraction is to assign single and meaningful responsibility to entities. However, when abstractions are created unnecessarily or for mere convenience, they have trivial or no responsibility assigned to them, and hence violate the principle of abstraction. Since the

abstraction is needlessly introduced in the design, this smell is named Unnecessary Abstraction.

3.5.2 POTENTIAL CAUSES

Procedural thinking in object-oriented languages

According to Johnson et al. [60], programmers from procedural background who are new to object-oriented languages tend to produce classes that "do" things instead of "being" things. Classes in such designs tend to have just one or two methods with data located in separate "data classes." Such classes created from procedural thinking usually do not have unique and meaningful responsibilities assigned to them.

Using inappropriate language features for convenience

Often, programmers introduce abstractions that were not originally intended in design for "getting-the-work-done" or just for "convenience." Using "constant interfaces"[3] instead of enums, for example, is convenient for programmers. By implementing constant interfaces in classes, programmers don't have to explicitly use the type name to access the members and can directly access them in the classes. It results in unnecessary interfaces or classes that just serve as placeholders for constants without any behavior associated with the classes.

Over-engineering

Sometimes, this smell can occur when a design is over-engineered. Consider the example of a customer ID associated with a `Customer` object in a financial application. It may be overkill to create a class named `CustomerID` because the `CustomerID` object would merely serve as holder of data and will not have any non-trivial or meaningful behavior associated with it. A better design choice in this case would be to use a string to store the customer ID within a `Customer` object.

3.5.3 EXAMPLES

Example 1

Consider the `java.util.FormattableFlags` class from JDK 7 that holds three flag values used in format specifiers; namely, "-," "S," and "#." These flags are encoded as integer values 1, 2, and 4 (respectively). Interestingly, this class was introduced in Java 1.5, which also saw the introduction of enumerations into the language. Since an enumeration could have been used instead of the public static int fields, the `java.util.FormattableFlags` class becomes unnecessary.

---

[3] Using the interface feature in Java as holder for constant values.

```
public class FormattableFlags {
  // Explicit instantiation of this class is prohibited.
  private FormattableFlags() {}
  /** Left-justifies the output. */
  public static final int LEFT_JUSTIFY = 1<<0;//'-'
  /** Converts the output to upper case */
  public static final int UPPERCASE = 1<<1;//'S'
  /** Requires the output to use an alternate form. */
  public static final int ALTERNATE = 1<<2;//'#'
}
```

Example 2

Consider the `javax.swing.WindowConstants` interface that defines four constants that are used to control the window-closing operations. Here is the code (documentation comments edited to conserve space):

```
public interface WindowConstants {
  /** The do-nothing default window close operation. */
  public static final int DO_NOTHING_ON_CLOSE = 0;
  /** The hide-window default window close operation */
  public static final int HIDE_ON_CLOSE = 1;
  /** The dispose-window default window close operation. */
  public static final int DISPOSE_ON_CLOSE = 2;
  /** The exit application default window close operation. */
  public static final int EXIT_ON_CLOSE = 3;
}
```

This interface is an example of "constant interface" and is a poor use of the interface feature provided by the language. Why would developers or designers use an interface to hold constants? First, enumerations were only introduced in Java 1.5, so developers had to use existing features. Second, it was convenient for classes to use inheritance rather than delegation to use constants defined in the interfaces. The reason is that the classes that implement that interface could conveniently access the constants defined in the interface without explicitly qualifying the constant values with the name of the interface! A natural question is: Why use interfaces to hold constants instead of using classes? If a class were to be used for defining constants, then its derived classes cannot extend any other class (note that Java does not support multiple class inheritance); hence, interfaces were preferred over classes for holding constants.

Having understood constant interfaces, note that there are classes such as `JFrame`, `JInternalFrame`, and `JDialog` that inherit the `WindowConstants` interface. Another such example of constant interface use is `java.io.ObjectStreamConstants` that is implemented by `ObjectInputStream` and `ObjectOutputStream` classes.

The approach of using a constant interface and implementing it suffers from the following problems:

- The derived classes are "polluted" with constants that may not be relevant to that derived class.

- These constants are implementation details and exposing them through an interface violates encapsulation.

- When constants are part of an interface, changes to the constants can break the existing clients.

To summarize, an interface serves as a protocol that the implementing classes must support. Defining an interface to use it as a holder of constants is an abuse of the abstraction mechanism.

Example 3

Consider the case of an e-commerce application that has two classes: namely, `Best-SellerBook` and `Book`. Whenever the client wants to create a best-seller book, it creates an instance of a `BestSellerBook`. Internally, `BestSellerBook` delegates all the method calls to the `Book` class and does nothing else. Clearly, the `BestSeller-Book` abstraction is unnecessary since its behavior is exactly the same as the `Book` abstraction.

3.5.4 SUGGESTED REFACTORING

The generic refactoring suggestions to address this smell include the following:

- As Fowler suggests [7], "a class that isn't doing enough to pay for itself should be eliminated."

- Consider applying "inline class" refactoring [7] to merge the class with another class.

- If a class or interface is being introduced to encode constants, check if you can use a more suitable alternative language feature such as enumerations instead.

Suggested refactoring for Example 1

The suggested refactoring is to make the `FormattableFlags` an enumeration and use it with `java.util.Formatter` class, which provides support for formatted output.

Suggested refactoring for Example 2

The suggested refactoring is to make the `WindowsConstants` an enumeration. With this refactoring, classes such as `JFrame`, `JInternalFrame`, and `JDialog` can use this enumeration instead. A similar refactoring applies to the `ObjectStreamConstants` example as well.

Suggested refactoring for Example 3

For the case of the e-commerce application that has two classes; namely, Best-SellerBook and Book, there are many possible refactoring solutions. One solution, for instance, is to remove the BestSellerBook class and instead add an attribute named isBestSeller (along with a getter and a setter) in the Book class. Now, when the client code wants to indicate if a book is a bestseller, it will set the attribute isBestSeller instead of creating an instance of the erstwhile BestSellerBook class.

3.5.5 IMPACTED QUALITY ATTRIBUTES

- **Understandability**—Having needless abstractions in the design increases its complexity unnecessarily and affects the understandability of the overall design.

- **Reusability**—Abstractions are likely to be reusable when they have unique and well-defined responsibilities. An abstraction with trivial or no responsibility is less likely to be reused in a different context.

3.5.6 ALIASES

This smell is also known in literature as:

- "Irrelevant class" [51]—This smell occurs when a class does not have any meaningful behavior in the design.

- "Lazy class"/"Freeloader" [7,62]—This smell occurs when a class does "too little."

- "Small class" [57,60]—This smell occurs when a class has no (or too few) variables or no (or too few) methods in it.

- "Mini-class" [63]—This smell occurs when a public, non-nested class defines less than three methods and less than three attributes (including constants) in it.

- "No responsibility" [65]—This smell arises when a class has no responsibility associated with it.

- "Agent classes" [51]—This smell arises when a class serve as an "agent" (i.e., they only pass messages from one class to another), indicating that the class may be unnecessary.

3.5.7 PRACTICAL CONSIDERATIONS

Delegating abstractions in design patterns

Some design patterns (e.g., Mediator, Proxy, Façade, and Adapter) that employ delegation have a class that may appear to be an Unnecessary Abstraction. For example, in case of the Object Adapter pattern, the Adapter class may appear to merely delegate client requests to the appropriate method on the Adaptee [54]. However, the primary intention behind the Adapter class is to fulfill the specific, well-defined responsibility of adapting the Adaptee's interface to the client needs. Hence, one has to carefully consider the context before deciding whether an abstraction that just performs delegation is unnecessary or not.

Accommodating variations

Consider the example of java.lang.Math and java.lang.StrictMath classes, which provide almost similar math-related functionality. The JavaDoc for StrictMath notes: "By default many of the Math methods simply call the equivalent method in StrictMath for their implementation." It may appear from the JavaDoc description that Math is an Unnecessary Abstraction that simply delegates calls to StrictMath. However, although both support math-related functionality, StrictMath methods return exactly the same results irrespective of the platform because the implementation conforms to the relevant floating-point standard, whereas Math methods may use native hardware support for floating-point numbers and hence return slightly different results. Here, note that Math is less portable but can result in better performance when compared to StrictMath. Therefore, it is a conscious design decision to create two abstractions to accommodate variation in objectives, i.e., portability and performance.

3.6 UNUTILIZED ABSTRACTION

This smell arises when an abstraction is left unused (either not directly used or not reachable). This smell manifests in two forms:

- **Unreferenced abstractions**—Concrete classes that are not being used by anyone

- **Orphan abstractions**—Stand-alone interfaces/abstract classes that do not have any derived abstractions

3.6.1 RATIONALE

One of the enabling techniques for applying the principle of abstraction is to assign a single and meaningful responsibility to an entity. When an abstraction is left unused in design, it does not serve a meaningful purpose in design, and hence violates the principle of abstraction.

Design should serve real needs and not imagined or speculative needs. Unrealized abstract classes and interfaces indicate unnecessary or speculative generalization, and hence are undesirable. This smell violates the principle YAGNI (You Aren't Gonna Need It), which recommends not adding functionality until deemed necessary [53]. Since the abstraction is left unutilized in the design, this smell is named Unutilized Abstraction.

3.6.2 POTENTIAL CAUSES

Speculative design

When designers attempt to make the design of a system "future-proof" or provide abstractions "just in case it is needed in future," it can lead to this smell.

Changing requirements

When requirements keep changing, the abstractions created for satisfying an earlier requirement often may not be needed anymore. However, when the abstraction continues to remain in the design, it becomes an Unutilized Abstraction.

Leftover garbage during maintenance

When maintenance or refactoring activities are performed without cleaning up the old abstractions, it could result in unreferenced abstractions.

Fear of breaking code

Often, one of the reasons why developers do not delete old code is that they are not sure if any other class in the code is still using it. This is especially true in large codebases where it is difficult to determine whether a piece of code is being used or not.

3.6.3 EXAMPLES

Example 1 (unreferenced abstractions)

This example is paraphrased from a bug report on unused classes in JDK.[4] The package sun.misc has classes that date back to early releases of JDK, and they were used by other classes in JDK internally. Later, many of the services provided by sun.misc package were provided as part of the public API. Eventually, the original clients of sun.misc package started using the services provided by the public API. Due to this, many of the original classes in sun.misc package became unreferenced abstractions. One such example is the internal class sun.misc.Service that was introduced in JDK 1.3, which was made redundant by the introduction of the class java.util.ServiceLoader in JDK version 1.6 (which is part of the public API). Hence, the original sun.misc.Service is an Unutilized Abstraction.

Example 2 (unreferenced abstractions)

In a large Java project that one of the authors was involved in, there was extensive use of concurrency. The code was developed using JDK 1.3 and contained several concurrent utilities such as a concurrent version of HashMap, a FIFO (First-In-First-Out) buffer that would block, and an array list implementation that used copy-on-write approach. When JDK 1.5 introduced java.util.concurrent package, developers started using the classes in this package without removing the original concurrent utilities which became Unutilized Abstractions.

Example 3 (orphan abstractions)

One of the authors was involved in the development of a visualization tool integrated into an Integrated Development Environment (IDE). The tool would

---

[4] See the original bug report "JDK-6852936: Remove unused classes from sun.misc" here: http://bugs.sun.com/bugdatabase/view_bug.do?bug_id=6852936.

visually show the data flow of potential bugs such as null-pointer access, divide-by-zero, etc. While developing the tool, the designer thought that it would be a useful feature to generate reports of the tool results. Since he planned to create PDF and HTML versions of the reports, he created the class hierarchy shown in Figure 3.12. All three were abstract classes and they did not have much code in it, because they were "placeholders" for future implementation. However, as the primary objective of the tool was to visualize data flow so that developers can view how a control-flow path can result in a defect, report generation was not of much importance. So, report generation, although likely to be a useful feature, was never implemented. For this reason, these three classes (shown in Figure 3.12) are Unutilized Abstractions. Note that the hierarchy (in Figure 3.12) may appear to suffer from Unnecessary Hierarchy (Section 6.2). However, in the case of Unnecessary Hierarchy the types in the hierarchy are utilized, which is not the case here.

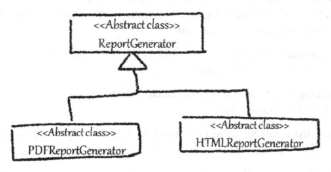

FIGURE 3.12

Unutilized report generation classes (Example 3).

ANECDOTE

During maintenance and refactoring, developers often refactor code bases that result in some of the old classes becoming obsolete. However, such code segments are often left in the code base (sometimes by mistake), making the source code bulge in size. Consider this documentation from the Java bug database for a set of classes in JDK source base (Check the original bug report "JDK-7161105: unused classes in jdk7u repository" here: http://bugs.sun.com/view_bug.do?bug_id=7161105):

"The ObjectFactory/SecuritySupport classes that were duplicated in many packages were replaced by a unified set under internal/utils. When the jaxp 1.4.5 source bundle was dropped, however, it was a copy of the source bundle on top of the original source, therefore leaving these classes behind unremoved."

The left-over code was later removed from the source base. What is the lesson that we can learn from this bug report? During refactoring or maintenance, it is important to ensure that old code is deleted from the code base to avoid its bloating due to dead code and unused classes.

3.6.4 SUGGESTED REFACTORING

The simplest refactoring is to remove the Unutilized Abstraction from the design. However, in the case of APIs, removing an abstraction is not feasible since there may be client code (or legacy code) that may be still referring to it. In these cases, such abstractions may be marked "obsolete" or "deprecated" to explicitly state that they must not be used by new clients.

Suggested refactoring for Example 1

All the uses of the `sun.misc.Service` class can be replaced by the use of `java.util.ServiceLoader` class. Therefore, for all practical purposes, there is no need for `sun.misc.Service` class and hence the suggested refactoring is to remove it from the code base. In fact, `sun.misc.Service` has been removed from JDK source code and JDK 9 will not have it.[5]

Suggested refactoring for Example 2

The following refactoring suggestions can be made for Example 2 considering the mapping between the project-specific concurrent utilities and the standard utilities introduced in Java 1.5 and later versions:

- The concurrent version of `HashMap` can be replaced with the use of `java.util.concurrent.ConcurrentHashMap`

- The blocking FIFO buffer can be replaced with the use of `java.util.concurrent.LinkedBlockingQueue`

- The array list implementation that used the copy-on-write approach could be replaced with the use of `java.util.concurrent.CopyOnWriteArrayList`

Note that performing the refactoring to make such replacements would require extensive code/design analysis and reviews in addition to extensive testing. This is because such replacements can result in subtle concurrency bugs that are hard to find, reproduce, or test.

Suggested refactoring for Example 3

Since report generation is a feature that is not needed and the hierarchy was added based on a speculated need, the suggested refactoring is to remove the entire hierarchy from the design.

---

[5] See the closed bug report 'JDK-8034776: Remove sun.misc.Service' in: http://bugs.java.com/bugdatabase/view_bug.do?bug_id=8034776.

ANECDOTE

Unutilized Abstraction is a commonly occurring smell across development organizations. Interestingly, the main reason behind the occurrence of this smell is changing requirements. In one instance that the authors are aware of, the project was following the Scrum process. In each sprint, suitable tasks would be identified from the backlog for development. Just like in other real-world projects, after a certain sprint, the customer changed his requirements, and consequently a new feature was expected to replace the old one.

Before the next sprint commenced, the allocation of tasks for the development of the new feature was done. It turned out that the new task was assigned to a different developer. This developer, instead of reusing the existing implementation, overlooked it and reinvented the wheel. In other words, he created new classes that were doing the same thing but the old classes were never removed and were left unused leading to the Unutilized Abstraction smell.

3.6.5 IMPACTED QUALITY ATTRIBUTES

- **Understandability**—Presence of unused abstractions in design pollutes the design space and increases cognitive load. This impacts understandability.

- **Reliability**—The presence of unused abstractions can sometimes lead to run-time problems. For instance, when code in unused abstractions gets accidentally invoked, it can result in subtle bugs affecting the reliability of the software.

3.6.6 ALIASES

This smell is also known in literature as:

- "Unused classes" [35,55]—This smell occurs when a class has no direct references and when no calls to that class's constructor are present in the code.

- "Speculative generality" [7]—This smell occurs when classes are introduced, speculating that they may be required sometime in future.

3.6.7 PRACTICAL CONSIDERATIONS

Unutilized Abstractions in APIs

Class libraries and frameworks usually provide extension points in the form of abstract classes or interfaces. They may appear to be unused within the library or framework. However, since they are extension points that are intended to be used by clients, they cannot be considered as Unutilized Abstractions.

3.7 DUPLICATE ABSTRACTION

This smell arises when two or more abstractions have identical names or identical implementation or both. The design smell exists in two forms:

- **Identical name**—This is when the names of two or more abstractions are identical. While two abstractions can accidentally have the same name, it needs to be analyzed whether they share similar behavior. If their underlying behavior is not related, the main concern is simply the identical names. This would impact understandability since two distinct abstractions have an identical name. However, in case the underlying behavior of the two abstractions is also identical, it is a more serious concern and could indicate the "identical implementation" form of Duplicate Abstraction.

- **Identical implementation**—This is when two or more abstractions have semantically identical member definitions; however, the common elements in those implementations have not been captured and utilized in the design. Note that the methods in these abstractions might have similar implementation, but their signatures might be different. Additionally, identical implementation occurring in siblings within an inheritance hierarchy may point to an Unfactored Hierarchy smell (see Section 6.3).

This design smell also includes the combination of these forms. We have come across designs with "duplicate" abstractions that have identical names, identical method declarations (possibly with different signatures), and similar implementation.

Identical implementation could occur in four forms following the nature of "code clones" (fragments of code that are very similar). The sidebar "types of code clones" summarizes these four forms.

TYPES OF CODE CLONES

Code clones can be similar textually in the code, or they could be similar in their functionally but could differ textually. Based on the level of similarity, code clones can be considered to be of four types [16]:

Textually Similar Clones

Type 1: Two code fragments are clones of type-1 when the fragments are exactly identical except for variations in whitespace, layout, and comments.

Type 2: Two code fragments are clones of type-2 when the fragments are syntactically identical except for variation in symbol names, whitespace, layout, and comments.

Type 3: Two code fragments are clones of type-3 when the fragments are identical except some statements changed, added, or removed, in addition to variation in symbol names, whitespace, layout, and comments.

Functionally Similar Clones

Type 4: Two code fragments are clones of type-4 when the fragments are semantically identical but implemented by syntactic variants.

3.7.1 **RATIONALE**

Avoid duplication is an important enabling technique for the effective application of the principle of abstraction.

If two or more abstractions have an identical name, it affects understandability of the design. Developers of client code will be confused and unclear about the choice of the abstraction that should be used by their code.

If two or more abstractions have identical implementation (i.e., they have duplicate code), it becomes difficult to maintain them. Often, a change in the implementation of one of these abstractions will need to be reflected across all other duplicates. This introduces not only an overhead but also the possibility of subtle difficult-to-trace bugs. Duplication should be avoided as much as possible to reduce the extent of change required.

In summary, this smell indicates a violation of the DRY (Don't Repeat Yourself) principle. The DRY principle mandates that every piece of knowledge must have a single unambiguous representation within a system. If the DRY principle is not followed, a modification of an element within the system requires modifications to other logically unrelated elements making maintainability a nightmare. Since there is duplication among abstractions in the design, this smell is named Duplicate Abstraction.

3.7.2 **POTENTIAL CAUSES**

A Duplicate Abstraction smell can arise due to many reasons. While some of these reasons are generic, some are specific to a particular programming paradigm or platform.

Copy-paste programming

The "get-the-work-done" mindset of a programmer leads him to copy and paste code instead of applying proper abstraction.

Ad hoc maintenance

When the software undergoes haphazard fixes or enhancements over many years, it leaves "crufts"[6] with lots of redundant code in it.

Lack of communication

Often, in industrial software, code duplication occurs because different people work on the same code at different times in the life cycle of the software. They are not aware of existing classes or methods and end up re-inventing the wheel.

Classes declared non-extensible

When a class that needs to be extended is declared non-extensible (for example, by declaring a class as final in Java), developers often resort to copying the entire code in a class to create a modified version of the class.

---

[6]Wikipedia: Cruft is jargon for anything that is left over, redundant and getting in the way. It is used particularly for superseded and unemployed technical and electronic hardware and useless, superfluous or dysfunctional elements in computer software.

3.7.3 EXAMPLES

JDK has numerous classes with identical names. Specifically, of the 4005 types in Java 7, 135 type names are duplicates, which is a substantial 3.3%! Let us discuss a few of these Duplicate Abstractions.

Example 1

There are three different classes with the name `Timer` in JDK. The description of these classes as per JDK documentation is as follows:

- `javax.swing.Timer` is meant for executing objects of type `ActionEvent` at specified intervals.

- `java.util.Timer` is meant for scheduling a thread to execute in the future as a background thread.

- `javax.management.timer.Timer` is meant for sending out an alarm to wake up the listeners who have registered to get timer notifications.

Since all three timers have similar descriptions (they execute something in future after a given time interval), choosing the right `Timer` class can be challenging to inexperienced programmers.

Example 2

Classes `java.util.Date` and its derived class `java.sql.Date` share the same name (see Figure 3.13)! The compiler does not complain that the base and derived classes have the same name because these classes belong to different packages. However, it is very confusing for the users of these classes. For example, when both these classes are imported in a program, it will result in a name ambiguity that must be resolved manually by explicitly qualifying the class names.

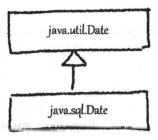

FIGURE 3.13

Classes with identical name 'Date' in JDK (Example 2).

Example 3

The `Scanner` class of `org.eclipse.jdt.internal.compiler.parser` package is almost a complete duplication of the `PublicScanner` class in `org.eclipse.jdt`.

core.compiler package. About 3500 lines of code are identical across these two classes. The JavaDoc description of the Scanner class says:

> "Internal Scanner implementation. It is mirrored in org.eclipse.jdt.core.compiler public package where it is API."

Both classes share identical public method signatures as well as implementation, and hence suffer from the "identical implementation" form of Duplicate Abstraction.

ANECDOTE

An very unusual problem was reported by one of the attendees during one of our guest lectures on design smells. The attendee was involved as a consultant architect in a large Java project. He found that the project team had spent several hours debugging the following problem.

While invoking a method from a third-party library, an exception named Missing-ResourceException was getting thrown at times. To handle that exception, one of the team members had added a catch handler for that exception and logged that exception using a logging library. However, what was frustrating to the team was that even after adding the catch handler, the application sometimes crashed with the same exception!

To aid debugging, the attendee suggested that the logging code be removed and the stack trace be printed on the console. This was done and the application was executed repeatedly. Eventually, when the crash occurred again, it was found that the exception thrown was not java.util.MissingResourceException which the code was handing, but was a custom exception named MissingResourceException that was defined in a package in the third-party library. Since these exceptions are RuntimeExceptions, the compiler did not issue any error for the catch block for catching an exception that could never get thrown from that code block!

Although this appeared to be a programming mistake, a deeper reflection revealed that it was in fact a design problem: the design specification did not mention specifically the type of exception that should have been handled. This, in combination with the identical names of the two exception classes resulted in the programmer handling the wrong exception.

This incident also highlighted how careful one should be when designing an API. In this case, since the name of an exception defined by the third-party API clashes with an existing JDK exception, it resulted in problems for the clients of the third-party API.

In summary, the important lessons that can be learned from this experience are:
- Design problems can cause hard-to-find defects
- Naming is important; avoiding duplicate names is especially important!

3.7.4 SUGGESTED REFACTORING

For identical name form, the suggested refactoring is to rename one of the abstractions to a unique name.

In the case of the identical implementation form of Duplicate Abstraction, if the implementations are exactly the same, one of the implementations can be removed. If the implementations are slightly different, then the common implementation in the duplicate abstractions can be factored out into a common class. This could be an existing supertype in the existing hierarchy (see refactoring for Unfactored Hierarchy (Section 6.3)) or an existing/new class which can be "referred to" or "used" by the duplicate abstractions.

Suggested refactoring for Example 1

For the Timer class example, since the main concern is identical name, the refactoring suggestion is to change their names so that they are unique. javax.swing.Timer is meant for executing objects of type ActionEvent, so it can be renamed as ExecutionTimer or EventTimer. Similarly, the Timer implementation from java.util can be renamed to AlarmTimer. The java.util.Timer can be retained as it is.

Suggested refactoring for Example 2

For the Date class example, let us take a look at the JavaDoc description for java.sql.Date.

> "To conform with the definition of SQL DATE, the millisecond values wrapped by a java.sql.Date instance must be 'normalized' by setting the hours, minutes, seconds, and milliseconds to zero in the particular time zone with which the instance is associated."

Following the hints from the words "wrapped by" in the JavaDoc description, a better design could be to "wrap" a java.util.Date instance in java.sql.Date, i.e., convert inheritance to delegation (see Broken Hierarchy in Section 6.8 for further details). Further since java.sql.Date conforms to SQL DATE, it is preferable to rename it as java.sql.SQLDate which will clearly differentiate it from the plain class name java.util.Date (see Figure 3.14).

FIGURE 3.14

Suggested refactoring for java.util.Date and java.sql.Date classes (Example 2).

Suggested refactoring for Example 3

With respect to the Scanner example, the classes Scanner and PublicScanner suffer from a high degree of identical implementation. A possible refactoring is to use inheritance but this would be appropriate only if the duplicate percentage is moderate and both the abstractions vary quite a bit. However, since the percentage of duplication is 99.9, a more appropriate solution is to delete one of the classes and make the other one compatible with the clients of the deleted class.

3.7.5 IMPACTED QUALITY ATTRIBUTES

- **Understandability**—Developers can become confused about which abstraction to use when there are two or more abstractions with identical names or implementation. Further, duplicate implementations bloat the code. These factors impact the understandability of the design.

- **Changeability** and **Extensibility**—Change or enhancement involving one abstraction potentially requires making the same modification in the duplicate abstractions as well. Hence, changeability and extensibility are considerably impacted.

- **Reusability**—Duplicate abstractions often have slightly different implementations (especially Type 3 and Type 4 clones). The differences in implementations are usually due to the presence of context-specific elements embedded in the code. This makes the abstractions hard to reuse in other contexts; hence, reusability of the abstractions is impacted.

- **Reliability**—When two abstractions have identical names, a confused developer may end-up using the wrong abstraction. For example, he may type cast to a wrong type, leading to a runtime problem. In case of abstractions with identical implementations, a modification in one of the abstractions needs to be duplicated across the other copies failing which a defect may occur.

3.7.6 ALIASES

This smell is also known in literature as:

- "Alternative classes with different interfaces" [7]—This smell occurs when classes do similar things, but have different names.

- "Duplicate design artifacts" [74]—This smell occurs when equivalent design artifacts are replicated throughout the architecture.

3.7.7 PRACTICAL CONSIDERATIONS

Accommodating variations

One reason why duplicate abstractions may exist is to support synchronized and unsynchronized variants. A synchronized variant of an abstraction may have used synchronization constructs heavily and this may lead to creating separate abstractions (that suffer from Duplicate Abstraction smell) corresponding to the two variants. An example of this is seen in `java.util.Vector` and `java.util.ArrayList` classes that have similar method definitions. The main difference between these classes is that the former is thread-safe and the latter is not thread-safe.

Duplicate type names in different contexts

It is hard to analyze and model large domains and create a unified domain model. In fact, "total unification of the domain model for a large system will not be feasible or cost-effective" [17]. One solution offered by Domain Driven Design is to divide the large system into "Bounded Contexts." In this approach, the resulting models in different contexts may result in types with same names. Since Bounded Context is one of the patterns that help deal with the larger problem of modeling large domains, such types with same names in different contexts is acceptable.

Lack of language support for avoiding duplication

Many methods and classes are duplicated in JDK because generics support is not available for primitive types. For example, the code for methods such as `binarySearch`, `sort`, etc. are duplicated seven times in the `java.util.Arrays` class because it is not possible to write a single generic method that takes different primitive type arrays. This results in the class suffering from a bloated interface.

Encapsulation Smells

4

The principle of encapsulation advocates separation of concerns and information hiding through techniques such as hiding implementation details of abstractions and hiding variations.

Consider the example of a car. Do you need to know exactly how the engine of the car works in order for you to be able to drive it? Is it really required for you to know how the anti-braking system (ABS) of your car works? Well, you may know these details (if you are an automobile engineer), but these details are not required for you to drive the car (Figure 4.1).

FIGURE 4.1

A car hides internal details (e.g., engine) from the its users.

This is precisely what the principle of Encapsulation does—it hides details that are not really required for the user of the abstraction (the abstraction in this case is the car). In addition, the principle of Encapsulation helps an abstraction to hide variation in the implementation details. For instance, whether your car has a petrol engine or a diesel engine, it does not change the way you drive your car.

The principle of encapsulation complements the principle of abstraction through information hiding. Encapsulation disallows (or "hides") the users of the abstraction from seeing internal details of the abstraction. In addition, encapsulation hides variation in implementation; the idea of hiding variation is explicitly stated by Gamma et al. [54]: "Encapsulate what varies." Hence, there are two techniques that enable effective application of the principle of encapsulation (see Figure 4.2):

• **Hide implementation details**. An abstraction exposes to its clients only "what the abstraction offers" and hides "how it is implemented." The latter,

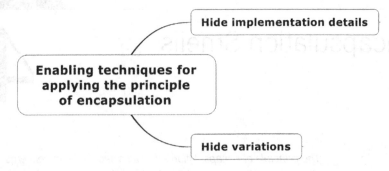

FIGURE 4.2

Enabling techniques for the principle of encapsulation.

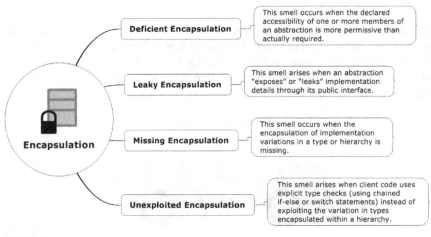

FIGURE 4.3

Smells resulting due to the violation of the principle of encapsulation.

that is, the details of the implementation include the internal representation of the abstraction (e.g., data members and data structures that the abstraction uses) and details of how the method is implemented (e.g., algorithms that the method uses).

- **Hide variations**. Hide implementation variations in types or hierarchies. With such variations hidden, it is easier to make changes to the abstraction's implementation without much impact to the clients of the abstraction.

All of the smells described in this chapter map to a violation of one of the above enabling techniques. Figure 4.3 gives an overview of the smells that violate the principle of encapsulation, and Table 4.1 provides an overview of mapping between the design smells and the enabling technique(s) that they violate. The Rationale

Table 4.1 Design Smells and the Violated Encapsulation Enabling Techniques

Design Smells	Violated Enabling Technique
Deficient Encapsulation (Section 4.1), Leaky Encapsulation (Section 4.2)	Hide implementation details
Missing Encapsulation (Section 4.3), Unexploited Encapsulation (Section 4.4)	Hide variations

subsection in each of the smell descriptions provides a detailed explanation of how a particular smell violates an enabling technique.

In the rest of this chapter, we will discuss specific smells that result due to the violation of the principle of encapsulation.

4.1 DEFICIENT ENCAPSULATION

This smell occurs when the declared accessibility of one or more members of an abstraction is more permissive than actually required. For example, a class that makes its fields public suffers from Deficient Encapsulation.

An extreme form of this smell occurs when there exists global state (in the form of global variables, global data structures, etc.) that is accessible to all abstractions throughout the software system.

4.1.1 RATIONALE

The primary intent behind the principle of encapsulation is to separate the interface and the implementation, which enables the two to change nearly independently. This separation of concerns allows the implementation details to be hidden from the clients who must depend only on the interface of the abstraction. If an abstraction exposes implementation details to the clients, it leads to undesirable coupling between the abstraction and its clients, which will impact the clients whenever the abstraction needs to change its implementation details. Providing more access than required can expose implementation details to the clients, thereby, violating the "principle of hiding."

Having global variables and data structures is a more severe problem than providing lenient access to data members. This is because global state can be accessed and modified by any abstraction in the system, and this creates secret channels of communication between two abstractions that do not directly depend on each other. Such globally accessible variables and data structures could severely impact the understandability, reliability, and testability of the software system.

Since this smell occurs when the internal state of an abstraction is inadequately hidden, we name this smell Deficient Encapsulation.

4.1.2 POTENTIAL CAUSES

Easier testability
Often developers make private methods of an abstraction public to make them testable. Since private methods concern implementation details of an abstraction, making them public compromises the encapsulation of the abstraction.

Procedural thinking in object oriented context
Sometimes, this smell occurs when developers from procedural programming background using an object oriented paradigm expose data as global variables when the data needs to be used by multiple abstractions.

Quick-fix solutions
Delivery pressures often force developers to take shortcuts (which happens to be one of the main causes of technical debt). For instance, in situations where the data is shared between only a couple of abstractions, developers find it easier to expose that data globally than to create an abstraction and pass it as a parameter to a method.

4.1.3 EXAMPLES

Example 1
A simple example of Deficient Encapsulation is from the `java.awt.Point` class. This class has public x and y fields in addition to public getter and setter methods for these fields (see Figure 4.4; only relevant members are shown in this figure). The class exhibits Deficient Encapsulation, since the accessibility of its members is more permissive (i.e., members are declared public) than actually required (i.e., they should have been declared private).

Interestingly, JDK has many examples of this smell in its implementation. In our analysis of JDK 7, we found 508 classes that have at least one public field, and hence

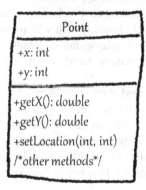

FIGURE 4.4

Public data members in java.awt.Point class (Example 1).

suffer from this smell. In fact, there are 96 classes that have five or more fields that are declared public. An extreme example is the class `com.sun.imageio.plugins.png.PNGMetadata` which has more than 85 public fields!

Example 2

Consider the class `SizeRequirements` from `java.swing.text` package in JDK 7. This class calculates information about the size and position of components that can be used by layout managers. Each `SizeRequirements` object contains information about either the width or height of a single component or a group of components.

Now consider the following public field in this class.

```
/** The alignment, specified as a value between 0.0 and 1.0,
inclusive. To specify centering, the alignment should be 0.5. */
public float alignment;
```

If the clients of `SizeRequirements` class were to directly access members like `alignment`, it would be difficult for the `SizeRequirements` class to ensure that the value of `alignment` remains valid as per the constraints specified in the comments (i.e., the value must be between 0.0 and 1.0).

CASE STUDY

It is common to observe rampant occurrences of Deficient Encapsulation smell in real-world projects. Although it is easy to understand why fields may be declared public, it is interesting to note in many real-world projects that methods that should have been declared private are instead made public.

When we questioned some development teams about this, most of them said that it was a conscious design choice: when methods are declared private, it is difficult to test them, so they are typically made public!

However, exposing all of the methods as public not only compromises design quality but can also cause serious defects. For instance, clients of the class will start directly depending on implementation details of the class. This direct dependency makes it difficult to change or extend the design. It also impacts the reliability, since clients can directly manipulate the internal details of the abstractions. Hence, ensuring the integrity of the internal state of the abstractions becomes difficult (if not impossible). In summary, making internal methods publicly accessible in the name of testability can have serious consequences.

So, how can we test classes without compromising their encapsulation?

There are many ways in which tests can be written without exposing methods as public. One way is to use reflection—tests can use reflection to dynamically load classes, examine their internals, and invoke methods (including private ones). Another way is to adopt a language such as Groovy that allows direct access to all the members (and ignores access specifiers) of a Java class.

Example 3

Consider the public classes `javax.swing.SwingUtilities`, `sun.swing.SwingUtilities2` and `sun.java.swing.SwingUtilities3` in Java 1.7. These utility classes provide services to the rest of the swing package. For instance,

`SwingUtilities3` class provides services for JavaFX applets. Since these classes are meant to be used only by the classes in swing package, they can be considered as "internal implementation details" of the swing package. In other words, the code in these utility classes is not meant to be used by the end-user applications.

In the context of Deficient Encapsulation, consider the documentation provided within `SwingUtilities2` and `SwingUtilities3` classes.

```
/**
 * A collection of utility methods for Swing.
 * <p>
 * WARNING: While this class is public, it should not be treated as.
 * public API and its API may change in incompatible ways between
 * dot dot releases and even patch releases.
 * You should not rely on this class even existing.
 */
```

Since these classes are declared public, they are accessible to client code that can directly use them. Such direct use of implementation-level methods of the swing package violates the principle of encapsulation, and hence these classes suffer from Deficient Encapsulation.

(On an unrelated note, it is clear that the classes are not named appropriately: the class names `SwingUtilities`, `SwingUtilities2`, and `SwingUtilities3` are quite general, and the difference between these classes is not evident from the class names.)

Example 4

Consider the following fields defined in `java.lang.System` class:

ANECDOTE

One of the authors was involved in reviewing an application for post-processing violations of static analyzers, clone detectors, and metric tools that was being developed at a start-up. The application generated summary reports that helped architects and project managers understand the code quality problems in their projects.

The application had three logical modules:
- `Parsing` module: Classes responsible for parsing the results from static analyzers, metric tools, and clone detectors.
- `Analytics` module: Classes responsible for analyzing the data such as aggregating them based on some criteria such as criticality of the violations.
- `Reporter` module: Classes responsible for generating reports and providing a summary to the architects and managers.

While inspecting the design and codebase, the author found an interesting class named `Data`. The main reason why this class existed is because the classes in `Reporting` module needed to know (for example, to create a summary report) the details resulting from the processing done by the `Parsing` and `Analytics` modules. To elaborate, the `Parsing` and `Analytics` modules provided direct and useful results that were used for summarizing the results in the `Reporting` module. The code in `Parsing` and `Analytics` module dumped the data structures into the `Data` class, and the code in `Reporting` module read this data from the `Data` class and created a summary as part of the final report that was generated. However, the way that this was realized was

ANECDOTE—Cont'd

by declaring all of the 23 fields of the Data class as public static (and non-final). The implication of such a design is that the details within Analytics module were unnecessarily available even to the Parsing module! This has an adverse impact on understandability and reliability. Such global data sharing provides an implicit form of coupling between the modules.

These members are declared final, but they can be "reset" using methods setIn, setOut, and setErr, respectively (these methods internally make use of native methods

```
public final static InputStream in = null;
public final static PrintStream out = null;
public final static PrintStream err = null;
```

to reset the final stream variables) provided in java.lang.System class. For instance, here is the declaration of the setOut method provided in java.lang.System class:

Since these fields are declared public, any code (i.e., other classes in JDK as well as application code) can access these fields directly. Hence, these fields are effec-

```
public static void setOut(PrintStream out)
```

tively global variables!

Common reason for making such fields public instead of providing getter methods is *performance*: since these fields are quite extensively used, it could considered as an unnecessary overhead to provide getter methods. However, providing such direct global access to fields is problematic. For illustration, let us consider one such problem.

The fields out and err are instances of type PrintStream. The PrintStream class was introduced in Java version 1.0 and supported only 8-bit ASCII values. Hence, to support Unicode, JDK 1.1.5 introduced PrintWriter class as a replacement to PrintStream class, which they intended to deprecate. However, fields of Print-Stream type such as System.out and System.err are directly used by most of the Java applications to access PrintStream's methods. For instance, every time we use System.out.println, we access the println method defined in PrintStream class! Hence, it is not possible to deprecate the entire PrintStream class.[1]

In summary, the deprecation of the PrintStream class was made difficult because of the Deficient Encapsulation smell in the System class which publicly exposed the data members out and err of type PrintStream.

---

[1] See Ref. [38] for an insightful discussion on the limited deprecation of the PrintStream class in JDK 1.1.5 and its later rollback in JDK 1.2.

CASE STUDY

Linux, a widely used open source operating system has attracted criticism from various quarters for its poor maintainability. One of the responsible factors for this is the large number of global variables in the source code. In a study, Yu et al. found that there are 99 global variables in version 2.4.20 of Linux [82]. Here, in particular, we are interested in a global variable named current.

This global variable was first introduced in version 1.0.0 of Linux and represents the currently running process. It is a pointer to a structure containing various fields that are used to describe the state of the process. Yu et al. [82] found that the global variable current is accessed (read and written) by 12 kernel modules and read by six other kernel modules. Furthermore, 1071 non-kernel modules have access to this global variable. The total number of read and write instances in kernel modules for this global variable is 382 and 114 respectively. Similarly, there are 6795 instances of read and 1403 instances of write for this global variable in non-kernel modules.

It is evident from the presented numbers that due to the global variable current, there is extremely strong coupling among various modules in Linux source code. This strong coupling makes it difficult to understand the functionality of the kernel and to debug the source code. This in turn makes changes to the source code error-prone.

The diagram (Figure 4.5) shows the strong coupling that exists due to the global variable current in Linux. It shows the coupling between kernel and non-kernel modules (files in C) due to the variable current. The arrows towards the box containing current are annotated. The annotation in the form of (x, y) indicates write and read instances for x and y, respectively. Similarly, annotation in the form of (x) indicates the number of read instances.

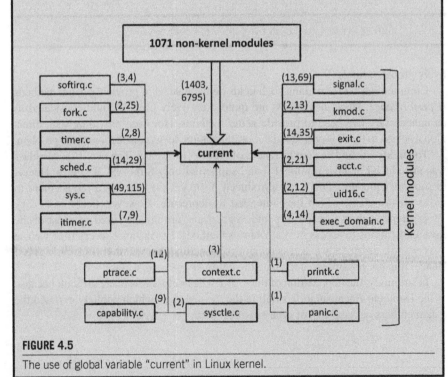

FIGURE 4.5

The use of global variable "current" in Linux kernel.

4.1.4 SUGGESTED REFACTORING

In the case of a public data member, "encapsulate field" refactoring can be applied to make the field private and provide accessor methods (i.e., get and set methods) as required. In case the methods that concern the implementation aspects of a class are made public, they must be made private (or protected if necessary).

Suggested refactoring for Examples 1 and 2

Make the data members in classes `Point` and `SizeRequirements` private and provide suitable accessor and mutator methods for the fields. For fields such as `alignment` in `SizeRequirements` class, provide the necessary validation for acceptable values in the mutator method.

Suggested refactoring for Example 3

Group the conceptually related methods in classes `SwingUtilities`, `SwingUtilities2`, and `SwingUtilities3` together in separate classes, and name the new classes based on the grouping, for example, `JavaFXUtilities`, `PaneUtilities`, `ComponentUtilities`, etc. Provide default access (i.e., package-private) access to these classes.

In the case of global variables, there are two variants possible:

- One or more members are made visible globally (by using `public static` in Java) even though only two or three classes access them
- One or more members are made visible globally (by using `public static` in Java) and a large number of classes access them

To refactor the first variant, passing the required variable as parameter could be considered. The second variant is more severe and trickier. One has to analyze existing abstractions and the responsibilities assigned to them to deal with this variant. It could be the case that the global variables have been introduced due to inappropriate abstractions and improper responsibility distribution. In such a case, the problem could be solved by identifying appropriate abstractions and encapsulating the variable within those abstractions. Now, clients can use these abstractions instead of globally visible data members.

Suggested refactoring for Example 4

To refactor this smell in `java.lang.System` class, one or more abstractions could be introduced to provide the functionality provided through the public members. For example, a class named, say, `Console`, could abstract the functionality that is provided by standard input, output, and error streams. This `Console` class could hide the implementation details (such as specific `Stream` classes used, kind of synchronization performed, etc.). Such a design would allow for changes in the implementation inside the `Console` abstraction, unlike the case in which data members (such as `out` and `err`) are directly exposed to the clients.

In fact Java 1.6 version introduced `java.io.Console` class that provides "methods to access the character-based console device." One can retrieve `Writer` or `Reader` objects associated with the `Console` object using `reader()` and `writer()` methods.

The class also provides methods such as `readLine()` and `printf()` for reading and writing strings to console, respectively. The readers and writers supported by this `Console` class wrap the actual input and output streams on which they operate. The `Console` class also uses locks internally to synchronize the reads and writes. In short, the `Console` class encapsulates the operations on input and output streams. This class is perhaps not meant to be a replacement of the original standard input, output, and error streams; however, it does illustrate what alternative design approach could be used instead of exposing streams directly to clients.

4.1.5 IMPACTED QUALITY ATTRIBUTES

- **Understandability**—One of the main objectives of the principle of encapsulation is to shield clients from the complexity of an abstraction by hiding its internal details. However, when internal implementation details are exposed, the view of the abstraction may become complex and impact understandability. In the case when global data or data structures are used, it is very difficult to track and differentiate between read and write accesses. Furthermore, since the methods operating on the global data/data structures are not encapsulated along with the data, it is harder to understand the overall design.

- **Changeability** and **Extensibility**—Since the declared accessibility of members of the abstraction is more permissive, the clients of the abstraction may depend directly upon the implementation details of the abstraction. This direct dependency makes it difficult to change or extend the design. In the case of global variables, since encapsulation is lacking, any code can freely access or modify the data. This can result in unintended side effects. Furthermore, when defect fixes or feature enhancements are made, it can break the existing code. For these reasons, Deficient Encapsulation negatively impacts changeability and extensibility.

- **Reusability**—In the presence of Deficient Encapsulation smell, clients may directly depend on commonly accessible state. Hence, it is difficult to reuse the clients in a different context, since this will require the clients to be stripped of these dependencies.

- **Testability**—Globally accessible data and data structures are harder to test, since it is very difficult to determine how various code segments access or modify the common data. Furthermore, the abstractions that make use of the global data structures are also difficult to test because of the unpredictable state of the global data structures. These factors negatively impact testability of the design.

- **Reliability**—When an abstraction provides direct access to its data members, the responsibility of ensuring the integrity of the data and the overall abstraction is moved from the abstraction to each client of the abstraction. This increases the likelihood of the occurrence of runtime problems.

4.1.6 ALIASES

This smell is also known in literature as:

- "Hideable public attributes/methods" [55]—This smell occurs when you see public attributes/methods that are never used from another class but instead are used within the own class (ideally, these methods should have been private).

- "Unencapsulated class" [57]—A lot of global variables are being used by the class.

- "Class with unparameterized methods" [57]—Most of the methods in class have no parameters and utilize class or global variables for processing.

4.1.7 PRACTICAL CONSIDERATIONS

Lenient access in nested or anonymous classes

It is perhaps acceptable to declare data members or implementation-level methods as public in case of nested/anonymous classes where the members are accessible only to the enclosing class.

Performance considerations

Some designers make a conscious choice to make use of public data members citing efficiency reasons. Consider the class Segment from java.swing.text package (slightly edited to save space):

```
/** A segment of a character array representing a fragment of
text. It should be treated as immutable even though the array
is directly accessible. This gives fast access to fragments of
text without the overhead of copying around characters. This is
effectively an unprotected String. */
public class Segment implements Cloneable, CharacterIterator,
CharSequence {
    /** This is the array containing the text of interest. This
    array should never be modified; it is available only for
    efficiency. */
    public char[] array;
    /** This is the offset into the array that the desired text
    begins. */
    public int offset;
    /** This is the number of array elements that make up the text
    of interest. */
    public int count;
    // other members elided ...
}
```

This Segment class and its public fields are widely used within the text package. This design compromise would be acceptable assuming that the designers of the Segment class carefully weighed the tradeoff between performance benefits and the qualities that are violated because of this smell.

In general, designers should be wary of making such a decision. Often developers tend to declare fields public because they believe that direct access to those fields will be faster than through the accessor (i.e., get and set) methods. However, since current compilers and JIT compilers inline accessor methods, the performance overhead of using accessor methods is usually negligible.

4.2 LEAKY ENCAPSULATION

This smell arises when an abstraction "exposes" or "leaks" implementation details through its public interface. Since implementation details are exposed through the interface, it not only is harder to change the implementation but also allows clients to directly access the internals of the object (leading to potential state corruption).

It should be noted that although an abstraction may not suffer from Deficient Encapsulation (Section 4.1) (i.e., the declared accessibility of its members are as desired), it is still possible that the methods in the pubic interface of the abstraction may leak implementation details (see examples in Section 4.2.3).

4.2.1 RATIONALE

For effective encapsulation, it is important to separate the interface of an abstraction (i.e., "what" aspect of the abstraction) from its implementation (i.e., "how" aspect of the abstraction). Furthermore, for applying the principle of hiding, implementation aspects of an abstraction should be hidden from the clients of the abstraction.

When implementation details of an abstraction are exposed through the public interface (i.e., there is a violation of the enabling technique "hide implementation details"):

- Changes made to the implementation may impact the client code.

- Exposed implementation details may allow clients to get handles to internal data structures through the public interface, thus allowing clients to corrupt the internal state of the abstraction accidentally or intentionally.

Since implementation aspects are not hidden, this smell violates the principle of encapsulation; furthermore, the abstraction "leaks" implementation details through its public interface. Hence, we term the smell Leaky Encapsulation.

4.2.2 POTENTIAL CAUSES

Lack of awareness of what should be "hidden"

It requires considerable experience and expertise to discern and separate the implementation and interface aspects of an abstraction from each other. Inexperienced designers often inadvertently leak implementation details through the public interface.

Viscosity

It requires considerable thought and effort to create "leak-proof" interfaces. However, in practice, due to project pressures and deadlines, often designers or developers resort to quick and dirty hacks while designing interfaces, which leads to this smell.

Use of fine-grained interface

Often, this smell occurs because fine-grained methods are directly provided in the public interface of a class. These fine-grained methods typically expose unnecessary implementation details to the clients of the class. A better approach is to have logical coarse-grained methods in the public interface that internally make use of fine-grained methods that are private to the implementation.

4.2.3 EXAMPLES

Example 1

Consider a feature-rich e-mail application similar to Microsoft® Outlook® or Mozilla Thunderbird®. One of the features that such an application supports is maintaining a list of to-do items. Assume that the content of each to-do item is maintained in a TodoItem class. The class TodoList maintains the list of TodoItems. Figure 4.6 outlines the members in TodoList class (distilled to a very simple form to maintain focus on the smell under discussion).

One of the methods in TodoList class is the public method getListEntries(), which returns the list of to-do items maintained by that object. The problem is with the return type of the method i.e., LinkedList. The method exposes the internal detail that the TodoList class uses a linked list as the mechanism for maintaining the list of TodoItems.

Presumably, the application may have mostly inserts and deletes, and hence the class designer may have chosen a LinkedList for implementation in TodoList class. In the future, if it is found that the application performs search operations more frequently

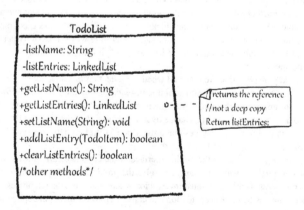

FIGURE 4.6

TodoList class exposing its internal use of linked list (Example 1).

than modifications to the list, it is better to change the implementation to use some other data structure such as an `ArrayList` or a `HashMap` (which provides faster lookup than a `LinkedList`). Furthermore, a new requirement tomorrow may require that at runtime the application should be able to switch to a specific implementation based on the context. However, since `getListEntries()` is a public method and returns `LinkedList`, changing the return type of this method may break the clients that are dependent on it. This suggests that it may be very difficult to support future modifications to the `TodoList` class.

Another serious problem with the `getListEntries()` method is that it returns a handle (i.e., reference) to the internal data structure. Using this handle, the clients can directly change the `listEntries` data structure bypassing the methods in `TodoList` such as `addListEntry()`.

To summarize, `TodoList` class "leaks" an implementation detail in its public interface, thereby binding the `TodoList` class to use a specific implementation.

ANECDOTE

A participant of the Smells Forum reported an example of this smell in an e-commerce application. In this application, the main logic involved processing of orders, which was abstracted in an `OrderList` class. The `OrderList` extended a custom tree data structure, since most use cases being tested by the team involved inserting and deleting orders.

When the application was first deployed, a customer filed a change request complaining that the application was not able to handle large number of orders and it "hanged." Profiling the application showed `OrderList` to be a "bottleneck class." The tree implementation internally used was not a self-balancing tree, and hence the tree often got skewed and looked more like a "list." To fix this problem, a developer quickly added a public method named `balance()` in the `OrderList` class that would balance the tree. He also ensured that the `balance()` method was invoked from the appropriate places in the application to address the skewing of the tree. When he tested the application, this solution appeared to solve the performance problem and so he closed the change request.

In a few months, more customers reported similar performance problems. Taking a relook at the class revealed that most of the time orders were being "looked-up" and not inserted or deleted. Hence the team now considered replacing the internal tree implementation to a hash-table implementation.

However, the `OrderList` class was tied to the "tree" implementation because it extended a custom `Tree` class. Furthermore, changing the implementation to use a more suitable data structure such as a hash table was difficult because the clients of the `OrderList` class used implementation-specific methods such as `balance()`! Although refactoring was successfully performed to use hash table instead of unbalanced tree in the `OrderList`, it involved making changes in many places within the application.

There are two key insights that are revealed when we reflect on this anecdote:
- Having the `OrderList` extend the custom tree instead of *using* the custom tree forced the `OrderList` to unnecessarily expose implementation details to the clients of the `OrderList` class. Due to the choice of using inheritance over delegation, the clients of the `OrderList` could not be shielded from the changes that arose when a different data structure, i.e., a hash table was used inside the `OrderList`.
- Adding `balance()` method in the public interface of the class is clearly a work-around. Such workarounds or quick-fix solutions appear to solve the problem, but they often backfire and cause more problems. Hence, one must invest a lot of thought in the design process.

Design smells such as Leaky Encapsulation can cause serious problems in applications, and we need to guard against such costly mistakes.

Example 2

Consider a class CustomListBox, which is a custom implementation of a ListBox UI control. One of the operations that you may perform on a ListBox object is to sort it. Figure 4.7 shows only the sort-related methods in CustomListBox class.

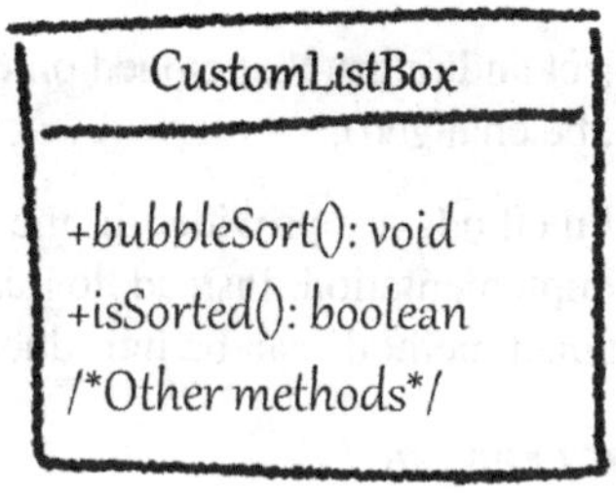

FIGURE 4.7

CustomListBox leaks the name of the sorting algorithm it uses (Example 2).

The problem with this class is that the name of the public method bubbleSort() exposes the implementation detail that the CustomListBox implementation uses "bubble sort" algorithm to sort the list. What if the sorting algorithm needs to be replaced with a different sorting algorithm, say, "quick sort" in the future? There are two possibilities:

- **Option 1**: Change the name of the algorithm to quickSort() and replace the algorithm accordingly. However, this change will break existing clients who are depending on the public interface of the class.

- **Option 2**: Replace only the implementation of the bubbleSort() method with the quick sort algorithm without changing the name of the existing method; i.e., the method name remains bubbleSort() but the method implements quick sort algorithm. The problem with this bad hack is that it will end up misleading the clients of this class that a "bubble sort" algorithm is being used because the name of the algorithm is mentioned in the method.

Thus both options are undesirable. In reflection, the root cause of the problem is that the name of the algorithm is "leaked" in the public interface of the class, thus leading to a Leaky Encapsulation smell.

4.2.4 SUGGESTED REFACTORING

The suggested refactoring for this smell is that the interface should be changed in such a way that the implementation aspects are not exposed via the interface. For example, if details of the internal algorithms are exposed through the public interface, then refactor the public interface in such a way that the algorithm details are not exposed via the interface.

It is also not proper to return a handle to internal data structures to the clients of a class, since the clients can directly change the internal state by making changes through the handle. There are a few ways to solve the problem:

- Perform deep copy and return that cloned object (changes to the cloned object do not affect the original object).

- Create an immutable object and return that cloned object (by definition, an immutable object cannot be changed).

If low-level fine-grained methods are provided in the public interface, consider making them private to the implementation. Instead, logical coarse-grained methods that make use of the fine-grained methods can be introduced in the public interface.

Suggested refactoring for Example 1

The suggested refactoring for the ToDoList example is to change the return type of the getListEntries() in such a way that it does not reveal the underlying implementation. Since List interface is the base type of classes such as ArrayList and LinkedList, one refactoring would be to use List as the return type of getListEntries() method. Or, a designer could choose to use Collection as the return type, which is quite general and does not reveal anything specific about the implementation.

However, it is also important to ensure that the clients of the ToDoList are not provided a handle to directly change its internal state. Therefore, consider returning a deep copy or a read-only copy of the internal list to the clients. At this point, let us take a step back and think about the clients of the TodoList class. Why would they be interested in getListEntries() method? If the end goal was to traverse the list and access each entry, then a better refactoring solution would be to return an Iterator instead. This kind of logical structured reasoning in practice will allow you to come up with a better and more effective design.

Suggested refactoring for Example 2

The suggested refactoring for the CustomListBox example is to replace the method name bubbleSort() with sort() (see Figure 4.8). With this, the sort() method can internally choose to implement any suitable sorting algorithm for sorting the

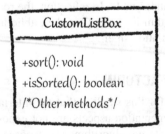

FIGURE 4.8

Suggested refactoring for CustomListBox (Example 2).

elements in the `CustomListBox`. For instance, the class `CustomListBox` can internally use Strategy pattern to employ the relevant algorithm at runtime.

Note that this class is part of the public API, so changing the method name will break the clients of the class. A work-around, to address this problem and the smell at the same time, is to introduce a new `sort()` method and deprecate the existing `bubbleSort()` method. Design is hard; API design is harder!

CASE STUDY

Consider the case of a software system in which a class implements operations on an image object. The operation to display an image completes in four steps that must be executed in a specific sequence, and the designer has created public methods corresponding to each of these steps: i.e., `load()`, `process()`, `validate()`, and `show()` in the `Image` class. Exposing these methods creates a constraint on using these four methods; specifically, the methods corresponding to these four steps—load, process, validate, and show—must be called in that specific sequence for the image object to be valid.

This constraint can create problems for the clients of the `Image` class. A novice developer may call `validate()` without calling `process()` on an image object. Each of the operations makes a certain assumption about the state of the image object, and if the methods are not called in the required sequence, then the operations will fail or leave the image object in an inconsistent state. Clearly, the `Image` class exposes "how" aspects of the abstraction as part of the public interface. It thus exhibits the Leaky Encapsulation smell.

How can this problem be addressed? One potential solution is to have a state flag to keep track of whether the operations are performed in a sequence. However, this is a really bad solution, since maintaining a state flag is cumbersome: if we maintain the state flag in the `Image` class, every operation must check for the proper transition and handle any exceptional condition.

At this juncture, we can take a step back and question why the four internal steps need to be exposed to the client who is concerned only with the display of the image. We can then see that the problem can be solved by exposing to the clients of the `Image` class only one method, say `display()`, which internally calls each of the four steps in sequence.

If we reflect upon this anecdote, we see that the underlying problem in this example is that the fine-grained steps were exposed as public methods. Hence, the key take-away here is that it is better to expose coarse-grained methods via the public interface rather than fine-grained methods that run the risk of exposing internal implementation details.

4.2.5 IMPACTED QUALITY ATTRIBUTES

- **Understandability**—One of the main objectives of the principle of encapsulation is to shield clients from the complexity of an abstraction by hiding its internal details. However, when internal implementation details are exposed in the case of a Leaky Encapsulation smell, the public interface of the abstraction may become more complex, affecting its understandability.

- **Changeability and Extensibility**—When an abstraction "exposes" or "leaks" implementation details through its public interface, the clients of the abstraction may depend directly upon its implementation details. This direct dependency makes it difficult to change or extend the design without breaking the client code.

- **Reusability**—Clients of the abstraction with Leaky Encapsulation smell may directly depend upon the implementation details of the abstraction. Hence, it is difficult to reuse the clients in a different context, since it will require stripping the client of these dependencies (for reference, see Command Pattern [54]).

- **Reliability**—When an abstraction "leaks" internal data structures, the integrity of the abstraction may be compromised, leading to runtime problems.

4.2.6 ALIASES

This smell is also known in literature as:

- Leaking implementation details in API [49]—This smell occurs when an API leaks implementation details that may result in confusing users or inhibiting freedom to change implementation.

4.2.7 PRACTICAL CONSIDERATIONS

Low-level classes

Consider an example of embedded software that processes and plays audio in a mobile device. In such software, the data structures that store metadata about the audio stream (e.g., sampling rate, mono/stereo) need to be directly exposed to the middleware client. In such cases, when public interface is designed purposefully in this way, clients should be warned that the improper use of those public methods might result in violating the integrity of the object. Also, it is important to ensure that such classes are not part of the higher-level API, such as the one that is meant for use by the mobile application software, so that runtime problems can be avoided.

4.3 MISSING ENCAPSULATION

This smell occurs when implementation variations are not encapsulated within an abstraction or hierarchy.

This smell usually manifests in the following forms:

- A client is tightly coupled to the different variations of a service it needs. Thus, the client is impacted when a new variation must be supported or an existing variation must be changed.

- Whenever there is an attempt to support a new variation in a hierarchy, there is an unnecessary "explosion of classes," which increases the complexity of the design.

4.3.1 RATIONALE

The Open Closed Principle (OCP) states that a type should be open for extension and closed for modification. In other words, it should be possible to change a type's behavior by extending it and not by modifying it (see case study below). When the variations in implementation in a type or a hierarchy are not encapsulated separately,

---

CASE STUDY ON OCP

Localization in Java is supported through the use of resource bundles (see `java.util.ResourceBundle` in Java 7). We can write code that is mostly independent of user's locale and provide locale-specific information in resource bundles.

The underlying process of searching, resolving, and loading resource bundles is complex. For most purposes, the default implementation provided by the `ResourceBundle` class is sufficient. However, for sophisticated applications, there may be a need to use a custom resource bundle loading process. For instance, when there are numerous heavyweight locale-specific objects, you may want to cache the objects to avoid reloading them. To support your own resource bundle formats, search strategy, or custom caching mechanism, `ResourceBundle` provides an extension point in the form of `ResourceBundle.Control` class. Here is the description of this class from JDK documentation:

"ResourceBundle.Control defines a set of callback methods that are invoked by the Resource-Bundle.getBundle factory methods during the bundle loading process... Applications can specify ResourceBundle.Control instances returned by the getControl factory methods or created from a subclass of ResourceBundle.Control to customize the bundle loading process."

In summary, `ResourceBundle` supports a default process for locating and loading resource bundles that is sufficient for most needs. Furthermore, the class also provides support for customizing this bundle locating and loading process by providing a separate abstraction in the form of `ResourceBundle.Control` class. Thus, this design by default supports the standard policy and provides an extension point to plug-in a custom policy. Such a design follows OCP.

This example is also an illustration of what Alan Kay (Turing award winner and co-creator of Smalltalk) said about design: "Simple things should be simple, complex things should be possible."

---

it leads to the violation of OCP.

One of the enabling techniques for Encapsulation is "hide variations." This is similar to the "Variation Encapsulation Principle (VEP)" which is advocated by Gamma et al. [54]. Thus, when a type (or hierarchy) fails to encapsulate the variation in the implementation, it implies that the principle of encapsulation has been either poorly applied or not applied at all. Hence, we term this smell Missing Encapsulation.

4.3.2 POTENTIAL CAUSES

Lack of awareness of changing concerns
Inexperienced designers are often unaware of principles such as OCP and can end up creating designs that are not flexible enough to adapt to changing requirements. They may also lack the experience to observe or foresee the concerns that could change in the future (based on the planned product roadmap); as a result, these concerns may not be properly encapsulated in the design.

Lack of refactoring
As existing requirements change or new requirements emerge, the design needs to evolve holistically to accommodate the change. This is especially crucial when

designers observe or foresee major problems such as explosion of classes. The lack
of refactoring in such cases can lead to this smell.

Mixing up concerns

When varying concerns that are largely orthogonal to each other are not separated
but instead aggregated in a single hierarchy, it can result in an explosion of classes
when the concerns vary.

Naive design decisions

When designers naively use simplistic approaches such as creating a class for every
combination of variations, it can result in unnecessarily complex designs.

4.3.3 EXAMPLES

Example 1

Assume that you have an existing `Encryption` class that needs to encrypt data using
an algorithm. There are various choices for such an algorithm including DES (Data
Encryption Standard), AES (Advanced Encryption Standard), TDES (Triple Data
Encryption Standard), etc. Figure 4.9 illustrates how the `Encryption` class encrypts
data using the DES algorithm. Suppose a new requirement is introduced that requires
data to be encrypted using the AES algorithm. A novice developer may come up with
the design shown in Figure 4.10, in which he introduces different methods such as
`encryptUsingDES()` and `encryptUsingAES()` in the `Encryption` class.

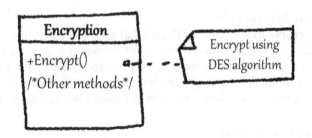

FIGURE 4.9

The class Encryption provides DES algorithm for encryption (Example 1).

There are many undesirable aspects of this design solution:

- The `Encryption` class becomes bigger and harder to maintain, since it implements
  multiple encryption algorithms even though only one algorithm is used at a time.

- It is difficult to add new algorithms and to vary the existing ones when a particular encryption algorithm is an integral part of the `Encryption` class.

- The algorithm implementations are tied to the `Encryption` class, so they cannot
  be reused in other contexts.

FIGURE 4.10

The class Encryption provides both DES and AES algorithms for encryption (Example 1).

In this example, encryption algorithms provide a service to the Encryption class. The Encryption class is tightly coupled to these services and is impacted when they vary.

Example 2

Consider a design that supports encrypting different kinds of content (such as images and text) as well as different kinds of algorithms (such as DES and AES). Figure 4.11 shows a commonly-seen simple design to model this solution.

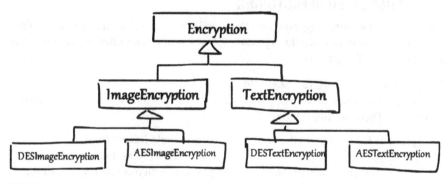

FIGURE 4.11

Hierarchy to support encryption of different kinds of content using different kinds of encryption algorithms (Example 2).

In this design, there are two variation points: the kind of content, and the kind of encryption algorithm that is supported. Every possible combination of these two variations is captured in a dedicated class. For instance, DESImageEncryption class deals with encrypting images using DES encryption algorithm. Similarly, AESTex-tEncryption class deals with encrypting text using AES encryption algorithm.

How does this design support a new type of content, a new encryption algorithm, or both? Figure 4.12 shows how the existing design will be extended to support TDES, a new encryption algorithm, and Data, a new type of content. Clearly, there

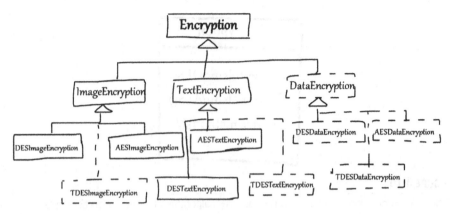

FIGURE 4.12

Class explosion in Encryption hierarchy when new kind of content and algorithm are added (Example 2).

is an explosion of classes. This is because the variations in the implementation are mixed together and have not been encapsulated separately, i.e., the design suffers from Missing Encapsulation smell.

4.3.4 SUGGESTED REFACTORING

The generic refactoring suggestion for this smell is to encapsulate the variations. This is often achieved in practice through the application of relevant design patterns such as Strategy and Bridge [54].

Suggested refactoring for Example 1

Let us consider what would happen if we were to use inheritance for refactoring Example 1. There are two options:

- **Option 1**: In this option, the Encryption class would inherit from DESEncryptionAlgorithm or AESEncryptionAlgorithm as needed and use the encrypt() method within. However, the problem with this solution is that the Encryption class would be tied to the specific encryption algorithm at compile time. A more serious problem is that the classes would not share an IS-A relationship, indicating a Broken Hierarchy smell (Section 6.8) (Figure 4.13).

- **Option 2**: Create subclasses named DESEncryption and AESEncryption that extend the Encryption class and contain implementation of DES and AES encryption algorithms, respectively. With this solution, the clients can hold reference to an Encryption class and point to the specific subclass object based on their need. By adding new subclasses, it is easier to add support for new encryption algorithms as well. However, the problem with this solution is that the DESEncryption and AESEncryption classes inherit other methods from the Encryption class. This reduces the reusability of the encryption algorithms in other contexts (Figure 4.14).

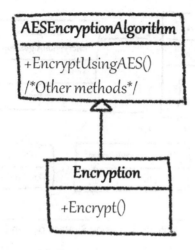

FIGURE 4.13

A possible refactoring for Example 1 (Option 1) which introduces Broken Hierarchy.

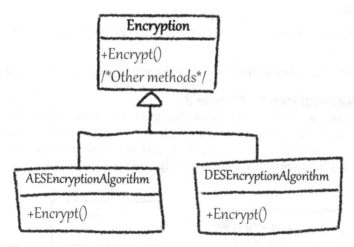

FIGURE 4.14

A possible refactoring for Example 1 (Option 2) using inheritance.

A better approach is to decouple the encryption algorithms from the Encryption class by employing the "factor out Strategy" refactoring [8]. The resulting design structure is shown in Figure 4.15.

In this design, an EncryptionAlgorithm interface is created. Classes named DESEncryptionAlgorithm and AESEncryptionAlgorithm implement the EncryptionAlgorithm interface and define the DES and AES algorithms, respectively. The Encryption class maintains a reference to the EncryptionAlgorithm interface.

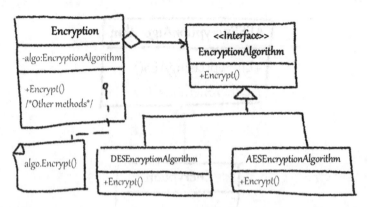

FIGURE 4.15

Suggested refactoring for Encryption class using Strategy pattern (Example 1).

This design structure offers the following benefits:

- An Encryption object can be configured with a specific encryption algorithm at runtime.

- The algorithms defined in the EncryptionAlgorithm hierarchy can be reused in other contexts.

- It is easy to add support for new encryption algorithms as and when required.

Suggested refactoring for Example 2

The main issue in the design (of Example 2) is that there are two orthogonal concerns that have been mixed up in the inheritance hierarchy. A refactoring suggestion is to use a structure similar to the Bridge pattern [54] and encapsulate the variations in these two concerns separately, as shown in Figure 4.16.

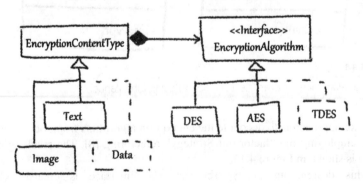

FIGURE 4.16

Suggested refactoring for supporting multiple kinds of content and algorithms (Example 2).

In this solution, the hierarchy rooted in `EncryptionContentType` class makes use of the algorithm implementations that are rooted in `EncryptionAlgorithm` interface. If a new content type named `Data` and a new encryption algorithm type TDES were to be introduced in this design, it would result in the addition of *only* two new classes (as shown in the Figure 4.16). In this way, the problem of explosion of the classes described in Example 2 can be addressed. Also, now, the encryption algorithm implementations rooted in `EncryptionAlgorithm` can be reused in other contexts.

4.3.5 IMPACTED QUALITY ATTRIBUTES

- **Understandability**—When there are numerous services (many of which may not be used) embedded in an abstraction, the abstraction becomes complex and difficult to understand. Furthermore, in cases where variation is not hidden in a hierarchy, the explosion of classes that results increases the complexity of design. These factors impact the understandability of the design.

- **Changeability** and **Extensibility**—When variations in implementation in a type or a hierarchy are not encapsulated separately, clients are tightly coupled to these different variations. This has two effects when a new or different variation must be supported. First, it is harder to change the clients when they need to use a different or new variation. Second, it may result in explosion of classes (see Example 2 above). If variations were to be encapsulated separately, the clients would be shielded from changes in the variations. In the absence of such encapsulation, changeability and extensibility are impacted.

- **Reusability**—When services are embedded within an abstraction, the services cannot be reused in other contexts. When two or more orthogonal concerns are mixed up in the hierarchy, the resulting abstractions that belong to the hierarchy are harder to reuse. For instance, in Example 2, when encryption content type and algorithm are mixed together, we no longer have specific algorithm classes that could be reused in other contexts. These factors impact the reusability of the type or hierarchy.

4.3.6 ALIASES

This smell is also known in literature as:

- "Nested generalization" [52]—This smell occurs when the first level in an inheritance hierarchy factors one generalization and the further levels "multiplies out" all possible combinations.

- "Class explosion" [22]—This smell occurs when number of classes explode due to extensive use of multiple generalizations.

- "Combinatorial explosion" [23]—This smell occurs when new classes need to be added to support each new family or variation.

4.3.7 PRACTICAL CONSIDERATIONS
None.

4.4 UNEXPLOITED ENCAPSULATION

This smell arises when client code uses explicit type checks (using chained if-else or switch statements that check for the type of the object) instead of exploiting the variation in types *already* encapsulated within a hierarchy.

4.4.1 RATIONALE

The presence of conditional statements (such as switch-case and if-else) in the client code that check a type explicitly and implement actions specific to each type is a well-known smell. Although this is a problem in general, consider the case when types are encapsulated in a hierarchy but are not leveraged. In other words, explicit type checks are being used instead of relying on dynamic polymorphism. This results in the following problems:

- Explicit type checks introduce tight coupling between the client and the concrete types, reducing the maintainability of the design. For instance, if a new type were to be introduced, the client will need to be updated with the new type check and associated actions.

- Clients need to perform explicit type check for all the relevant types in the hierarchy. If the client code misses checking one or more of the types in the hierarchy, it can lead to unexpected behavior at runtime. If runtime polymorphism were to be used instead, this problem could be avoided.

Such explicit type checks are an indication of the violation of the enabling technique "hide variations" and the principle of "encapsulate what varies" [54]. In the case of this smell, even though variation in types has been encapsulated within a hierarchy, it has not been exploited by the client code. Hence, we name this smell Unexploited Encapsulation.

4.4.2 POTENTIAL CAUSES

Procedural thinking in object-oriented language

Procedural languages such as C and Pascal do not support runtime polymorphism. Developers from procedural background think in terms of encoding types and use switch or chained if-else statements for choosing behavior. When the same approach is applied in an object-oriented language, it results in this smell.

Lack of application of object-oriented principles

Inexperienced software developers may be aware of object-oriented design principles, but they do not have a firm enough grasp of these concepts to actually put them into practice. For instance, they may be familiar with the concept of hierarchy and polymorphism, but may not be aware of how to exploit these concepts properly to create a high-quality design. As a result, they may introduce type checks in their code.

4.4.3 EXAMPLE

In JDK, the hierarchy rooted in the abstract class `DataBuffer` is designed to wrap data arrays of various primitive types. `DataBuffer`'s subclasses `DataBuffer-Byte`, `DataBufferDouble`, `DataBufferFloat`, `DataBufferInt`, `DataBufferShort`, `DataBufferUShort` provide support for data arrays of specific primitive type (see Figure 4.17). The class `DataBuffer` also defines the constants `TYPE_BYTE`, `TYPE_DOUBLE`, `TYPE_FLOAT`, `TYPE_INT`, `TYPE_SHORT`, `TYPE_UNDEFINED`, and `TYPE_USHORT`. The JavaDoc comment for this class states, "the Java 2D API image classes use TYPE_BYTE, TYPE_USHORT, TYPE_INT, TYPE_SHORT, TYPE_FLOAT, and TYPE_DOUBLE DataBuffers to store image data."

What is interesting about encoding these data types is that these data types are used extensively in the `java.awt` package code base that supports images. Explicit type checking using a switch statement is also performed extensively for these data types (all the classes mentioned here are from `java.awt.image` package). For instance, `ComponentColorModel` class has 16 switch statements with case statements for some of these data types. Similarly, `Raster` class has 13 instances and `DirectColorModel` has 11 instances of switch-based explicit type checks. Classes `BandedSampleModel`, `ColorModel`, `ComponentSampleModel`, `IndexColorModel`, `MultiPixelPackedSampleModel`, `SampleModel`, and `SinglePixelPackedSample-Model` have at least one instance of switch-based explicit type check of these data types.

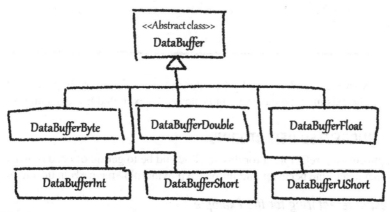

FIGURE 4.17

Explicit type checking is performed for the classes belonging to DataBuffer hierarchy.

Here is an example of how the explicit type check using a switch statement on concrete types is used in `ColorModel` class:

```
switch (transferType) {
  case DataBuffer.TYPE_BYTE:
    byte bdata[] = (byte[])inData;
    pixel = bdata[0] & 0xff;
    length = bdata.length;
    break;
  case DataBuffer.TYPE_USHORT:
    short sdata[] = (short[])inData;
    pixel = sdata[0] & 0xffff;
    length = sdata.length;
    break;
  case DataBuffer.TYPE_INT:
    int idata[] = (int[])inData;
    pixel = idata[0];
    length = idata.length;
    break;
  default:
    throw new
    UnsupportedOperationException("This method has not been "+
    "implemented for transferType" + transferType);
}
```

In this code, a data member `transferType` is defined as follows:

```
/**
* Data type of the array used to represent pixel values.
*/
protected int transferType;
```

This extensive use of encoded type values instead of employing polymorphism to exploit the existing type hierarchy indicates an Unexploited Encapsulation smell.

4.4.4 SUGGESTED REFACTORING

A straight-forward refactoring for this smell would be to get rid of conditional statements that determine behavior and introduce polymorphic methods in the hierarchy.

Suggested refactoring for the Example
We describe here a potential refactoring for the `ColorModel` class that was discussed above. The refactoring here could be that instead of the `ColorModel`

class holding the `transferType` variable of type `int`, we could use a `DataBuffer` instance instead. Thus,

```
protected int transferType;
```

refactors to:

```
protected DataBuffer dataBuffer;
```

The appropriate type of `DataBuffer` could be provided via a constructor of the `ColorModel`. Methods such as `getPixel()` and `getSize()` could be defined in the types belonging to the `DataBuffer` hierarchy, and the whole switch along with associated cases can be reduced to the following two statements:

```
pixel = dataBuffer.getPixel();
length = dataBuffer.getSize();
```

Since the `dataBuffer` reference will point to the `DataBuffer` type that was passed through the constructor, the appropriate `getPixel()` and `getSize()` methods within that particular type will be invoked. The `ColorModel` class does not have to be aware of the actual type of `DataBuffer` anymore.

(Please note that the client code that instantiates `ColorModel` has to provide the specific type of `DataBuffer` in the `ColorModel` constructor. Therefore, this client code is responsible for checking the type of input data and creating the corresponding `DataBuffer` type. For this, a switch-case statement may be needed either in the client code or in a factory class [54]. However, unlike the original code in which switch-case statements were spread all over the codebase, only one such switch-case is needed in the entire codebase.)

This solution brings multiple benefits to the design. First, since `ColorModel` is not aware of the type of `DataBuffer` anymore, it is more loosely coupled to the `DataBuffer` hierarchy. Thus, it is not impacted if there is a change in any of the types or if a new type is added. Second, the refactored design is cleaner and leaner, since the unnecessary conditional statements and type checks have been removed.

4.4.5 IMPACTED QUALITY ATTRIBUTES

- **Changeability** and **Extensibility**—A hierarchy helps encapsulate variation, and hence it is easy to modify existing variations or add support for new variations within that hierarchy without affecting the client code. With type-based switches, the client code needs to be changed whenever an existing type is changed or a new type is added. This adversely impacts changeability and extensibility.

- **Reusability**—Since the client code does type checks and executes certain functionality according to the type, reusability of the types in the hierarchy is impacted. This is because since some functionality is embedded in the client code, the types in the hierarchy do not contain all of the relevant functionality that may be needed to consider them as "reusable" units.

- **Testability**—When this smell is present, the same code segments may be replicated across the client code. This results in increased effort to test these fragments when compared to the effort if the code were to be provided within a hierarchy.

- **Reliability**—A common problem when using type-based checking is that programmers may overlook some of the checks. Such missing checks may manifest as defects.

ANECDOTE

The authors heard an interesting story at a software engineering conference from one of the attendees who worked for a telecommunications company. In one of his projects, he came across a class named Pulse which has an association with a hierarchy rooted in Phone. There are two subclasses of the Phone class namely CellPhone and LandPhone. While analyzing the design fragment, he realized that the code in the Pulse class was performing explicit type checks for types in the Phone hierarchy.

When he asked a project team member about this explicit type checking, the team member revealed that earlier they were making a polymorphic call to the Phone hierarchy to compute the pulse charges. However, a later requirement necessitated the computation of the data charges incurred by a cell phone. This required the CellPhone class to additionally support computation of data charges.

Now, in this project, the ownership of the Phone hierarchy was with the Device Team and the ownership of the Pulse class was with the Billing Team. These two teams were geographically distributed across two continents. To prevent sweeping changes to critical portions of the code, it was decided that changes to the critical portions could be made only by the teams responsible for them. Thus, any changes to the Phone hierarchy (and this included the change to CellPhone to support computation of data charges) could be made only by the Device Team. Upon receiving the requirement, the Billing Team (which was responsible for the Pulse class) requested the Device Team to make changes to the CellPhone class. Since the Device Team already had a huge backlog of change requests, they could not fulfill this requirement in time for the product release. Left with little choice and under time pressure, the Billing Team implemented the requirement by explicitly checking for the type of Phone and calling existing methods of CellPhone to compute data charges in the Pulse class itself! This implementation led to the Unexploited Encapsulation smell.

The key learning from this anecdote is how the dynamics of two teams working on the same product may introduce smells. A proper coordination between the Device and Billing teams could have avoided this problem. Furthermore, it is understandable that the inefficient solution adopted by the Billing Team was necessary, given the time pressure, but adequate measures should have been taken to document it and ensure that this problem was rectified later. A follow-up should have been done after the product release to ensure that the CellPhone and Pulse classes were modified appropriately and the Unexploited Encapsulation smell was removed. However, over and over again, project teams forget about the shortcuts that they have used and fail to rectify their mistakes. This negligence builds up technical debt over time and eventually results in steep increase in maintenance costs for the project.

4.4.6 ALIASES

This smell is also known in literature as:

- "Simulated polymorphism" [28]—This smell occurs when the code does conditional checks and chooses different behavior based on the type of the object to simulate polymorphism.

- "Improper use of switch statement" [7]—This smell occurs when switch statements are used instead of employing runtime polymorphism.

- "instanceof checks" [26]—This smell occurs when code has concentration of instanceof operators in a code block.

4.4.7 PRACTICAL CONSIDERATIONS

None.

Modularization Smells

5

*The principle of modularization advocates the creation of cohesive
and loosely coupled abstractions through techniques such as localization
and decomposition.*

To understand what modularization means and why it is important, let us consider the very case of this book! Let us imagine that we rewrite this book and explain it like one long story without any breaks. The resulting book will not have chapters, sections, or subsections. Each smell will be described in an ad hoc manner and there will be no definite order to the discussion of smells in the book. Further, there will be no cross references between smells (Figure 5.1).

How would readers react to such a book? Would this be an easy read? Clearly, readers would find it difficult to distinguish between smells. They will have to flip pages back and forth to gain a comprehensive understanding of smells. Further, they will be unable to gain a proper understanding of the various design principles

FIGURE 5.1

A book with no chapters and sub-sections is difficult to read.

because the principles would be intermingled and the description of those principles spread throughout the book. In summary, these problems would give readers a harrowing experience and reduce the usefulness of the book.

However, the current book organizes and aggregates smells based on the principles that are violated. The book "decomposes" the subject material into three logical parts, namely, the introduction and background, the catalog of smells, and the reflections. Additionally, each part is divided into several chapters that deal with a specific topic. This allows readers to quickly navigate to the particular design principle and the smells that are "categorized" under that principle. Additionally, most discussions about a design principle are "localized" in the introductory section of the concerned chapter, which allows readers to access all the information about a particular design principle at a single place in the book. In other words, the current book demonstrates the application of techniques such as decomposition and localization to achieve good modularization.

Similarly, it is important to follow the principle of modularization during software design. It should be pointed out that while modularization is generally considered to be a system-level concern (and concerns how we package abstractions to create logical modules), we use the term *module* here to mean *abstractions at the class level*, specifically, concrete classes, abstract classes, and interfaces. Thus, the goal behind modularization in the context of this book is to create cohesive and loosely coupled abstractions.

Figure 5.2 shows the enabling techniques that help apply the principle of modularization. These are:

- **Localize related data and methods.** Each abstraction should be cohesive in nature, i.e., the abstraction should keep related data and associated methods together.

- **Decompose abstractions to manageable size.** Break large abstractions into smaller ones that are moderate in size (i.e., neither too small, nor too large in size). For instance, a huge class not only makes it difficult for the reader to understand it, but also makes changes difficult because of possible interweaved responsibilities implemented by the class.

- **Create acyclic dependencies.** Abstractions should not be cyclically-dependent on each other. In other words, if a dependency graph is created, it should be free

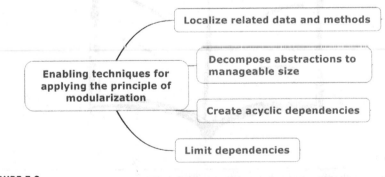

FIGURE 5.2

Enabling techniques for the principle of modularization.

of cycles. Otherwise, a change in an abstraction may result in a ripple effect across the entire design.

- **Limit dependencies.** Create abstractions with low fan-in and fan-out. *Fan-in* refers to the number of abstractions that are dependent on a given abstraction. Thus, a change in an abstraction with high fan-in may result in changes to a large number of its clients. *Fan-out* refers to the number of abstractions on which a given abstraction depends. A large fan-out indicates that any change in any of these abstractions may impact the given abstraction. Thus, to prevent a ripple effect due to potential changes, it is important to reduce the number of dependencies between abstractions in the design.

Each smell described in this chapter maps to a violation of an enabling technique. Figure 5.3 provides an overview of the smells that violate the principle of modularization and Table 5.1 provides an overview of mapping between the design smells and the

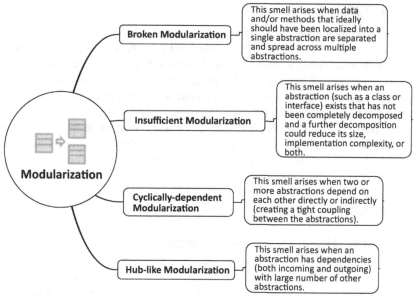

FIGURE 5.3

Smells resulting from the violation of the principle of modularization.

Table 5.1 Design Smells and Corresponding Violated Enabling Technique

Design Smells	Violated Enabling Technique
Broken modularization (5.1)	*Localize related data and methods*
Insufficient modularization (5.2)	*Decompose abstractions to manageable size*
Cyclically-dependent modularization (5.3)	*Create acyclic dependencies*
Hub-like modularization (5.4)	*Limit dependencies*

enabling technique(s) they violate. A detailed explanation of how these smells violate enabling techniques is discussed in the Rationale subsection of each smell description.

In the rest of this chapter, we discuss the specific smells that result due to the violation of the principle of modularization.

5.1 BROKEN MODULARIZATION

This smell arises when data and/or methods that ideally should have been localized into a single abstraction are separated and spread across multiple abstractions.

This smell commonly manifests as:

- Classes that are used as a holder for data but have no methods operating on the data within that class.

- Methods in a class that are more interested in members of other classes.

5.1.1 RATIONALE

One of the key enabling techniques for modularization is to "localize related data and methods." Lanza and Marinescu [21] recommend that "data and operations should collaborate harmoniously within the class to which they semantically belong." An abstraction suffering from this smell violates this enabling technique when the abstraction has only data members and the methods operating on the data are provided in some other abstraction(s).

When members that should ideally belong in a single abstraction are spread across multiple abstractions, the result is a tight coupling among the abstractions. Hence, this smell violates the principle of modularization. Since related members are "broken" and are made part of different abstractions, this smell is named Broken Modularization.

5.1.2 POTENTIAL CAUSES

Procedural thinking in object-oriented languages

Procedural languages provide language features such as "structs" (in C) and "record" (in Pascal) that hold data members together. Functions process the common data stored in structs/records. When developers from procedural language backgrounds such as C or Pascal move to an object-oriented language, they tend to separate data from functions operating on it, thereby resulting in this smell.

Lack of knowledge of existing design

Large real-world projects have a complex design and have a codebase that is spread over numerous packages. In such projects, developers usually work on a small part of the system and may not be aware of the other parts of the design. Due to this, while implementing a new feature, developers may be unaware of the most appropriate classes where data/methods should be placed; this may lead to members being misplaced in the wrong classes.

5.1.3 EXAMPLES

Example 1

Consider an application that manages peripheral devices remotely over a network. In this application, data related to a device is stored in a class named DeviceData. The methods for processing the device data are provided in a class named Device. What is interesting about these two classes is that DeviceData only has public data members with no methods, and device class holds an object of type DeviceData and provides methods for accessing and manipulating that data member (Figure 5.4). Clearly, since the data and methods that ideally should have been localized in a single class have been separated across Device and DeviceData classes, this design fragment is an instance of a Broken Modularization smell.

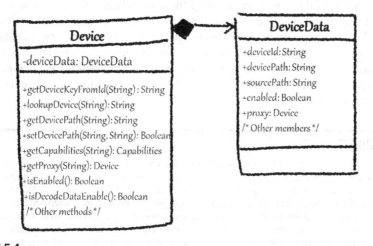

FIGURE 5.4

Class diagram in a device management application (Example 1).

Example 2

In an application for customer order processing, a key class was named as Order. Figure 5.5 shows the simplified version of this Order class; other classes interacting with the Order class such as Customer, Payment, ShoppingCart, LineItem, and Product are not shown in this figure. What was interesting about this design was that the Order class had only data members and the code operating on the data such as code that validates the order, calculates tax, and changes the order status was dispersed throughout the application. Clearly, the Order class along with its associated classes exhibits the Broken Modularization smell.

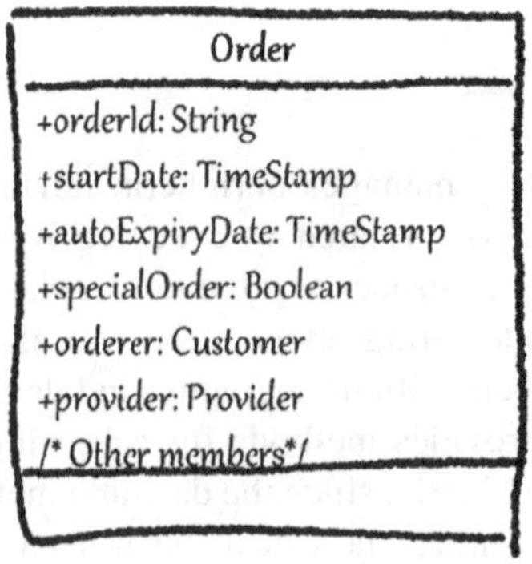

FIGURE 5.5

Order class that contains only public data members (Example 2).

As a result of this smell, maintaining the code related to Orders was a nightmare—for a fix or an enhancement, the code needed to be changed in multiple places. Further, since the members were public, any client code could change an Order object and trigger illegal state transitions. For instance, if a valid order state transition were to be "new" -> "paymentreceived" -> "processing" -> "shipped" -> "delivered" -> "closed", a client code could directly modify the Order object to move its state from "new" state to "closed" state.

ANECDOTE

During a lecture on software architecture and design that one of the authors was delivering one of the participants shared an experience from his project. This participant was associated with the development of a multiversion configuration tool for devices. This tool included a Graphical User Interface (GUI) editor, which first allowed the user to input configuration parameters and then invoked "checks" to verify whether the input data were acceptable. The software architecture was typical—there was a User Interface (UI) layer, a Business Logic layer, a Data layer, and a cross-cutting Utility layer. In version 1.0 of the editor, the "checks" were coded in the UI layer. In version 1.2, additional "checks" were added in the Utility layer. The new version 2.0 finally had "check" functionality in the UI, Business Logic, and Utility layer.

Unfortunately, there was no refactoring planned or executed to ensure quality of design as the software evolved. The lack of refactoring during the subsequent versions resulted in a design where the check functionality was dispersed across multiple components across layers. Every time a change or fix was needed in the check functionality, one would need to inspect all three layers where the functionality was implemented. Needless to say, it became extremely complex to manage and extend the check functionality. Eventually, due to lack of *localization* of these checks in a single layer, maintaining the check functionality resulted in massive effort and delays.

Even though this anecdote talks about an architectural problem, it is very relevant to this book:

- It highlights how even small design decisions can have a huge impact on the architecture and the project.
- It underlines the importance of adhering to fundamental principles and techniques such as localization, separation of concerns, and high cohesion and low coupling.

5.1.4 SUGGESTED REFACTORING

When the design is procedural in style, and has numerous data classes, apply "convert procedural design to objects" refactoring [7]. In this refactoring, we move the data members and the behavior associated with the data members into the same class.

- If a method is used more by another class (Target class) than by the class in which it is defined (Source class), apply "move method" refactoring and move that method from Source class to the Target class (see Figure 5.6).

- If a field is used more by another class (Target class) than the class in which it is defined (Source class), apply "move field" refactoring and move that field from Source class to the Target class (see Figure 5.6).

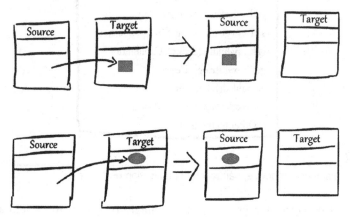

FIGURE 5.6

Suggested refactoring for Broken Modularization smell.

Suggested refactoring for Example 1

Since data and behavior for the same responsibility are split across DeviceData and Device, a natural refactoring is to combine them together in a single class (see Figure 5.7).

Suggested refactoring for Example 2

The following set of refactorings can be applied to refactor the example:

- Order class has multiple responsibilities. So, it needs to be broken into multiple classes such as OrderItem, OrderDetail, and Payment.

- Data members in Order need to be made private.

- Methods operating on the Order members need to be provided within the Order class itself. For example, validateOrder() could be a method in this class.

- Members not directly relating to Order should be moved to appropriate classes.

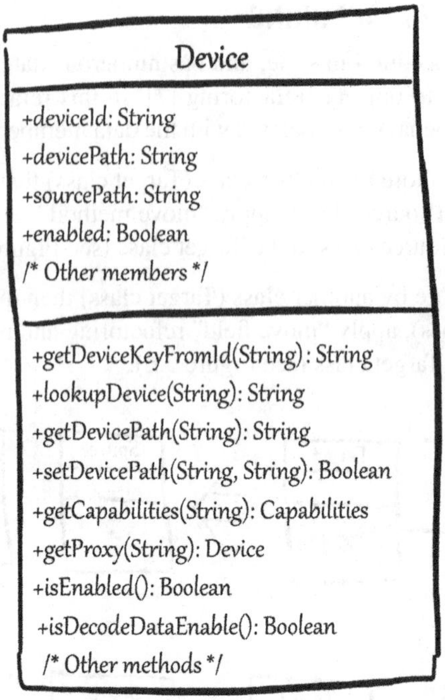

FIGURE 5.7

Suggested refactoring in device management application (Example 1).

It should be noted that grouping all seemingly related methods into a single abstraction to address Broken Modularization can lead to a Multifaceted Abstraction (Section 3.4) or Insufficient Modularization (Section 5.2) smell. Hence, due caution needs to be exercised while refactoring this smell.

5.1.5 IMPACTED QUALITY ATTRIBUTES

- **Understandability**: In case of Broken Modularization smell, to understand how a particular functionality is realized, one needs to understand all the associated methods and data that are spread across abstractions. This impacts understandability of the design.

- **Changeability** and **Extensibility:** When members that should ideally belong to an abstraction are separated across abstractions, supporting changes or enhancements becomes difficult because modifications may need to be made across multiple abstractions. This impacts changeability and extensibility of the design.

- **Reusability** and **Testability:** In the case of this smell, when we want to reuse or test a particular functionality, we have to use multiple abstractions together instead of a single abstraction. This impacts reusability and testability of the design.

- **Reliability:** When data and methods operating on that data are split across abstractions, encapsulation of those abstractions may be compromised and implementation details could get exposed. Further, when methods are misplaced in other abstractions, those methods are exposed to the implementation details (such as data structures and algorithms) of the abstractions in which they are placed. These factors could lead to defects affecting reliability.

5.1.6 ALIASES

This smell is also known in literature as:

- Class passively stores data [59]: This smell occurs when a class passively stores data and does not provide methods to operate on the data.

- Data class [7, 10, 57, 76]: This smell occurs when a class is used as a "dumb" data holder without complex functionality (but the class is usually heavily relied upon by other classes in the system).

- Data records [77]: This smell occurs when classes contain only data members without any methods.

- Record (class) [78]: This smell occurs when a class looks and feels much like Pascal record types; in this case, the class has all of its fields public and has no methods other than constructors and methods inherited from `Object` class.

- Data container [25]: This smell occurs when one class holds all the necessary data (and is called the Data Container), whereas the second class interacts with other classes implementing functionality related to the data of the first class.

- Misplaced operations [8]: This smell occurs when unexploited cohesive operations are outside (i.e., in other classes) instead of inside the same class.

- Feature envy [7, 76]: This smell occurs when there is a method that seems more interested in a class other than the one it is actually in.

- Misplaced control [30]: This smell occurs when a piece of functionality is unjustifiably separated from the data on which it operates.

5.1.7 PRACTICAL CONSIDERATIONS

Auto-generated code
The code generated from auto-code generators (from higher level models) often consists of a number of data classes. In the context of auto-generated code, it is not a recommended practice to directly change the generated code, since the models will be out-of-sync with the code. Hence, it may be acceptable to live with such data classes in generated code.

Data Transfer Objects (DTOs)

Often, a Data Transfer Object (DTO) is used to transfer data between processes to reduce the number of calls that would have been otherwise required in the context of remote interfaces. DTOs aggregate data and lack behavior; this is done consciously to facilitate serialization [84].

5.2 INSUFFICIENT MODULARIZATION

This smell arises when an abstraction exists that has not been completely decomposed, and a further decomposition could reduce its size, implementation complexity, or both.

There are two forms of this smell:

- **Bloated interface:** An abstraction has a large number of members in its public interface.

- **Bloated implementation:** An abstraction has a large number of methods in its implementation or has one or more methods with excessive implementation complexity.

The smell could also appear as a combination of these two forms, i.e., "bloated interface and implementation."

5.2.1 RATIONALE

Modularization concerns the logical partitioning of a software design so that the design becomes easy to understand and maintain. One of the key enabling techniques for effective modularization is to "decompose abstractions to manageable size." In this context, Lanza and Marinescu [21] recommend that "operations and classes should have a harmonious size, i.e., they should avoid both size extremities." When an abstraction has complex methods or a large number of methods, it violates this enabling technique and the principle of modularization. Since the abstraction is inadequately decomposed, we name this smell Insufficient Modularization.

MULTIFACETED ABSTRACTION VERSUS INSUFFICIENT MODULARIZATION

Note that Multifaceted Abstraction smell (Section 3.4) is different from Insufficient Modularization smell. In Multifaceted Abstraction, an abstraction addresses more than one responsibility, thereby violating the Single Responsibility Principle (SRP). In Insufficient Modularization, an abstraction violates the Principle of Decomposition, indicating that the abstraction is large, complex, or both. Interestingly, these two smells often occur together: It is common to see a large and complex abstraction that has multiple responsibilities. However, they are different smells: An abstraction could have a single responsibility, but could still be large and complex. Similarly, an abstraction could be small, but could still have multiple responsibilities.

5.2.2 **POTENTIAL CAUSES**

Providing centralized control
A typical cause of bloated implementation is centralizing control and assigning a large amount of work to a single abstraction or a method in an abstraction.

Creating large classes for use by multiple clients
Often, software developers create a large abstraction so that it can be used by multiple clients. However, creating a single large abstraction that fits the needs of multiple clients leads to many problems, such as reduced changeability and extensibility of the design (see the Impacted Quality Attributes section).

Grouping all related functionality together
Often, inexperienced developers tend to group together and provide all related functionality in a single class or interface without understanding how the Single Responsibility Principle (SRP) should be properly applied. This results in bloated interfaces or classes.

5.2.3 **EXAMPLES**

Example 1: bloated implementation
An example of Insufficient Modularization with bloated implementation is `java.net.SocketPermission` in JDK 1.7. The problem with the `SocketPermission` class is that the sum of Cyclomatic complexities of its methods[1] is 193! In particular, one of its private methods `getMask()` has a Cyclomatic complexity of 81 due to its complex conditional checks with nested loops, conditionals, etc.

Example 2: bloated interface and implementation
The `java.awt.Component` class is an abstraction for graphical objects such as buttons and checkboxes. This abstract class is an example of Insufficient Modularization that has bloated interface as well as bloated implementation. It is a massive class with 332 methods (of which 259 are public), 11 nested/inner classes, and 107 fields (including constants) (see Figure 5.8). The source file of this class spans 10,102 lines of code! The sum of Cyclomatic complexity of its methods is 1143, indicating that the implementation is dense. Many methods belonging to the class have high Cyclomatic complexity; for example, the method `dispatchEventImpl(Event)` has a Cyclomatic complexity of 65.

Other examples from JDK 1.7 that exhibit bloated interface and implementation include:

- `java.swing.JTable` (Figure 5.9) has 44 attributes and 203 methods, and 9608 lines of code (as of JDK version 1.7).

- `java.lang.BigInteger` has 28 fields and 103 methods.

- `java.util.Calendar` has 81 fields and 71 methods.

---

[1] The sum of Cyclomatic complexity of methods in a class is also known by the metric name Weighted Method per Class (WMC).

ANECDOTE

One of the participants at the Smells Forum shared her experience that highlighted how the viscosity of the environment can lead to the introduction of Insufficient Modularization smell. She had just joined a globally distributed software development project concerning a critical clinical workflow product. The ownership of the code base was with the central team located in Country A, and she was a part of the offshore development team located in Country B.

In the first few weeks of her involvement, she realized that there were a number of smells in the design and code. For instance, she came across a class in the source code that was very long and dense – it had around 40,000 source lines of code and the Weighted Methods per Class - i.e., the sum of Cyclomatic complexities of the methods of a class – exceeded 2000! In other words, this class was a clear example of Insufficient Modularization. When she approached her team members, she realized that they were already aware of the size and complexity of this class. In fact, she also came to know that this class was prone to defects and was subjected to frequent changes.

Being new to the project, she was puzzled about why this class was so huge and why no refactoring had been performed on it so far. Upon further probing, she found out that the real problem was due to the process being followed in the project! There were two aspects that contributed to this problem. First, to prevent unwarranted modifications to the critical product, the project relied on a stringent process to control changes to the source code. As per this process, whenever a new class was introduced by the team in Country B, it needed to be approved by the central team in Country A because it owned the code base. This approval process was a long and arduous affair requiring multiple email and telephone interactions to champion the need for adding a new class.

Second, the project management was understandably very concerned about the timely release of this product in the market and continuously pressurized the team in Country B to finish coding and bug-fixing activities as early as possible. Naturally, in such a situation, the team in Country B wanted to avoid the time-consuming approval process for new classes. Consequently, the team decided not to introduce any new classes and instead decided to merge all new code in existing classes. This led to the bloating of existing classes in the design.

The nature of the change approval process also discouraged refactoring. For instance, refactoring the class with 40000 lines would require breaking it up into several smaller cohesive classes. Since the approval for all these newly-created classes would require a long time, the team in Country B was not keen to refactor such large and complex classes. Since refactoring was not taken up at regular intervals, even during the maintenance phase, the existing classes continued to bloat and became increasingly bug-prone.

There are two key take-aways from this anecdote:

- Although software processes are meant to facilitate the creation of higher quality software, if they are difficult to follow or not user-friendly, people will either bypass the process, or avoid it completely, or take short-cuts thus affecting the quality of software. Organizations should, therefore, strive to make software processes user-friendly.
- Project management is often unaware of the impact of software processes. In the above case, if the project management were to be aware of the nature of the change approval process and its impact on the schedule, they could have taken appropriate steps to avoid incurring technical debt. For instance, they could have optimized the change approval process (perhaps by having it done in the same country) so that the schedule is met. Alternately, they could have modified the schedule to ensure that the team in Country B feels encouraged to follow good design practices and the change approval process set in place.

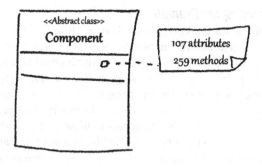

FIGURE 5.8

java.awt.Component class is large and dense (Example 2).

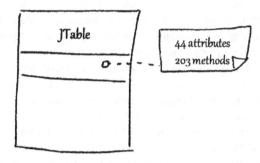

FIGURE 5.9

java.swing.JTable class is large and dense (Example 2).

5.2.4 SUGGESTED REFACTORING

Refactoring for bloated interface

- If a subset of the public interface consists of closely related (cohesive) members, then extract that subset to a separate abstraction.

- If a class consists of two or more subsets of members and each set of members is cohesive, split these subsets into separate classes.

- If the class interface serves multiple clients via client-specific methods, consider applying the Interface Segregation Principle (ISP) to separate the original interface into multiple client-specific interfaces.

Refactoring for bloated implementation

- If the method logic is complex, introduce private helper methods that help simplify the code in that method.

- In case an abstraction has both Multifaceted Abstraction smell as well as Insufficient Modularization smell, encapsulate each responsibility within separate (new or existing) abstractions.

Suggested refactoring for Example 1

Create helper methods for the complex methods such as getMask() in java.net. SocketPermission. For example, the private getMask() method has code for skipping whitespace in the passed string argument, which could be extracted to a new helper method. Interestingly, getMask() method also has duplicate blocks of code for checking characters in four known strings: CONNECT, RESOLVE, LISTEN, and ACCEPT. One possible refactoring is to create a helper method named matchForKnownStrings() that checks for the characters in these four strings. Now, the code within the getMask() method can be simplified by making four calls to matchForKnownStrings() instead of duplicating code four times for making these checks.

Suggested refactoring for Example 2

The abstract class Component provides default functionality to create lightweight components that can be defined by extending the Component class. It assembles all the required default functionality that a new component may reuse. It covers a number of concerns such as event listening, component layout and positioning, focus, fonts, and graphics configuration, which makes the class huge.

Hence, a suggested refactoring is to separate out these concerns into different abstractions and make the Component class use these abstractions via delegation. For instance, event listening can be separated out as an interface (say, ComponentEvents) and a default implementation (say, DefaultComponentEvents class) of the event listening functionality for components can be provided by realizing this interface. The Component class can now use DefaultComponentEvents class via delegation for listening to events. Any custom support for event listening can now be realized by providing a suitable implementation of the ComponentEvents interface.

Additionally, methods such as getFontMetrics(), createImage(), createVolatileImage() can be moved to FontMetrics, Image, and VolatileImage classes, respectively. To summarize, by suitably extracting abstractions or moving methods to classes, the Insufficient Modularization smell in Component class can be addressed.

5.2.5 IMPACTED QUALITY ATTRIBUTES

- **Understandability:** Clients find bloated interfaces hard to comprehend and use. Similarly, it is difficult for developers to understand and maintain an abstraction with bloated implementation. The complexity of the abstraction thus impacts its understandability.

- **Changeability** and **Extensibility:** When an abstraction has a bloated interface, typically there are numerous clients accessing it. Dependency of the clients on such an interface imposes a constraint on the interface's changeability and extensibility, since changes to the interface (or sometimes even its implementation) have the potential to affect the large number of clients that are coupled to it. Further, when an abstraction has bloated implementation, it becomes difficult to figure out the places in the abstraction that need be modified to accommodate a change or enhancement.

- **Testability:** An abstraction with this smell poses considerable challenges to testing that abstraction. For instance, a complex method implementation with high Cyclomatic complexity requires a proportionate number of test cases to exercise all its paths (Note: Cyclomatic complexity of a method corresponds to the number of paths in that method, and hence the number of minimum test cases needed for testing that method).

- **Reliability:** It is also well known that complexity breeds defects. Thus, a class with complex methods is likely to harbor many runtime problems thus impacting it's reliability.

5.2.6 ALIASES

This smell is also known in the literature as:

- God class [28]: This smell occurs when a class has 50 or more methods or attributes.

- Fat interface [79]: This smell occurs when the interface provided by the class is not cohesive.

- Blob class [76]: This smell occurs when a class is very large and has a high complexity.

- Classes with complex control flow [59]: This smell occurs when a class has a very high Cyclomatic complexity.

- Too much responsibility [65]: This smell occurs when a class has "too much" responsibility.

- Local breakable (class) [77]: This smell occurs when a class has excessive responsibility and has many local dependencies.

5.2.7 PRACTICAL CONSIDERATIONS

Key classes

Key classes [52] abstract most important concepts in a system and tend to be large, complex, and coupled with many other classes in the system. While it is difficult to avoid such classes in real-world systems, it is still important to consider how they could be decomposed so that they become easier to maintain.

Auto-generated code

Often, classes that are created as part of automatically generated code have complex methods. For example, tools for generating parsers usually create complex code with extensive conditional logic. In practice, it is difficult to change the generator tool or manually refactor such complex code.

5.3 CYCLICALLY-DEPENDENT MODULARIZATION

This smell arises when two or more abstractions depend on each other directly or indirectly (creating a tight coupling between the abstractions).

5.3.1 RATIONALE

A cyclic dependency is formed when two or more abstractions have direct or indirect dependencies on each other. Cyclic dependencies between abstractions violate the Acyclic Dependencies Principle (ADP)[79] and Ordering Principle [80]. In the presence of cyclic dependencies, the abstractions that are cyclically-dependent may need to be understood, changed, used, tested, or reused together. Further, in case of cyclic dependencies, changes in one class (say A) may lead to changes in other classes in the cycle (say B). However, because of the cyclic nature, changes in B can have ripple effects on the class where the change originated (i.e., A). Large and indirect cyclic dependencies are usually difficult to detect in complex software systems and are a common source of subtle bugs. Since this smell is a result of not adhering to the enabling technique, "create acyclic dependencies," we name this smell Cyclically dependent Modularization.

A special form of cyclic dependency is sometimes exhibited within an inheritance hierarchy. A subtype has a dependency on its supertype because of the inheritance relationship. However, when the supertype also depends on the subtype (for instance, by having an explicit reference to the subtype), it results in a cyclic dependency. We refer to this special form of cyclic dependency as Cyclic Hierarchy smell, and discuss it in detail in Section 6.10.

UNDERSTANDING CYCLES

To better understand the impact of cyclic dependencies, let us first understand some terms related to cycles. A *dependency diagram* is a directed graph that shows the dependency relationship among abstractions. In a dependency diagram, if you start from one abstractions and reach the same abstraction by following one or more path(s) formed by the dependency edges, the abstractions in the followed path form a *cycle*. A *tangle* consists of more than one cycle. When abstractions are tightly coupled by a large number of direct or indirect cyclic dependencies, they form a *tangled design*, and the dependency graph looks unpleasantly complex.

Figure 5.10 shows a tangle between six abstractions in java.util package. In this graph, you can see cycles of various lengths. (It should be noted that the graph also shows Cyclic Hierarchy smell.)

In this design, any change to an abstraction involved in this dependency chain has the potential to affect other abstractions that depend on it, causing ripple effects or cascade of changes. A designer must, therefore, strive for designs that do not consist of tangles.

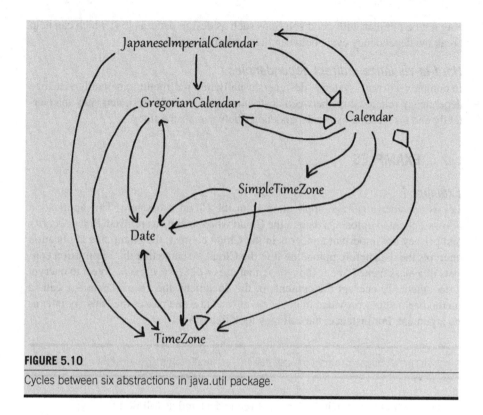

FIGURE 5.10

Cycles between six abstractions in java.util package.

5.3.2 POTENTIAL CAUSES

Improper responsibility realization

Often, when some of the members of an abstraction are wrongly misplaced in another abstraction, the members may refer to each other, resulting in a cyclic dependency between the abstractions.

Passing a self reference

A method invocation from one abstraction to another often involves data transfer. If instead of explicitly passing only the required data, the abstraction passes its own reference (for instance, via "this") to the method of another abstraction, a cyclic dependency is created.

Implementing call-back functionality

Circular dependencies are often unnecessarily introduced between two classes while implementing call-back[2] functionality. This is because inexperienced developers

---

[2] A call-back method is one that is passed as an argument to another method, and is invoked at a later point in time (for instance, when an event occurs).

may not be familiar with good solutions such as design patterns [54] which can help break the dependency cycle between the concerned classes.

Hard-to-visualize indirect dependencies

In complex software systems, designers usually find it difficult to mentally visualize dependency relationships between abstractions. As a result, designers may inadvertently end up creating cyclic dependencies between abstractions.

5.3.3 EXAMPLES

Example 1

Let us consider a storage application from the Cloud ecosystem. This application allows a client to upload its data to the Cloud where it can be archived. Since security and privacy are important concerns in the Cloud context, the client-side application encrypts the data before uploading it to the Cloud. Assume that this application consists of a class named SecureDocument that uses a DESEncryption[3] object to encrypt a document. To encrypt the contents of the document, the SecureDocument calls a method encrypt() provided in DESEncryption class and passes the "this" pointer as its argument. For instance, the call may look like this:

```
SecureDocument encryptedDocument = desEncryption.encrypt(this);
```

The method encrypt in DESEncryption is declared as follows:

```
SecureDocument encrypt(SecureDocument docToEncrypt)
```

Using the "this" pointer within the encrypt method, the DESEncryption object fetches the contents of the document, encrypts it, and returns an encrypted document object. Thus, SecureDocument and DESEncryption know about each other, leading to the Cyclically-dependent Modularization smell between them, as shown in Figure 5.11.

Example 2

Consider the case of a medical application that supports encryption of scanned images before storing them on a drive. This application consists of a SecurityManager class that fetches an encrypted image from an Image class (Figure 5.12). The Image class, in turn, uses an Encryption class to encrypt its contents; during this process, the Image class passes the "this" pointer to the encrypt() method within the Encryption class. When invoked, the encrypt() method within the Encryption

---

[3]DES stands for Data Encryption Standard; it is a well-known symmetric key algorithm for encrypting data.

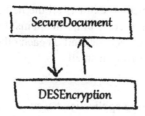

FIGURE 5.11

Cyclic dependency between SecureDocument and DESEncryption (Example 1).

FIGURE 5.12

Cyclic dependency between Image and Encryption classes (Example 2).

class fetches the `Image` contents, and returns the contents after encryption. Here, the `Image` and `Encryption` classes are dependent on each other, hence this design exhibits the Cyclically-dependent Modularization smell.

Example 3

Consider an order-processing module in an e-commerce application. In this application, assume that you have two classes named `Order` and `OrderImpl` that provide support for order processing (Figure 5.13). The `Order` class maintains information about an order and the associated information about the ordered items. The method `getAmount()` in `Order` class uses `computeAmount()` method of `OrderImpl` class. In

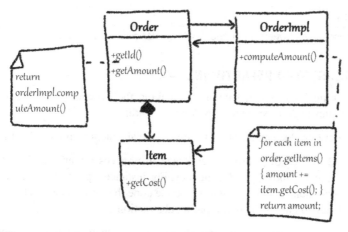

FIGURE 5.13

Cyclic dependency between Order and OrderImpl classes (Example 3).

turn, the `computeAmount()` method extracts all the items associated with the `Order` object and computes the sum of costs of all the items that are a part of the order. In effect, classes `Order` and `OrderImpl` depend on each other, hence the design has the Cyclically-dependent Modularization smell.

Example 4

Assume that an order-processing application has an `Order` class encapsulating information about an order such as `name`, `id`, and `amount`. The `getAmount()` method of the `Order` class uses `computeAmount()` method of `TaxCalculator` class. The `computeAmount()` method fetches all the items associated with the `Order` object and computes a summation of each item cost. In addition, it calls `calculateTax()` method, adds the computed tax with the running amount, and returns it. In this case, classes `Order` and `TaxCalculator` depend on each other, as shown in Figure 5.14. Clearly, the design fragment shows the Cyclically-dependent Modularization smell.

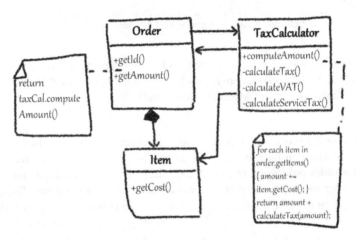

FIGURE 5.14

Cyclic dependency between Order and TaxCalculator classes (Example 4).

5.3.4 SUGGESTED REFACTORING

The refactoring for this smell involves breaking the dependency cycle. There are many strategies to do this; some important ones are:

- **Option 1:** Introduce an interface for one of the abstractions involved in the cycle.

- **Option 2:** In case one of the dependencies is unnecessary and can be safely removed, then remove that dependency. For instance, apply "move method" (and "move field") refactoring to move the code that introduces cyclic dependency to one of the participating abstractions.

- **Option 3:** Move the code that introduces cyclic dependency to an altogether different abstraction.

- **Option 4:** In case the abstractions involved in the cycle represent a semantically single object, merge the abstractions into a single abstraction.

As an illustration, consider the direct cyclic dependency between class A and class B (Figure 5.15). Figure 5.16, Figure 5.17, Figure 5.18, and Figure 5.19 respectively show the four options for refactoring to remove the cycle.

Suggested refactoring for Example 1

For the storage application from the Cloud ecosystem, a suggested refactoring is to introduce an interface IEncryption and have the class DESEncryption implement the interface. The SecureDocument class now depends on IEncryption interface instead of depending on the concrete DESEncryption class. This results in a design that removes the cyclic dependency. Interfaces are less likely to change than a concrete type, thus the resultant design is more stable than the original design with cyclic dependency. For instance, a

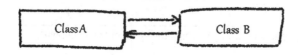

FIGURE 5.15

Cyclic dependency between classes A and B.

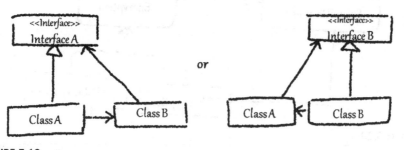

FIGURE 5.16

Breaking a cyclic dependency by introducing an interface (Option 1).

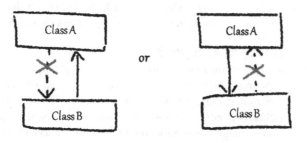

FIGURE 5.17

Breaking a cyclic dependency by removing a dependency (Option 2).

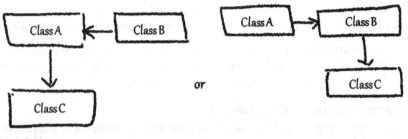

FIGURE 5.18

Breaking a cyclic dependency by introducing another abstraction (Option 3).

FIGURE 5.19

Breaking a cyclic dependency by merging the abstractions (Option 4).

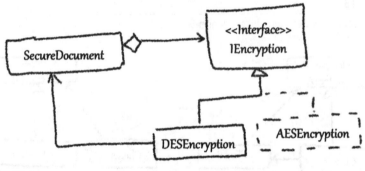

FIGURE 5.20

Suggested refactoring for cyclic dependency between SecureDocument and DESEncryption (Example 1).

new class such as AESEncryption (that supports the AES[4] encryption algorithm) can be added to the design without affecting the SecureDocument class (Figure 5.20).

Suggested refactoring for Example 2

For the healthcare application that requires image encryption, a suggested refactoring is to shift the responsibility of encrypting an image object from Image class to SecurityManager class to break the cycle. In the refactored design, SecurityManager class depends on Image and Encryption classes. SecurityManger class directly invokes image encryption on Encryption class by providing the

---

[4] Advanced Encryption Standard.

Image object. The Encryption class, in turn, uses the Image object reference provided by the SecurityManager to fetch the content of the image object, encrypt the content, and return the encrypted content to SecurityManager. Here, by removing the dependency from Image class to Encryption class, the cyclic dependency is broken (Figure 5.21).

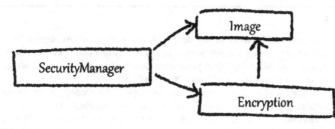

FIGURE 5.21

Suggested refactoring for cyclic dependency between Image and Encryption (Example 2).

Suggested refactoring for Example 3

In the case of the Order example, classes Order and OrderImpl are tightly coupled to each other, and they semantically represent an order abstraction. Since the OrderImpl class has only one method, this class could be merged into the Order class. When we apply this refactoring, the cyclic dependency disappears, since there is only one class (Figure 5.22).

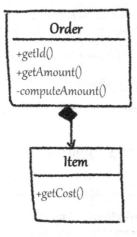

FIGURE 5.22

Suggested refactoring for cyclic dependency in order-processing module (Example 3).

Suggested refactoring for Example 4

To refactor the `Order` example with the `TaxCalculator` class, we can employ "move method" refactoring. The `computeAmount()` originally belonging to `TaxCalculator` class can be moved to `Order` class. By moving this method, we eliminate the dependency from `TaxCalculator` to `Order` class (Figure 5.23).

ANECDOTE

One of the authors was working as a software design consultant for a startup company. The product that the company was developing was originally designed by an experienced architect, but he had recently quit the company. Most developers in the team were fresh engineers, a company strategy intended to keep costs low until they could get further funding.

With lack of experienced designers or architects, development proceeded without any focus on architecture or design quality. The management prided itself on its pragmatic view and pushed the development team to meet functional requirements and get the product to the market on time.

In this process, the author noticed that numerous compromises were made in the design. For instance, the original design was a layered architecture with strict separation of concerns. However, with no architect or designer to oversee the development, developers started introducing business logic in UI classes such as `Buttons` and `Panels`. Worse, low-level utility classes such as `GraphUtilities` also directly referred to GUI classes. These aspects clearly indicate violation of the layering style.

To demonstrate the extent of the problems to management, the author ran dependency analysis tools and found innumerable dependency cycles across layers. He also used visualization tools to demonstrate how the whole codebase was excessively tangled. It was evident that touching code in any class could potentially break the working software. Due to the extent of the problem and the impending release, management could not take immediate remedial steps.

While the product was well received by the customers when it was launched, the design was so brittle that even small changes would break the working software. Upon the recommendation of the author, the management recruited an experienced designer as the architect. All further development was frozen, and considerable refactoring was performed to clean up the design. After a few months of refactoring, the design quality significantly improved to an extent that development tasks could commence. However, because the technical debt had to be repaid through extensive refactoring, the second release was delayed considerably from its originally scheduled date.

Key take-aways from this experience are:
- It is important to have a designated architect who actively ensures that architectural erosion or design decay does not happen.
- If the technical debt is not repaid through periodic refactoring, it will eventually stall the project.

5.3.5 IMPACTED QUALITY ATTRIBUTES

- **Understandability:** Since all the abstractions that are cyclically-dependent can be understood only together, it impacts the understandability of the design.

- **Changeability** and **Extensibility:** Making changes to an abstraction that is part of a cycle can cause ripple effects across classes in the dependency chain (including the original abstraction). This makes it difficult to understand, analyze, and implement new features or changes to any abstraction that is part of a

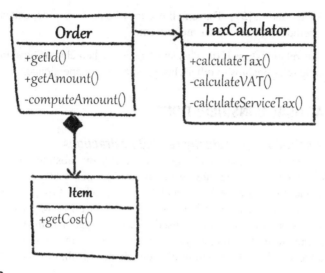

FIGURE 5.23

Suggested refactoring for cyclic dependency between Order and TaxCalculator (Example 4).

dependency cycle. Hence, this smell impacts the changeability and extensibility of the design.

- **Reusability:** The abstractions in a dependency cycle can only be reused together. Hence, this smell impacts reusability of the design.

- **Testability:** Since it is difficult to independently test the abstractions participating in the cycle, this smell impacts testability.

- **Reliability:** In a dependency chain, changes to any abstraction can potentially manifest as runtime problems across other abstractions. For instance, consider the case where a value is represented as a double in a class and that the class is part of a long cycle. If the value is changed to float type in the class, the impact of this change on other classes may not be evident at compile-time; however, it is possible that it manifests as a floating-point error at runtime in other classes.

5.3.6 ALIASES

This smell is also known in literature as:

- Dependency cycles [72, 73, 74]: This smell occurs when a class has circular references.

- Cyclic dependencies [71, 75, 76]: This smell occurs when classes are tightly coupled and mutually dependent.

- Cycles [9]: This smell occurs when one of the (directly or indirectly) used classes is the class itself.

- Bidirectional relation [57]: This smell occurs when two-way dependencies between methods of two classes are present.

- Cyclic class relationships [70]: This smell occurs when classes have improper or questionable relationships to other classes, such as codependence.

5.3.7 PRACTICAL CONSIDERATIONS

Unit cycles between conceptually related abstractions

Cycles of size one (i.e., cycles that consist of exactly two abstractions) are known as *unit cycles*. Often, unit cycles are formed between conceptually related pairs. For instance, consider the classes `Matcher` and `Pattern` (both part of `java.util.regex` package) that are cyclically-dependent on each other (see Figure 5.24). These two classes are almost always understood, used, or reused together. In real-world projects, it is common to find such unit cycles. However, since the unit cycle is small, it is easier to understand, analyze, and implement changes within the two abstractions that are part of the cycle.

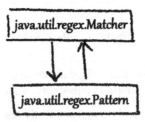

FIGURE 5.24

Cyclic dependency between Matcher and Pattern.

However, large cycles and tangles (which are commonly observed in large real-world software systems) make it considerably difficult to maintain the software. It is, therefore, important for software designers in real-world projects to focus on reducing cyclic dependencies between abstractions.

5.4 HUB-LIKE MODULARIZATION

This smell arises when an abstraction has dependencies (both incoming and outgoing) with a large number of other abstractions.

5.4.1 RATIONALE

"High cohesion and low coupling" is the basis for effective modularization. Meyer's "few interfaces" rule for modularity says that "every module should communicate with as few others as possible." [24] For effective modularization, we must follow the enabling technique "limit dependencies." When an abstraction has large number of incoming and outgoing dependencies, the principle of modularization is violated.

When an abstraction has a large number of incoming dependencies and outgoing dependencies, the dependency structure looks like a hub, hence we name this smell Hub-like Modularization.

5.4.2 POTENTIAL CAUSES

Improper responsibility assignment (to a hub class)
When an abstraction is overloaded with too many responsibilities, it tends to become a hub class with a large number of incoming as well as outgoing dependencies. In other words, most classes in the design will talk to this hub class, and this hub class also communicates with most other classes.

"Dump-all" utility classes
Classes that provide supporting functionality often grow very large and get coupled with a large number of other classes. Consider the `javax.swing.SwingUtilities` class that is used by numerous other classes in the swing package. This is not surprising given the fact that it is a utility class. However, what is surprising is the number of UI classes in swing package it refers back to—such a large number of incoming and outgoing dependencies makes this class a hub class. In our experience, we have seen that utility classes often become common "dump-all-ancillary-functionality-here" classes that turn out to be hub classes.

5.4.3 EXAMPLES

Example 1
The `java.awt.Font` class represents fonts and supports functionality to render text as a sequence of glyphs on `Graphics` and `Component` objects. This class has 19 incoming dependencies and 34 outgoing dependencies, as shown in Figure 5.25. Note that these do not include dependencies from method implementations within this class.

Example 2
`java.util.Component` class abstracts graphical objects that can be displayed on the screen, such as buttons and scrollbars. This class has 498 incoming dependencies and 71 outgoing dependencies, as shown in Figure 5.26. Note that these do not include dependencies from method implementations within this class.

5.4.4 SUGGESTED REFACTORING

A refactoring solution for this smell may involve applying one or more of the following:

- If the hub class has multiple responsibilities, indicating improper responsibility assignment, the refactoring suggestion is to split up the responsibilities across multiple new/old abstractions so that the number of incoming and outgoing dependencies is reduced.

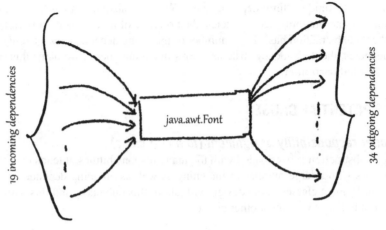

FIGURE 5.25

Incoming and outgoing dependencies of java.awt.Font class (Example 1).

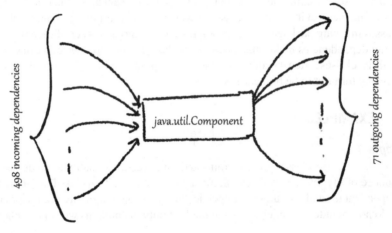

FIGURE 5.26

Incoming and outgoing dependencies of java.awt.Component class (Example 2).

- If the dependencies are caused due to misplaced members in the hub class, the refactoring suggestion is to assign those members to appropriate abstractions.

- Sometimes the Chain of Responsibility [54] pattern can be used to reduce the number of incoming dependencies on a hub class. For example, in the scenario where a number of candidate receivers are interested in value or data held by the hub class, the number of incoming dependencies on the hub class will be high. To address this, one possible refactoring is to connect all the receivers via a Chain of Responsibility and have the hub class notify only the first receiver in the chain about the change in value. The receiver would, in turn, cascade the notification to other receivers in the chain. With this refactoring, the number of incoming dependencies on the hub class drastically reduces.

Refactoring for Example 1

The `java.awt.Font` class has some members that could be assigned to more suitable classes. For instance, consider the overloaded versions of the `createGlyphVector()`

```
public GlyphVector createGlyphVector(FontRenderContext frc.
CharacterIterator ci) {
  return (GlyphVector)new StandardGlyphVector(this, ci, frc);
}
```

methods; see one definition of the method below:

The method definition of `createGlyphVector()` shows that the `Font` class has direct knowledge of `GlyphVector` class. Although, conceptually, glyphs are related to fonts, glyph-related functionality need not belong to `Font` class, and could be moved to `GlyphVector` class. Now, any client code that originally depended on the `Font` class for glyph related functionality can directly use the `GlyphVector` class. Such refactorings can help reduce some of the incoming as well as outgoing dependencies of the `Font` class.

Refactoring for Example 2

Considering the size, complexity, and number of dependencies of `java.awt.Component` class, different kinds of refactorings (such as move method, split class, extract class, and extract method) may be performed. To illustrate how a "move method" refactoring can be applied, consider the following public methods of this class:

```
FontMetrics getFontMetrics(Font font)
Image createImage(ImageProducer producer)
Image createImage(int width, int height)
VolatileImage createVolatileImage(int width, int height)
VolatileImage createVolatileImage(int width, int height,
ImageCapabilities caps)
```

It can be argued that these are ancillary or supportive methods that do not belong to `Component` class. If we move these methods to relevant classes such as `FontMetrics`, `Image`, and `VolatileImage`, the related dependencies would also move to these classes. This, in turn, would help reduce the number of incoming and outgoing dependencies of the `Component` class.

5.4.5 IMPACTED QUALITY ATTRIBUTES

- **Understandability:** For understanding a hub class, one may have to look up and understand many other classes that the class depends on. Further, the presence of a hub class may make it difficult to understand dependencies among various classes. These factors impact understandability of the design.

- **Changeability, Extensibility,** and **Reliability:** When an abstraction is depended upon by numerous other abstractions, any modification to that abstraction has the potential to affect all the other abstractions that depend on it. For this reason, modifying a hub class is difficult. Similarly, when an abstraction depends on numerous other abstractions, it is subject to ripple effects from the modifications to any of these abstractions. For this reason, a hub class can be affected by numerous other abstractions, and can in turn affect abstractions that depend on that hub class. In other words, designs with hub classes are prone to ripple effects of changes done to the design, impacting the changeability and extensibility of the design. Sometimes (as previously discussed in the case of Cyclically-dependent Modularization), these ripple effects may manifest as runtime problems, impacting reliability.

- **Reusability** and **Testability:** Given the large number of outgoing dependencies that the hub class has with other classes in the design, it is difficult to decouple the hub class to reuse it in other contexts or test it independently.

5.4.6 ALIASES

This smell is also known in literature as:

- Bottlenecks [55, 71]: This smell occurs when a class refers to many other classes and is used by many other classes.

- Local hubs [77]: This smell occurs when a type has many immediate dependencies and many immediate dependents.

- Man-in-the-middle [25]: This smell occurs when the design has a central class that serves as a kind of a mediator for many other classes or even other modules.

5.4.7 PRACTICAL CONSIDERATIONS

Core abstractions

If you analyze large object oriented applications, you will find that there are a few "core abstractions" that play a central role in the design. From our experience, we find that it is usually difficult to keep the number of incoming as well as outgoing dependencies low for such core abstractions. For instance, consider the class java.lang.Class in JDK. This class represents all classes and interfaces in a Java application, and hence is a core abstraction in JDK. Since the java.lang.Class has more than 1000 incoming dependencies and 40 outgoing dependencies, it has Hub-like Modularization smell. However, limiting the number of incoming and outgoing dependencies of such core abstractions is difficult (if not impossible).

Hierarchy Smells

6

The principle of hierarchy advocates the creation of a hierarchical organization of abstractions using techniques such as classification, generalization, substitutability, and ordering.

Did you know that our planet houses more than 8.7 million species? Imagine trying to study all these species and figuring out how they are unique and how they differ from each other. How can we deal with this large-scale bio-diversity?

Carl Linnaeus, also known as the Father of Taxonomy, dealt with this complex bio-diversity by proposing a taxonomy for the species [32]. This taxonomy helped organize all the species through a hierarchical classification which consists of kingdoms which are divided into classes which in turn are divided into orders, families, genus, and species. Figure 6.1 shows how "human species" would be classified under this taxonomy.

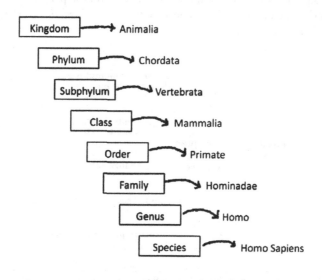

FIGURE 6.1

Linnaeus' taxonomy showing the hierarchical classification of the human species.

In summary, a hierarchical organization offers a powerful tool for dealing with complex diversity in real-world entities. It helps order the entities, deal with similarities and differences, and think in terms of generalizations and specializations.

Modern software is extremely complex and requires a way to understand, reason about, and analyze the relationships between a large number of real-world entities. Organizing these entities in a hierarchy is one of the key tools that help deal with this complexity during software development.

Object-oriented languages support two kinds of hierarchies: type hierarchy (is-a relationship) and object hierarchy (part-of relationship) [47]. In this chapter, we concern ourselves with type hierarchies and use the term hierarchy synonymously with type hierarchy.

So, now that we understand the importance and benefit of the principle of hierarchy, how do we apply this principle in software design? We list below some key enabling techniques that we have gleaned from our experience that allow us to apply the principle of hierarchy in software design (see Figure 6.2).

- **Apply meaningful classification**. Classify types to create a hierarchical organization using the following two steps:

    - Identify commonalities and variations among types. The commonalities are captured in a new abstraction which is referred as a supertype (this process is known as generalization). The variations are encapsulated in subtypes that inherit common behavior from supertypes. For a meaningful application of classification, the focus during this step should be more on capturing the commonalities and variation in the *behavior* of types rather than their data.

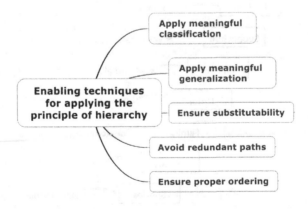

FIGURE 6.2

Enabling techniques for the principle of hierarchy.

- Classify the supertypes and subtypes in levels to create a hierarchy. The resulting hierarchy should have general types towards the root and the specialized types towards the leaves.

- **Apply meaningful generalization**. As described in the previous enabling technique, generalization is the process wherein common behavior and elements between the subtypes are identified and factored out in supertypes. Meaningful generalization helps enhance reusability, understandability, and extensibility of the design. Further, generalization also helps reduce (or altogether eliminate) code duplication within types in the hierarchy.

- **Ensure substitutability**. Ensure that the types in the hierarchy follow the Liskov's Substitution Principle (LSP); in other words, a reference of a supertype can be substituted with objects of its subtypes without altering the behavior of the program. Adherence to this principle allows object-oriented programs to leverage dynamic polymorphism. This improves the changeability, extensibility, and reusability of the design.

- **Avoid redundant paths**. An inheritance hierarchy allows us to explicitly express the logical relationship between related types. When there are redundant paths in an inheritance hierarchy, it unnecessarily complicates the hierarchy. This affects the understandability of the hierarchy and can also lead to runtime problems.

- **Ensure proper ordering**. The key benefit of a hierarchical organization stems from its ability to provide us with a means to address the complex relationships among types. Hence, it is critical to express these relationships in an orderly fashion and maintain them consistently within the hierarchy. For example, in an inheritance hierarchy, it is intuitive to understand that a subtype depends on a supertype; however, when a supertype depends on its subtype(s), it is harder to understand the design since the ordering of dependencies is violated.

The smells described in this chapter map to violation of one or more of these enabling technique(s). Figure 6.3 gives an overview of the smells that violate the principle of hierarchy and Table 6.1 provides an overview of mapping between the design smells and the enabling technique(s) they violate. A detailed explanation of how these smells violate enabling techniques is discussed in the Rationale subsection of each smell description.

In the rest of this chapter, we'll discuss the specific smells that result due to the violation of the principle of hierarchy.

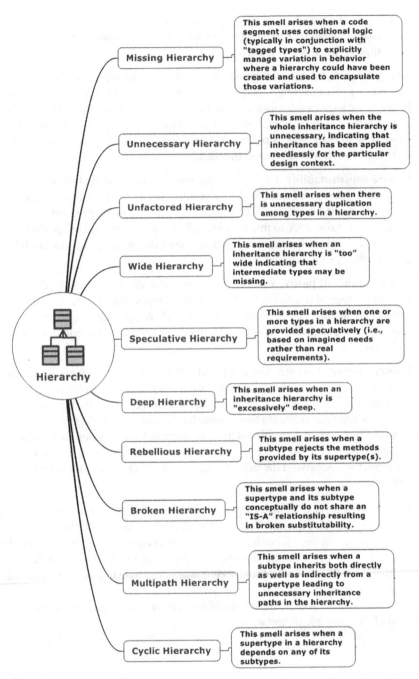

FIGURE 6.3

Smells resulting due to the violation of principle of hierarchy.

Table 6.1 Design Smells and the Hierarchy Enabling Techniques They Violate

Design Smell(s)	Violated Enabling Technique
Missing Hierarchy (see Section 6.1), Unnecessary Hierarchy (see Section 6.2)	Apply meaningful classification
Unfactored Hierarchy (see Section 6.3), Wide Hierarchy (see Section 6.4), Speculative Hierarchy (see Section 6.5), Deep Hierarchy (see Section 6.6)	Apply meaningful generalization
Rebellious Hierarchy (see Section 6.7), Broken Hierarchy (see Section 6.8)	Ensure substitutability
Multipath Hierarchy (see Section 6.9)	Avoid redundant paths
Cyclic Hierarchy (see Section 6.10)	Ensure proper ordering

6.1 MISSING HIERARCHY

This smell arises when a code segment uses conditional logic (typically in conjunction with "tagged types") to explicitly manage variation in behavior where a hierarchy could have been created and used to encapsulate those variations.

6.1.1 RATIONALE

Switch-based-on-type-codes (or chained if-else statements) is one of the most well-known design smells. When type information is encoded (for example, using an enumeration, an integral value, or a string), variation in behavior is not encapsulated properly. Further, the commonality among those types is also left unexploited. In addition, the switch (or chained if-else) statements will be repeated in multiple places violating "Don't Repeat Yourself" (DRY) principle and causing difficulties in maintenance.

Using "tagged types" or conditional logic to handle variation in behavior clearly indicates that the enabling technique "apply meaningful classification" was not employed and as a result a hierarchy is "missing" in the design. Hence, we name this smell Missing Hierarchy.

6.1.2 POTENTIAL CAUSES

Misguided simplistic design

Inexperienced designers often adopt encoded type values that are used in conjunction with conditional statements and (wrongly) believe that it results in a "straightforward" or "simple" design.

Procedural approach to design

In C-like procedural languages, the main way to handle variation in behavior is to use encoded types and conditional logic. Following such a design approach while programming in object-oriented languages is a common cause of this smell.

Overlooking inheritance as a design technique

We have come across many cases where developers were unaware of the benefits inheritance can bring to design when used correctly. Due to this, developers often rely on explicit conditional logic for handling variation instead of creating and using a hierarchy.

6.1.3 EXAMPLES

Example 1

Consider the following code segment from `java.swing.plaf.windows.XPStyle.java`:

```java
public Insets getBorderInsets(Component c, Insets insets){
    Insets margin = null;
    //
    // Ideally we'd have an interface defined for classes which
    // support margins (to avoid this hackery), but we've
    // decided against it for simplicity
    //
    if (c instanceof AbstractButton) {
        margin = ((AbstractButton)c).getMargin();
    } else if (c instanceof JToolBar) {
        margin = ((JToolBar)c).getMargin();
    } else if (c instanceof JTextComponent) {
        margin = ((JTextComponent)c).getMargin();
    }
    // rest of the code elided ...
```

The chained if-else code block has explicit type checks for `AbstractButton`, `JToolBar`, and `JTextComponent`. The code where the `getMargin()` method is called is the same within all the conditions. As one can observe from the inline comments, the concerned developer consciously chose a hack, and in that process introduced this smell in design. Note that the explicit type checks as shown above is repeated in two other places in the same source file.

Example 2

Consider the class `javax.sound.sampled.AudioFormat` that can be used to determine the audio format and interpret data from a sound stream. This class has a field named "encoding" that "tags" the kind of audio encoding that the sound stream uses:

```
public class AudioFormat {
  /**
   * The audio encoding technique used by this format.
   */
  protected Encoding encoding;
  // ...
}
```

Now, `javax.sound.sampled.AudioFormat.Encoding` is a class that declares encoding types (code slightly edited to save space):

```
public static class Encoding {
    // Specifies signed, linear PCM data.
    public static final Encoding PCM_SIGNED
    = new Encoding("PCM_SIGNED");
    // Specifies unsigned, linear PCM data.
    public static final Encoding PCM_UNSIGNED = new Encoding("PCM_
UNSIGNED");
    // Specifies floating-point PCM data.
    public static final Encoding PCM_FLOAT = new Encoding("PCM_
FLOAT");
    // Specifies u-law encoded data.
    public static final Encoding ULAW = new Encoding("ULAW");
    // Specifies a-law encoded data.
    public static final Encoding ALAW = new Encoding("ALAW");
    // Encoding name.
    private String name;
    // definitions of the constructor, equals, hashCode and
    // toString methods elided ...
}
```

The client code makes extensive use of these encoding values to determine behavior. To give an idea of a sample usage of this class, here is the code from `com.sun.media.sound.FloatFormatConverter`:

```
if (targetEncoding.equals(Encoding.PCM_FLOAT))
  bits = 32;
if (targetEncoding.equals(Encoding.PCM_SIGNED))
    formats.add(new AudioFormat(Encoding.PCM_SIGNED,
    AudioSystem.NOT_SPECIFIED, 8, channels, channels,
    AudioSystem.NOT_SPECIFIED, false));
if (targetEncoding.equals(Encoding.PCM_FLOAT)) {
    formats.add(new AudioFormat(Encoding.PCM_FLOAT,
    AudioSystem.NOT_SPECIFIED, 32, channels, channels * 4,
    AudioSystem.NOT_SPECIFIED, false));
```

Such conditional statements make the code brittle and hard to read. Since this code uses conditional checks instead of encapsulating the variations within a hierarchy, this code has Missing Hierarchy smell.

6.1.4 SUGGESTED REFACTORING

Consider the following refactoring for this smell depending on the context:

- If two or more implementations within the condition checks have common method calls, relevant interfaces can be introduced to abstract that common protocol.

- If the code has conditional statements that can be transformed into classes, "extract hierarchy" refactoring can be applied to create a hierarchy of classes wherein each class represents a case in the condition check. This hierarchy can now be exploited via runtime polymorphism.

Suggested refactoring for Example 1

For the `java.swing.plaf.windows.XPStyle.java` example, a potential refactoring is provided in the code comment itself: *"Ideally we'd have an interface defined for classes which support margins (to avoid this hackery)."* Clearly, a refactoring suggestion would be to create an interface that declares methods such as `getMargin()` and `setMargin()`. Classes such as `AbstractButton`, `JToolBar`, and `JTextComponent` that support the concept of margins can implement that interface (Figure 6.4).

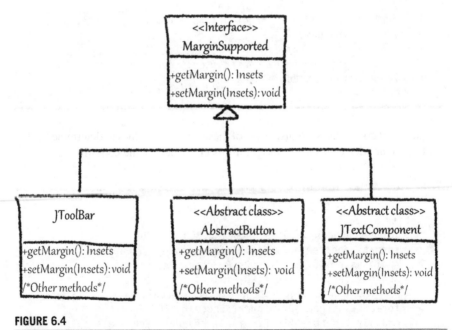

FIGURE 6.4

Suggested refactoring for AbstractButton, JTextComponent, and JToolBar classes (Example 1).

With this change, the relevant code within the `java.swing.plaf.windows.XPStyle.java` class will be transformed to:

```
public Insets getBorderInsets(Component c, Insets insets){
    Insets margin = null;
    if(c instanceof MarginSupported) {
        margin = c.getMargin();
    }
    // rest of the code elided.
}
```

The `c.getMargin()` will be a polymorphic call and will be bound to the dynamic type of the component "c." The ideal refactoring would be to replace the first argument of `getBorderInsets()` method from `Component` type to `MarginSupported` type. However, since `getBorderInsets()` is a public method, we cannot change the signature of this method without breaking backward compatibility. Hence, we have to resort to using an explicit type check for `MarginSupported`.

Suggested refactoring for Example 2

For the `AudioFormat` example, the refactoring suggestion is to first create classes such as `SignedPCMEncoding`, `UnsignedPCMEncoding`, `FloatPCMEncoding`, `ULAWEncoding`, and `ALAWEncoding`. Next, introduce a hierarchy where all these classes extend the abstract `Encoding` class. Finally, methods such as `getBitSize()` can be introduced in the `Encoding` class and can be overridden by the derived classes (Figure 6.5). With this change, client code such as this

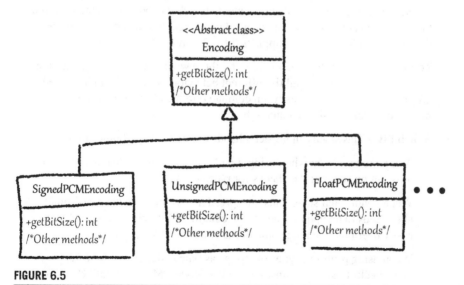

FIGURE 6.5

Suggested refactoring for audio format example (Example 2).

```
if (targetEncoding.equals(Encoding.PCM_FLOAT))
    bits = 32;
```

can be refactored to a more readable and maintainable code like this:

```
bits = targetEncoding.getBitSize();
```

The idea here is to exploit runtime polymorphism to return the bit size depending upon the kind of `targetEncoding`.

6.1.5 IMPACTED QUALITY ATTRIBUTES

- **Understandability**—When compared to the equivalent code that makes use of runtime polymorphism through a hierarchy, using switch-based-on-type-codes and tagged types increases the complexity of the code base and thus impacts the understandability of the design.

- **Changeability** and **Extensibility**—A hierarchy helps encapsulate variation and hence it is easy to modify existing types or add support for new types within that hierarchy without affecting the client code. On the other hand, with type-based switches, the client code needs to be changed whenever an existing type is changed or a new type is added. This adversely impacts changeability and extensibility of the design.

- **Reusability**—Consider the encoding example (discussed in Example 2) where the type information is provided in a tagged type in a class and the behavior is spread across the conditional statements in the client code. Since the type and the associated behavior are not encapsulated together, it is hard to reuse the design. Therefore, this smell impacts the reusability of the design.

- **Testability**—When this smell is present, there would be numerous conditional statements in code with slightly different behavior. This results in increased effort to test these fragments when compared to the effort if the code were to be provided within classes in a hierarchy.

- **Reliability**—This smell can impact reliability in many ways. Some of the ways are:

  - A common problem when using type-based checking is that a developer may miss out on some of the checks for type codes.

  - When conditional statements are spread across the code base, and functionality needs to be updated across the conditional statements, a developer may easily overlook updating some of the conditional statements.

  - When using primitive types or strings as type codes, a developer has to provide checks to guard against invalid type codes. Missing guard checks can lead to unexpected behavior and defects.

6.1.6 ALIASES

This smell is also known in literature as:

- "Tag class" [61]—This smell occurs when a class has a tag field that indicates the flavor of the instance.

- "Missing inheritance" [8]—This smell occurs when duplicated code or "switch-case" statements are used instead of inheritance.

- "Collapsed type hierarchy" [20]—This smell occurs when a non-trivial class contains at least two switch or equivalent if-else constructs; these conditional checks are used to determine behavior.

- "Embedded features" [20]—This smell occurs when class uses attributes that represent on/off switches for optional features of the class; these attribute values are checked to determine behavior.

6.1.7 PRACTICAL CONSIDERATIONS

Interacting with the external world

File formats usually "mark" the data content within the file to indicate the type of the data (for instance, the file format for .class in Java). This encoding helps read data from the flat-file: the program needs to first check the type information of the data and then process the data. In this case, explicit type checks in the form of switch statements or chained if-else statements may be needed to read the data and convert that data into objects. However, once data is processed, there is no need for explicit type checks. To understand this better, consider the following example from `java.io.ObjectStreamClass`:

```
private void computeFieldOffsets() throws InvalidClassException {
    primDataSize = 0;
    numObjFields = 0;
    int firstObjIndex = -1;
    for (int i = 0; i < fields.length; i++) {
            ObjectStreamField f = fields[i];
            switch (f.getTypeCode()) {
                    case 'Z':
                    case 'B':
                            f.setOffset(primDataSize++);
                            break;
                    case 'C':
                    case 'S':
                            f.setOffset(primDataSize);
                            primDataSize += 2;
                            break;
    // rest of the code elided to save space...
```

The class supports object serialization and the type codes for serialized data are described in `ObjectStreamField` class. For example, codes "Z", "B", "C", and "S" refer to the types `Boolean`, `Byte`, `Character`, and `Short` respectively. For serialization, the type of data needs to be "encoded" as values and it is natural to employ chained if-else or switch statements to use them.

Our experience also shows that it is difficult to avoid conditional logic when an application interacts with entities from the external world, as in the following cases:

- Reading a configuration file to alter the runtime configuration of an application.

- Instantiating objects using a factory based on the application requirement.

So, in such contexts, "switch-based-on-type-code" may be required irrespective of whether a hierarchy that maps to the type codes already exists in the design or not.

6.2 UNNECESSARY HIERARCHY

This smell arises when the whole inheritance hierarchy is unnecessary, indicating that inheritance has been applied needlessly for the particular design context.

6.2.1 RATIONALE

For effective application of the principle of hierarchy, it is important to adhere to the enabling technique "apply meaningful classification." For a "meaningful" application of classification, the focus should be more on capturing the commonalities and variation in *behavior* rather than data. When this enabling technique is violated, it can result in an inheritance hierarchy that is "unnecessary" and which needlessly complicates the design. Hence, we name this smell Unnecessary Hierarchy.

6.2.2 POTENTIAL CAUSES

Subclassing instead of instantiating
Let us take a simple example of representing roses with different color such as red, pink, and white. Assume that these different kinds of roses differ only in their color and not in their *behavior*. Hence, it will be inappropriate to create a `Rose` supertype with subtypes such as `RedRose`, `PinkRose`, and `WhiteRose`. Instead of creating subclasses, a better design would be to create objects of type `Rose` with an attribute named `color` that can take values such as red, pink, and white.

Taxonomy mania
Some designers tend to overuse inheritance and sometimes force-fit it as a design solution in unwarranted contexts. Meyer calls this "taxonomy mania" [66]. Such overuse of inheritance leads to unnecessary hierarchies in design.

6.2.3 EXAMPLES

Example 1

Consider the case of a text editor that supports multiple fonts. In this application, when the user selects the font, the editor just passes this information to the underlying OS which renders the text in the selected font. Figure 6.6 shows how inheritance can be used to support multiple fonts in such an editor - Font is the supertype and fonts such as Arial and Calibri are supported via Font's subtypes named ArialFont and CalibriFont. However, if we were to reflect on this design, we will realize that since the editor does not change its behavior based on the font, classifying the types of fonts within a hierarchy is unnecessary. Hence, this design suffers from Unnecessary Hierarchy smell.

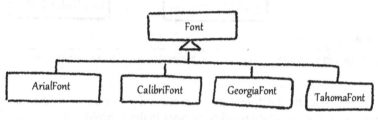

FIGURE 6.6

Font class hierarchy in a text editor (Example 1).

Example 2

Consider a GUI application which provides rich support for drawing graphical objects. One of the features of this editor is its support for drawing lines with different styles such as double line, thick thin line, thin thick line, and triple line. Further, you can draw lines with different dash or dot styles (see Figure 6.7). When the user

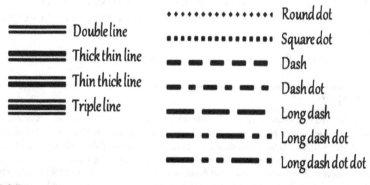

FIGURE 6.7

Kinds of line types and dot types supported in a drawing application (Example 2).

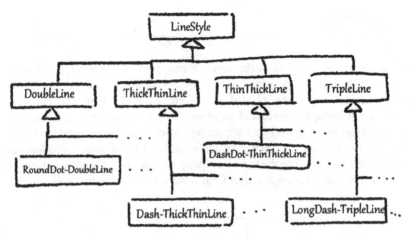

FIGURE 6.8

Class explosion in the LineStyle hierarchy to support multiple line styles (Example 2).

selects a line style, the GUI application passes this information to the underlying Operating System (OS) which renders the lines in the selected style.

One way to model this is to use an inheritance hierarchy (see Figure 6.8). But is this an effective design? In fact, there are two main problems with adopting such an inheritance hierarchy based approach for this example:

- As Blaha and Rumbaugh [52] observed, classification is meaningful if there are some significant subclasses that have more specialized behavior when compared to the base class. In this example, since the actual rendering of the line with different styles is performed by the underlying OS, the supertype and its subtypes do not differ in behavior. Clearly, modeling this relationship as generalization-specialization relationship is "over-engineering."

- If a new kind of style support is needed, then the number of derived classes can grow exponentially. In other words, the design can suffer from "class explosion" problem.

For these reasons, this design suffers from Unnecessary Hierarchy smell.

CASE STUDY

A "data buffer" is a temporary place to store data when we move data from one place to another. There are many uses of data buffer. For instance, we may want to use a buffer to read data from a text file into memory and cache it for performance reasons. There are different kinds of data that a buffer can handle; for instance, one can use a character buffer for reading a text file.

Now, consider a (partial) class hierarchy of the class `java.nio.Buffer` (see Figure 6.9). What is unusual about this hierarchy is that the subclasses correspond to the primitive types available in Java!

Intrigued by this Unnecessary Hierarchy, we set about searching for the source code for these classes. What we found was a single file named "X-Buffer.java.template"! Here is a code fragment from this file:

CASE STUDY—cont'd

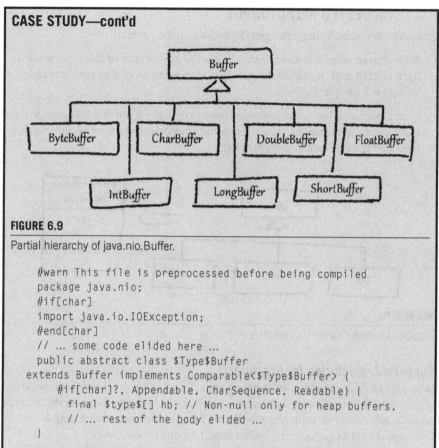

FIGURE 6.9

Partial hierarchy of java.nio.Buffer.

```
#warn This file is preprocessed before being compiled
package java.nio;
#if[char]
import java.io.IOException;
#end[char]
// ... some code elided here ...
public abstract class $Type$Buffer
extends Buffer implements Comparable<$Type$Buffer> {
    #if[char]?, Appendable, CharSequence, Readable} {
     final $type$[] hb; // Non-null only for heap buffers.
     // ... rest of the body elided ...
}
```

From this source code (especially from the explicit #warn comment "This file is preprocessed before being compiled"), it is clear that the JDK code must have used a preprocessor internally to generate type-specific source files that are later processed by the Java compiler.

Before we discuss this example further, it is important to note that Java's support for generics is limited:

1. You cannot instantiate a generic type with a primitive type. For the generic type List<T>, you cannot instantiate List<int> because int is a primitive type. However, you may use List<Integer> because Integer is a reference type (wrapper for int primitive type) in Java.

2. Java generics does not support template specializations like in C++. The template specialization feature in C++ allows one to override the default template implementation to handle a particular type in a different way.

Coming back to the Buffer example, note that the source code does use generics, as in Comparable<$Type$Buffer>. However, due to the limitations of Java generics (i.e., lack of support for instantiating primitive types and template specialization), the designers of the Buffer hierarchy probably had to use "work-arounds" such as using an internal preprocessor.

To summarize, when subclasses are created for specific primitive types, it is an Unnecessary Hierarchy. The feasibility of avoiding this smell depends on the extent of language support available (e.g., templates in C++ or generics in Java/C#).

6.2.4 SUGGESTED REFACTORING

Consider these refactoring strategies depending on the context:

- When instances of a type are instead modeled as subtypes of that type, remove the hierarchy and transform the subtypes into instances of that type (see refactoring for Example 1).

- If an inheritance hierarchy is created instead of using a suitable language feature (such as an enumeration), then remove the Unnecessary Hierarchy and use that language feature instead (Figure 6.10).

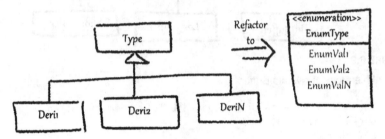

FIGURE 6.10

Suggested Refactoring for Unnecessary Hierarchy.

Suggested refactoring for Example 1

In the case of Font hierarchy, the suggested refactoring solution is to make the subtypes of Font into objects of Font, such as Arial and Calibri objects. But note that another possible refactoring is to model this list of fonts as an enumeration (Figure 6.11). Choosing the correct refactoring option would depend on the context.

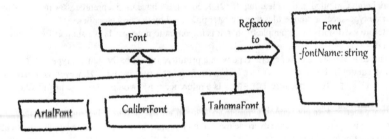

FIGURE 6.11

Suggested refactoring for the Font class hierarchy (Example 1).

Suggested refactoring for Example 2

A potential refactoring for the LineStyles example is to use two enumerations namely LineStyleEnum and DashDotStyleEnum instead of the hierarchy (see Figure 6.12). The `LineStyleEnum` will hold constants representing `Double-Line`, `ThickThinLine`, etc. Similarly, `DashDotStyleEnum` will hold constants representing `RoundDot`, `SquareDot`, etc. Now, the `Line` class can refer to values of `LineStyleEnum` and `DashDotStyleEnum` for drawing a line. If a new line style or dash dot style needs to be supported in the design, the enumerations can be easily extended. In this way, this refactoring addresses the "class explosion" problem found in the earlier design.

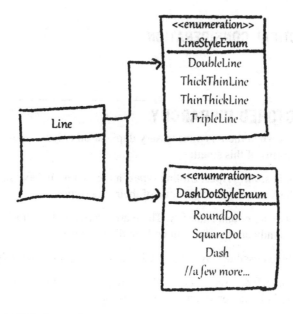

FIGURE 6.12

Suggested refactoring to support multiple line styles (Example 2).

6.2.5 IMPACTED QUALITY ATTRIBUTES

- **Understandability**—If a hierarchy is created unnecessarily, it complicates the design. Hence, this smell impacts understandability of the design.

- **Extensibility**—Consider Example 2 wherein the number of types in a hierarchy can grow exponentially when new combinations need to be supported in the design. This complicates the design and increases the effort required to support new combinations. Therefore, Unnecessary Hierarchy impacts the extensibility of the design.

- **Testability**—It requires more effort to test numerous types in an Unnecessary Hierarchy when compared to testing an alternative solution (e.g., one that uses an enumeration or a class). This impacts the testability of the overall design.

6.2.6 ALIASES

This smell is also known in literature as:

- "Taxomania" [66]—This smell (an abbreviation of "taxonomy mania") occurs when an inheritance structure is provided instead of providing simple boolean properties or properties that have fixed values.

- "Object classes" [51]—This smell occurs when subclasses are created instead of creating instances of their parent class.

6.2.7 PRACTICAL CONSIDERATIONS

None.

6.3 UNFACTORED HIERARCHY

This smell arises when there is unnecessary duplication among types in a hierarchy. There are two forms of this smell:

- *Duplication in sibling types*: Sibling types in the hierarchy have similar code segments that can be moved into one of their supertypes.

- *Duplication in super and subtypes*: There are similar code segments in super and subtypes indicating redundant code in the subtypes.

  There are three possible ways this smell manifests within a hierarchy in a design:

- *Unfactored interface*: Across types, there are public methods with similar signatures that could be factored out into a supertype.

- *Unfactored implementation*: Across types, there are methods with similar implementations that could be factored out into a supertype.

- *Unfactored interface and implementation*: Across types, there are public methods with similar signatures and implementations that could be factored out into a supertype.

6.3.1 RATIONALE

One of the motivations behind the usage of inheritance is to avoid redundancy by applying generalization, i.e., by factoring out the commonalities from types to a supertype in the inheritance hierarchy. This has two main advantages:

- If the common interface across types is elevated in the hierarchy, clients can depend on this common interface rather than the concrete implementation aspects of the subtypes. This allows the internals of the subtypes to change without impacting clients.

- If duplicated implementation across types in the hierarchy is removed by elevating the implementation to a supertype, unnecessary duplication across the types is avoided.

This smell violates the Don't Repeat Yourself (DRY) principle which advocates avoiding redundant code and the enabling technique "apply meaningful generalization." Since the commonalities in the types are not factored out, we name this smell Unfactored Hierarchy.

6.3.2 POTENTIAL CAUSES

Copying subtypes

We have seen developers copy the code of a subtype and paste it as a renamed new subtype with necessary changes. Of course, this would "get the work done," but this duplication will introduce this smell. This often occurs when excessive focus is placed on just completing the work without due attention to design quality.

Improper handling of outliers

Consider an example wherein a superclass named Bird has derived classes such as Pigeon, Crow, and Sparrow. The superclass Bird has a method fly(). Now, if a new subclass Penguin (which is a non-flying bird) needs to be supported in the design, then we need to force-fit the Penguin class in the hierarchy by providing an empty body for fly() or rejecting the method, such as by throwing an exception. However, this will result in a Rebellious Hierarchy smell (Section 6.7).

An alternative solution for this is to remove the fly() method in the Bird class and instead define fly() method in all subclasses except Penguin. However, this leads to unnecessary duplication of fly() method in the sibling classes in the hierarchy. Thus, in order to support outliers in the hierarchy (Penguin class in this case) and avoid Rebellious Hierarchy smell, designers often end up introducing this smell in the design.

Note that a better design solution that exhibits neither Unfactored Hierarchy or Rebellious Hierarchy is possible. For example, we could introduce intermediate classes FlyingBird and NonFlyingBird as subclasses of Bird class, and have only the FlyingBird class support the fly() method. Then, the classes Pigeon, Crow, and Sparrow become subtypes of FlyingBird and the Penguin class becomes a subtype of NonFlyingBird class.

6.3.3 EXAMPLES

Example 1

The abstract class java.text.NumberFormat in JDK 7 provides support for formatting and parsing numbers in any locale. It has two subclasses: ChoiceFormat and DecimalFormat. With ChoiceFormat, we can attach a format to a range of numbers and with `DecimalFormat`, we can format decimal numbers for any locale (see Figure 6.13).

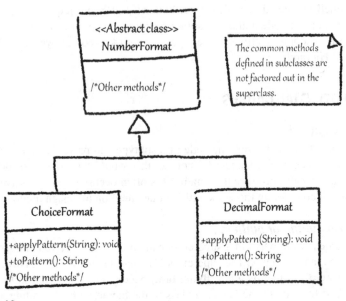

FIGURE 6.13

NumberFormat class hierarchy (Example 1).

The classes in the `NumberFormat` hierarchy support the use of a pattern for formatting. For example, in the pattern "###,###.##," the symbol "#" stands for a digit, the comma is the thousands-separator and the period represents the decimal point.

A formatting pattern can be set in the classes `ChoiceFormat` and `DecimalFormat` using the public method `applyPattern()`. Similarly, a set pattern can be retrieved using the public method `toPattern()`. The signature of these two methods are same but they have different implementations in the sibling classes. Since the method signatures in the subtypes are duplicated and are not factored out into the supertype, this hierarchy has Unfactored Hierarchy smell.

Example 2

The classes `AbstractQueuedSynchronizer` and `AbstractQueuedLongSynchronizer` both derive directly from `AbstractOwnableSynchronizer` (all these classes are part of `java.util.concurrent.locks` package). These two subclasses have considerable code duplication: 1278 lines out of 2110 raw lines in each of these files are duplicated! (See Figure 6.14—note that only a partial list of methods is shown in the figure for space reasons).

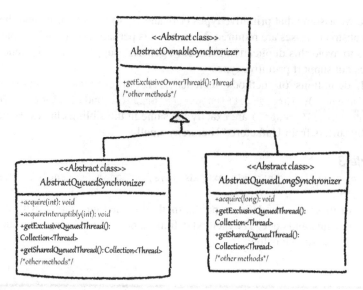

FIGURE 6.14

Unfactored methods in subtypes of AbstractOwnableSynchronizer (Example 2).

The JavaDoc comment for `AbstractQueuedLongSynchronizer` reads:

"A version of AbstractQueuedSynchronizer in which synchronization state is maintained as a long. This class has exactly the same structure, properties, and methods as AbstractQueuedSynchronizer with the exception that all state-related parameters and results are defined as long rather than int. This class may be useful when creating synchronizers such as multilevel locks and barriers that require 64 bits of state."

In fact, the code comment inside `AbstractQueuedLongSynchronizer` reads:

```
/*
To keep sources in sync, the remainder of this source file is
exactly cloned from AbstractQueuedSynchronizer, replacing class
name and changing ints related with sync state to longs. Please
keep it that way.
*/
```

So, it is clear that the code in these two classes is duplicated exactly except that `long` is used instead of `int` in `AbstractQueuedLongSynchronizer`.

Here we assume that primitive types (int and long) must be used and these two derived abstract classes are required. Note that it is perhaps not feasible to have used generics to avoid this duplication since Java generics supports only reference types and does not support primitive types.

Still, definitions of methods such as Collection<Thread> getExclusive-QueuedThreads(), Thread getFirstQueuedThread(), and Collection<Thread> getSharedQueuedThreads() are exactly the same in the sibling classes. Hence, this hierarchy suffers from Unfactored Hierarchy smell.

Example 3

The class java.awt.Rectangle extends java.awt.geom.Rectangle2D class (see Figure 6.15).

Both of these classes define a public method named outcode() with the same method signature and code. The method definition of outcode() from the superclass Rectangle2D is shown below:

```
public int outcode(double x, double y) {
    /*
     * Note on casts to double below. If the arithmetic of
     * x+w or y+h is done in float, then some bits may be
     * lost if the binary exponents of x/y and w/h are not
     * similar. By converting to double before the addition
     * we force the addition to be carried out in double to
     * avoid rounding error in the comparison.
     *
     * See bug 4320890 for problems that this inaccuracy causes.
     */
    int out = 0;
    if (this.width <= 0) {
        out |= OUT_LEFT | OUT_RIGHT;
    } else if (x < this.x) {
        out |= OUT_LEFT;
    } else if (x > this.x + (double) this.width) {
        out |= OUT_RIGHT;
    }
    if (this.height <= 0) {
        out |= OUT_TOP | OUT_BOTTOM;
    } else if (y < this.y) {
        out |= OUT_TOP;
    } else if (y > this.y + (double) this.height) {
        out |= OUT_BOTTOM;
    }
    return out;
}
```

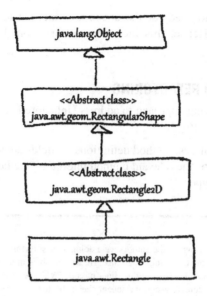

FIGURE 6.15

Partial inheritance hierarchy of java.awt.Rectangle class (Example 3).

Though the `outcode()` method definitions are exactly the same in both the super-class `Rectangle2D` as well as the subclass `Rectangle`, the comments within these definitions have diverged. Here is the comparison of comments in `Rectangle2D` class (left hand side) and `Rectangle` class (right hand side); the part that differs in comment is <u>underlined</u> in this box:

<pre>/*
* Note on casts to double
below. If the arithmetic of
* x+w or y+h is done in
float, then some bits may be
* lost if the binary exponents
of x/y and w/h are not
* similar. By converting to
double before the addition
* we force the addition to be
carried out in double to
* avoid rounding error in the
comparison.
*
* see bug 4320890 for
problems that this inaccuracy
causes.
*/</pre>

<pre>/*
* Note on casts to double
below. If the arithmetic of
* x+w or y+h is done in <u>int</u>,
<u>then we may get integer</u>
* <u>overflow</u>. By converting to
double before the addition
* we force the addition to
be carried out in double to
* avoid <u>overflow</u> in the
comparison.
*
* See bug 4320890 for
problems that this <u>can</u>
<u>cause</u>.
*/</pre>

Clearly, there is no need for the `outcode()` method to be duplicated in the subtype `Rectangle`. Hence, this hierarchy suffers from Unfactored Hierarchy smell.

6.3.4 SUGGESTED REFACTORING

The high-level refactoring approach to address Unfactored Hierarchy is to apply the principle of "factoring" [67,52]:

- If the method signatures, method definitions, or fields are same across sibling types, then "pull-up" the relevant method interfaces, method definitions, or fields to the supertype.

ANECDOTE

At one of the design forums where the authors were doing a guest lecture on design smells, one of the participants shared the following experience. He was involved in the review of a Java-based application with a code base close to a million lines of code. While reviewing the code he observed that the code base made extensive use of instanceof checks for the subclasses. The instanceof checks were for wide range of classes and he couldn't easily figure out why these checks were needed.

Since the review was tool driven, he analyzed the code base using PMD Copy Paste Detector (a code clone detector tool). He found that many of the clones reported by the tool were from sibling classes in hierarchies. A quick inspection of these classes showed that the hierarchies had both interface and implementation duplicated in the subclasses. Clearly, these hierarchies had Unfactored Hierarchy smell.

Armed with this new information about the presence of Unfactored Hierarchies in the code base, he went back and checked whether this was somehow related to the instanceof checks he had found earlier. Now the root cause of instanceof checks became evident! There were public methods with similar signatures in the subclasses that had not been factored out into the relevant supertypes. Hence, when the clients had a handle only to the supertypes, they were forced to perform runtime checks to determine the dynamic types of the objects, perform downcasts, and then access the methods provided in the subtypes.

The project team really liked this finding on how the Unfactored Hierarchy smell caused extensive runtime type checks in the rest of the code. They took up refactoring tasks to "pull up" common method declarations and definitions in the hierarchy. Once the refactoring was complete, most of the instanceof checks could also be removed.

Reflecting on this anecdote reveals two important insights:
- Tools are very useful for finding design smells especially in large code bases. However, as in the anecdote above, it is important for designers to manually check if the smells reported by tools are real design problems or false alarms, check how the smells relate to each other, and derive insights by analyzing their relationships. In general, combining the use of automated analysis tools with manual assessment by experts in a powerful and useful technique to identify smells in design.
- Smells are related to each other. Taking a holistic look at smells in a code base and understanding their relationships provides a better and bigger picture on the underlying problem than if smells are considered independent of each other. We discuss this in detail in Chapter 7.

- If methods defined across sibling types are similar but differ in some ways, apply relevant techniques to factor out the commonality to the supertype. For instance, if the method implementations in sibling subtypes share steps that are performed in the same order but the actual steps differ in their implementation, then consider applying Template Method pattern [54].

Suggested refactoring for Example 1

In the case of NumberFormat example, the signature of two methods is the same in the subclasses and their implementations are different. Hence, a suggested refactoring is to introduce abstract methods applyPattern() and toPattern() in the supertype NumberFormat (see Figure 6.16).

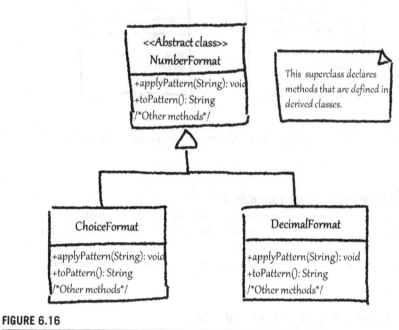

FIGURE 6.16

Suggested refactoring for NumberFormat hierarchy (Example 1).

Suggested refactoring for Example 2

In the case of AbstractOwnableSynchronizer example, since the method definitions are duplicated in subtypes, the suitable refactoring is to apply "pull-up method" and move the common method definitions to the supertype AbstractOwnableSynchronizer. It should be noted that we cannot "pull-up" methods that differ on the primitive type (int or long) they operate on. However, other common methods such as getQueuedThreads() that are duplicated in both the subclasses can be "pulled up" into the supertype (see Figure 6.17).

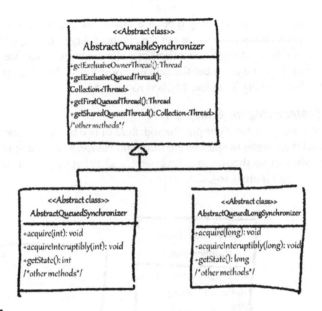

FIGURE 6.17

Suggested refactoring for AbstractOwnableSynchronizer hierarchy (Example 2).

Suggested refactoring for Example 3

In the case of `Rectangle` example, the code for the public method `outcode()` in the supertype `Rectangle2D` and the subtype `Rectangle` is exactly the same. Since the subtype anyway inherits the `outcode()` method from the supertype, the refactoring in this case is to remove the method definition from the subtype `Rectangle`.

6.3.5 IMPACTED QUALITY ATTRIBUTES

- **Understandability**—Duplication within the hierarchy unnecessarily bloats the code and increases the cognitive load on developers. This impacts understandability of the hierarchy and design.

- **Changeability** and **Reliability**—A change to the code that is common across a set of types needs to be replicated across all those types, failing which a defect may occur. This impacts changeability and reliability of the design.

- **Extensibility**—When this smell exists in a hierarchy, introducing a new subtype in the hierarchy can require more work. Since commonality is not exploited in the hierarchy, it is possible that fields, methods, or interface may need to be duplicated in the new subtype. This impacts the extensibility of the design.

- **Reusability**—In the case of unfactored interface, as in Example 1, common public interface across subtypes is not provided in the supertype and hence clients cannot exploit runtime polymorphism. This impacts the reusability of the design.

- **Testability**—In case of duplicate method implementations, it takes more effort to test the same code duplicated in multiple subtypes. This impacts the testability of the design.

6.3.6 ALIASES

This smell is also known in literature as:

- "Orphan sibling method/attribute" [28]—This smell occurs when members are provided in more than 50% or at least 10 of the direct subclasses, without being defined in any of the subclasses' ancestors.

- "Incomplete inheritance" [68]—This smell occurs when siblings of subclasses are similar and share a substantial amount of code.

- "Repeated functionality" [69]—This smell occurs when code is duplicated in two or more classes, instead of being abstracted into a common superclass.

- "Redundant variable declaration" [57]—This smell occurs when subclasses inheriting from the base class have the same data.

- "Significant sibling duplication" [76]—This smell occurs when there is duplication between siblings in an inheritance hierarchy.

6.3.7 PRACTICAL CONSIDERATIONS

Inadequate language support to avoid duplication

Consider a hierarchy where two sibling classes have a duplicate implementation. We could factor out the common implementation to their superclass, but we have to make sure that we don't introduce other smells in the process or make the design overly complex. For instance, if the implementation that is factored out to a superclass is rejected by other subtypes, then it would lead to a Rebellious Hierarchy smell (Section 6.7). As an alternative, if could try to factor out the common implementation to a new superclass; however, many object-oriented languages do not support multiple class inheritance (such as Java and C#). Thus, this alternative is not feasible in Java and C#. Hence, a designer may be forced to live with Unfactored Hierarchy smell due to inadequate language support.

Another example is the limited or lack of support for generics in a language. When the language does not support generics, duplication may be required to support an abstraction that differs only by type. For example, primitive types cannot be used as generic type parameters in Java. For this reason, in Java, when abstractions differ by the primitive type they support, duplication may be inevitable (as discussed in Example 2).

6.4 WIDE HIERARCHY

This smell arises when an inheritance hierarchy is "too" wide indicating that intermediate types may be missing.

6.4.1 RATIONALE

A wide inheritance hierarchy can indicate the violation of the enabling technique "apply meaningful generalization." When generalization is inadequately applied and consequently intermediate types are missing, it can result in the following problems:

- Missing intermediate types may force the clients of that hierarchy to directly refer to the subtypes. This dependency affects the changeability and extensibility of the hierarchy.

- There may be unnecessary duplication within types (since commonality cannot be properly abstracted due to lack of intermediate types).

For effective design of inheritance hierarchies, we need to "maintain moderation in size." If there are a large number of subtypes at the same level, it becomes harder to understand and use the hierarchy. Since the hierarchy is "too wide," this smell is named Wide Hierarchy. Based on our experience, we consider a hierarchy wide if any type in the hierarchy has more than 9 immediate subtypes.

Both Wide Hierarchy and Unfactored Hierarchy (Section 6.3) are similar in one aspect: both violate the enabling technique "apply meaningful generalization." However, the difference is that Wide Hierarchy arises when there are "too" many immediate subtypes for a supertype (indicating that intermediate types may be missing), whereas Unfactored Hierarchy arises when there is duplication in the hierarchy. In fact, both of them often occur together as can be seen from the anecdote below—wide hierarchies usually have duplication that can be factored out by introducing intermediate abstractions.

ANECDOTE

One of the participants in the Smells Forum shared this experience. He was associated with the development of a software product for monitoring devices connected to a network. In the earlier stages of the project, the software system was small. To have a common abstraction for devices present in the network, a class named `Device` was introduced with members such as `getDeviceId()`, and `isConnected()`.

Due to the success of the initial version of the product, it was decided to build a new version of the software for large networks. This required the software system to evolve to support new types of devices. Classes such as `FireAlarmDevice` and `CameraDevice` were created by extending the common superclass `Device`. Over time, the `Device` class became a superclass of a large number of such subclasses that each corresponded to a specific device type. This resulted in a Wide Hierarchy smell.

During a design review, it was found that the `Device` class hierarchy had considerable code duplication in its subclasses. Since the commonality between the sibling classes was not factored out, this hierarchy had Unfactored Hierarchy smell. However, the project was nearing a deadline, so a refactoring task was created for addressing this smell in the next release.

After the release, refactoring was performed to address both the smells. The `Device` class was made abstract and new intermediate classes such as `VideoDevice`, `AlarmDevice`, `Sensor-Device` etc., were introduced to factor out the commonality between erstwhile sibling classes. With this refactoring of the hierarchy rooted in `Device` class, the code duplication was drastically reduced and resulted in a decrease in the number of immediate subclasses of `Device` class.

This anecdote again highlights the fact that evolving a code base without taking up necessary refactoring tasks can result in the accumulation of technical debt (which is evident when we observe new design smells getting introduced in the design). When project teams are busy adding new functionality driven by deadlines, they don't often get time to reflect on the existing design. However, it is important to schedule the refactoring tasks during lean times in the project to keep technical debt under control.

6.4.2 POTENTIAL CAUSES

Ignoring generalization

Often developers introduce subtypes into an existing hierarchy without checking whether relevant intermediate supertypes would be needed in the hierarchy to better accommodate those subtypes. This lack of attention to the enabling technique "apply meaningful generalization" can result in a Wide Hierarchy smell.

Lack of refactoring

Often when a hierarchy is first designed, it is moderate in size. However, as the application evolves and more types are added to the hierarchy, lack of periodic refactoring can lead to a Wide Hierarchy smell.

6.4.3 EXAMPLE

Consider the `java.util.EventObject` class which is the superclass of 36 immediate subclasses. The partial hierarchy of this class is shown in Figure 6.18! Since this hierarchy has a large number of sibling classes, it exhibits the Wide Hierarchy smell.

6.4.4 SUGGESTED REFACTORING

In case of Wide Hierarchy, check if intermediate abstractions are missing in the hierarchy. If so, apply "extract superclass" refactoring [7] and introduce intermediate abstractions (see Figure 6.19).

Suggested refactoring for the Example

An interesting characteristic of the `EventObject` hierarchy is that some of the subclasses are at a different level of abstraction compared to their sibling classes. For example, when compared to the classes `PrintEvent`, `AWTEvent`, and `CaretEvent`, the classes `TreeExpansionEvent`, `TreeModelEvent`, and `TreeSelectionEvent` are

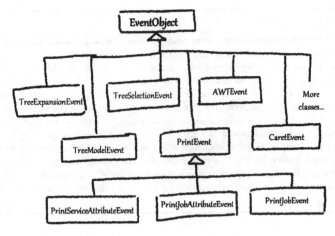

FIGURE 6.18

Partial hierarchy of EventObject class.

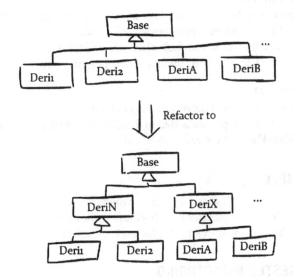

FIGURE 6.19

Refactoring Wide Hierarchy by introducing intermediate types.

arguably at a lower-level of abstraction. In fact, `PrintEvent` has three subclasses: `PrintJobAttributeEvent`, `PrintJobEvent`, and `PrintServiceAttributeEvent`. This gives us a clue that perhaps the classes `TreeExpansionEvent`, `TreeModelEvent` and `TreeSelectionEvent` could be made as subtypes of a common supertype `TreeEvent` (when we introduce `TreeEvent` class, it is at the same abstraction level as `PrintEvent` and `AWTEvent`, which indicates it is a good refactoring suggestion).

Figure 6.20 shows the refactored hierarchy wherein TreeEvent is introduced as an intermediate class.

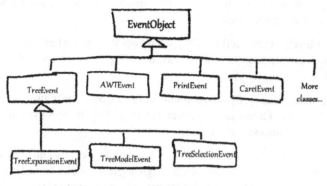

FIGURE 6.20

Suggested refactoring for EventObject hierarchy.

6.4.5 IMPACTED QUALITY ATTRIBUTES

- **Understandability**—Consider the EventObject hierarchy discussed in the Example section. When a programmer tries to understand the relationships between EventObject and its subclasses, he will be surprised to see classes such as PrintEvent and AWTEvent are at the same level as "lower-level" classes (i.e., more specific classes) such as TreeExpansionEvent, TreeModelEvent, and TreeSelectionEvent. In other words, when intermediate abstractions are missing, the sibling classes are not at the same level of abstraction and the programmer has to do a "logical leap" to move from higher levels of abstraction to much lower levels of abstraction. This impacts the understandability of the hierarchy.

- **Changeability**—When hierarchies lack intermediate abstractions, the clients are forced to depend directly on lower-level abstractions. Since lower-level abstractions are more susceptible to change, there is a higher possibility that the client code may also get impacted. Hence, in the presence of this smell, changeability of the hierarchy is impacted.

- **Extensibility**—One of the advantages of a properly designed hierarchy is that the types serve as "hook points" or "placeholders" for future extensions. Since some intermediate types are missing in the hierarchy, it affects the extensibility of the hierarchy.

- **Reusability**—An advantage of a properly designed hierarchy is that the types serve as interfaces to client code. Since some intermediate abstractions are missing in a Wide Hierarchy, it reduces the reusability of the hierarchy.

6.4.6 ALIASES

This smell is also known in literature as:

- "Wide inheritance hierarchy" [59]—This smell occurs when a superclass has more than four direct subclasses.

- "Missing levels of abstraction" [70]—This smell occurs when levels of class abstraction are missing (in other words, more expansion of levels is needed near the root of the hierarchy).

- "Coarse hierarchies" [70]—This smell occurs when a hierarchy has large number of members in a few classes instead of spreading the members among a set of intermediate ancestor classes.

- "Getting away from abstraction" [57]—This smell occurs when number of operations added by a subclass is very high suggesting that some intermediate classes between the subclass and its superclass could be missing.

6.4.7 PRACTICAL CONSIDERATIONS

Language or library could require extending a type

When a language, library, or framework forces classes to implement a specific class, it could result in a Wide Hierarchy. To give an example, consider the class `java.util.ListResourceBundle` that manages resources for a locale (in the context of localization). 443 classes within JDK that provide locale-specific resources directly extend `java.util.ListResourceBundle` class. Though a Wide Hierarchy smell exists in this case, it is probably acceptable in the current form because the library design forces the classes to directly extend `java.util.ListResourceBundle` class (or in general, the classes rooted in `java.util.ResourceBundle`) to support localization in their applications.

Using an interface for specifying a protocol

In general, interfaces in Java/C# or pure abstract base classes in C++ are useful for specifying a generic protocol (such as serialization) that a type has to implement. Naturally, the number of direct subtypes deriving from such interfaces could be very high and the resulting hierarchy should not be considered to suffer from a Wide Hierarchy smell.

6.5 SPECULATIVE HIERARCHY

This smell arises when one or more types in a hierarchy are provided speculatively (i.e., based on imagined needs rather than real requirements).

6.5.1 **RATIONALE**

One of the key enabling techniques for the effective application of the principle of hierarchy is "apply meaningful generalization." Generalization should be performed for exploiting commonalities in existing types. Further, in addition to current needs, generalization should also take into account the planned future needs of the product. However, when this is not followed and generalization is applied purely based on *imagined requirements*, the resulting hierarchy may have supertypes that aren't needed at all. The importance of not adding anything speculatively is also supported by the YAGNI ("You Ain't Gonna Need It") principle [33]. Since this smell arises when generalization is applied "speculatively" in a hierarchy, this smell is named Speculative Hierarchy.

6.5.2 **POTENTIAL CAUSES**

Future-proofing

This design smell often arises due to attempts to make the design of the system "future-proof," i.e., a design that can accommodate *all* changes one could imagine will happen in future.

Over-engineering

When designers over-engineer a design and provide generalized types that aren't actually needed to address the real requirements, it can lead to a Speculative Hierarchy smell.

6.5.3 **EXAMPLE**

Consider the inheritance hierarchy given in Figure 6.21. What is interesting about this hierarchy is that the supertypes have exactly one subtype (making it look like a "list").

This hierarchy was part of a code analyzer tool that statically analyzed the source code and reported potential defects in the source code. One of the features of this tool was its support for generating HTML reports. It was also planned that this tool would support reports in other formats (such as .doc, .rtf, and .pdf) in the future.

During the process of design, the designer speculated that the reports may need the "annotation feature" to be supported in the future even though it was not planned. For this reason, he introduced an intermediate type in the hierarchy as a placeholder to support annotation feature, as shown in Figure 6.21. Since the AnnotatedReport is provided based on an imagined need, this hierarchy suffers from Speculative Hierarchy smell.

6.5.4 **SUGGESTED REFACTORING**

When one or more supertypes are created speculatively, apply "collapse hierarchy" refactoring [7] to remove the concerned supertype(s).

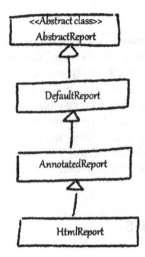

FIGURE 6.21

HtmlReport hierarchy.

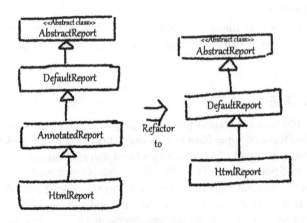

FIGURE 6.22

Refactoring for the HtmlReport hierarchy.

Suggested refactoring for the Example

In the discussed example, the current need for the tool is the ability to generate HTML reports. Since the AnnotatedReport type is based on a speculated need, it could be removed from the hierarchy (refer Figure 6.22). It should be pointed out that it is acceptable to have the AbstractReport and DefaultReport in the hierarchy because the support for different types of reports is part of the product roadmap.

6.5.5 IMPACTED QUALITY ATTRIBUTES

- **Understandability**—If one or more types in a hierarchy are added speculatively, it unnecessarily complicates the design. Hence, this smell impacts the understandability of the design.

- **Testability**—It may require more effort to test unnecessary generic types in the hierarchy when compared to testing a hierarchy without speculative types. This impacts the testability of the overall design.

6.5.6 ALIASES

This smell is also known in literature as:

- "Extra sub-class" [57]—This smell occurs when there is an abstract base class that is extended by only one derived class.

- "Speculative general types" [31]—This smell occurs when a supertype has at most one direct subtype; further, the type has features (either locally defined or inherited) that are never accessed.

- "Speculative generality" [7]—This smell occurs when design has hooks and special cases to handle things that aren't required for present needs. This sometimes results in abstract classes that aren't doing much.

- "List-like inheritance hierarchies" [35]—This smell occurs when each class possesses a maximum number of one subclass; such hierarchies often point to speculative generalizations.

6.5.7 PRACTICAL CONSIDERATIONS

None.

6.6 DEEP HIERARCHY

This smell arises when an inheritance hierarchy is "excessively" deep.

6.6.1 RATIONALE

One of the key techniques for effective design of inheritance hierarchies is "apply meaningful generalization." Instead, when we apply generalization excessively and create a large number of unnecessary intermediate supertypes, it results in a Deep Hierarchy smell.

A hierarchy that is excessively deep significantly increases the difficulty in predicting the behavior of code in a leaf type since the type inherits a relatively large number of methods from its supertypes. Consider the following examples that illustrate this problem:

- A method from a supertype close to the root may be overridden many times in the hierarchy; hence, in the leaf types, the semantics of the inherited method may not be clear.

- A field defined in a supertype may be hidden in one of the methods in the subtypes (e.g., a local variable name is provided in a derived method, which happens to be same as a field name inherited from the supertype).

Both these cases can confuse a developer which in turn may lead to the introduction of defects in the software. In other words, a hierarchy that is deep makes the design more complex which leads to poor understandability and a greater possibility of design or implementation errors. Hence, it is important to avoid hierarchies that are excessively deep. Since the hierarchy is excessively deep, this smell is named Deep Hierarchy.

The question that arises here is: How do I know if my hierarchy is deep or not? A rule-of-thumb is if the inheritance hierarchy is deeper than six levels, it can be considered deep [83].

Often, a hierarchy that is deep may have one or more intermediate supertypes that have been added because of imagined future needs. Thus, it is common to see a hierarchy that has a Deep Hierarchy also suffer from a Speculative Hierarchy smell. However, note that they are different smells - a hierarchy that has a Speculative Hierarchy smell need not also have a Deep Hierarchy smell, and vice versa.

6.6.2 POTENTIAL CAUSES

Excessive focus on reuse
Sometimes, developers may indulge in needless generalization to create intermediate types that can be reused. Such excessive focus on reuse at the cost of understandability and usability can lead to the occurrence of a Deep Hierarchy smell.

Speculative generalization
When designers speculatively add supertypes in a hierarchy for imagined future needs, the hierarchy tends to become deep.

6.6.3 EXAMPLES

Example 1
Consider the inheritance hierarchy of `java.nio.channels.DatagramChannel` class which abstracts "a selectable channel for datagram-oriented sockets" (see Figure 6.23). The depth of interface inheritance tree of this hierarchy is equal to seven and the depth

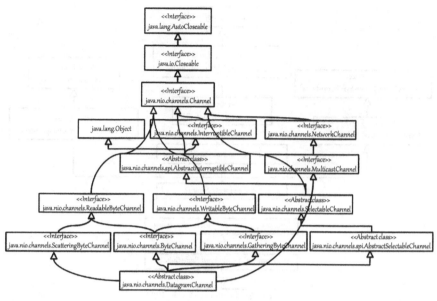

FIGURE 6.23

DatagramChannel hierarchy in java.nio.channels (Example 1).

of class inheritance is equal to four. Clearly this hierarchy is deep and difficult to understand, and suffers from Deep Hierarchy smell.

Example 2

Consider the following hierarchy of SynthCheckBoxUI in the javax.swing.plaf.synth package of Java 7. This class provides Synth (which is a "skinnable look and feel in which all painting is delegated") and Look & Feel (L & F) UI delegate for javax.swing.JCheckBox.

As can be seen from the Figure 6.24, this is a deep and "list-like" hierarchy. Starting from the root class, each level progressively adds only a few new methods. At some levels, methods are overridden as well. Even though at the SynthCheckBoxUI level we get only 34 methods (excluding methods inherited from the Object class), it is hard to understand the semantics of the inherited methods since they are overridden at intermediate levels.

6.6.4 SUGGESTED REFACTORING

If the hierarchy that is deep has one or more intermediate abstractions introduced unnecessarily or speculatively, apply "Collapse Hierarchy" [7] refactoring (see Figure 6.25).

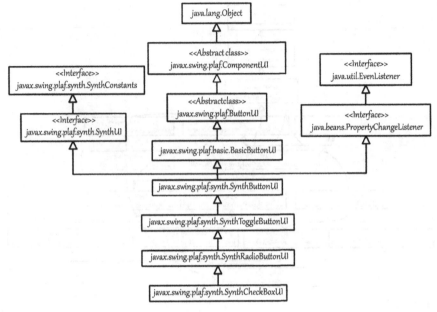

FIGURE 6.24

Hierarchy of SynthCheckBoxUI class (Example 2).

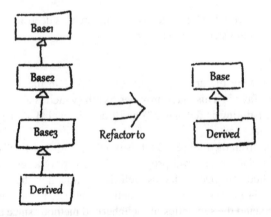

FIGURE 6.25

Applying collapse hierarchy refactoring for Deep Hierarchy smell.

Suggested refactoring for Example 1

In the case of the `DatagramChannel` class hierarchy, the suggested refactoring is to "collapse" some interfaces and classes. For instance, consider the interface `java. nio.channels.InterruptibleChannel` interface. It is a "marker interface" i.e., the interface essentially serves as a tag that can be checked at runtime (using instance of check) to test whether the implementing class supports a certain functionality or protocol. Here is the JavaDoc comment for this interface[1]:

```
A channel supports asynchronous closing and interruption if,
and only if, it implements this interface. This can be tested at
runtime, if necessary, via the instanceof operator.
```

However, with the introduction of annotations feature in Java 1.5, there is no need for marker interfaces. Hence, ideally this interface could be safely replaced with an annotation. By performing such refactorings, the depth of the inheritance hierarchy given in this example can be reduced.

Suggested refactoring for Example 2

For the SynthBoxUI example, an in-depth analysis of all the types in the hierarchy will reveal intermediate types that can be removed. For instance, consider the class definition of ButtonUI, an intermediate type in this hierarchy:

```
/**
 * Pluggable look and feel interface for JButton.
 */
public abstract class ButtonUI extends ComponentUI {
}
```

The abstract class ButtonUI has no members and perhaps serves the purpose of "tagging" a type as a ButtonUI. If so, a possible refactoring is to replace this class with an annotation (as described in the refactoring for previous example).

6.6.5 IMPACTED QUALITY ATTRIBUTES

- **Understandability**—As the hierarchy becomes deep, it significantly increases the difficultly in predicting the behavior of a leaf class since the class inherits a large number of methods. Further, it makes the design more complex. These factors impact the understandability of the design.

- **Changeability** and **Extensibility**—When a hierarchy is deep, it is difficult to figure out what types to modify within the hierarchy to implement change or enhancement requests. Further, when any modification is done in types closer to the root of the hierarchy, it is difficult to determine the ripple effects of the

---

[1] The source code for java.nio.channels.InterruptibleChannel interface contains declaration of a method with the signature "public void close() throws IOException;". But the base interface java.nio.channels.Channel declares this method, and hence is redundant.

change on its descendant types since the hierarchy is deep. This impacts the changeability and extensibility of the design.

- **Testability**—It may require more effort to test unnecessary intermediate types in a hierarchy that is deep (when compared to testing a hierarchy without those intermediate types). Further, because some methods in the hierarchy that is deep could have been overridden multiple times, it is harder to test the overridden methods in the hierarchy. These factors impact the testability of the hierarchy.

- **Reliability**—A method from a supertype close to the root of the hierarchy may be overridden many times in the hierarchy. Hence, in the leaf types, the semantics of the inherited method may not be clear. In a similar vein, a field defined in a supertype may be hidden (or shadowed) in one of the methods in the subtypes. Confusion that ensues from overriding or hiding often leads to runtime problems, impacting the reliability of the design.

ANECDOTE

One of the authors was called in as a consultant to help address the poor performance of a viewer application. This application allowed a control center operator to remotely visualize the status of devices and equipments deployed in the field. This application explicitly represented each physical device with an equivalent class in the design so that graphical objects corresponding to each device could be drawn in a network diagram in the viewer. These classes or types were organized in a hierarchy based upon the nature of the devices and the commonalities that they shared with each other.

When the author investigated the performance problem, he traced the root cause to an unusual problem: the depth of the hierarchy! There were two reasons why this hierarchy was deep. First, there were a large number of devices and equipments that needed to be modeled. Second, there were a number of different types of a particular device (i.e., they needed to be modeled as subtypes of a base device type). Every time, a new kind of specialized device was added in the field, the hierarchy used to grow deeper.

Whenever a leaf class belonging to this hierarchy was instantiated, the resulting object naturally included member variables that belonged to *all* the ancestors of the leaf class. In fact, some leaf objects contained hundreds of data members many of which were data structures (such as arrays) that were pre-initialized. Due to this, each object had a memory footprint in the order of several 100 KBs. Since there were thousands of device objects were being created by the application, it was running out of memory. This led to its poor performance.

As the author continued to explore the hierarchy and the types within, he realized that many leaf classes were not using the member variables that they were inheriting from their superclasses. It became evident that some leaf classes were forced to inherit member variables from intermediate superclasses because of the existing hierarchy. He, in collaboration with the development team, therefore, focused his effort on refactoring this hierarchy so that inheritance of unnecessary data members in the leaf classes could be avoided.

A key take-away that emerges from this anecdote is that the structure of the design impacts runtime qualities. In this particular case, the Deep Hierarchy smell combined with careless design of intermediate supertypes resulted in the application suffering from poor performance. It should be pointed out that this problem occurred in a graphical application running on powerful machines in a control center. One can only imagine how cautious designers must be when designing applications for systems with acute memory constraints.

6.6.6 ALIASES

This smell is also known in literature as:

- "Distorted hierarchy" [76]—This smell arises when an inheritance hierarchy is unusually narrow and deep.

6.6.7 PRACTICAL CONSIDERATIONS

Promoting reuse

Deep inheritance hierarchies promote reuse, and hence many widely used mature frameworks and libraries have deep hierarchies. Therefore, a designer must carefully consider the context and weigh the pros (e.g. reuse) and cons (e.g. understandability, changeability, extensibility, reliability, and performance) before creating a hierarchy that is deep. Thus, if the goal is to actively promote reuse, a designer may purposely create a deep hierarchy.

6.7 REBELLIOUS HIERARCHY

This smell arises when a subtype rejects the methods provided by its supertype(s).

In this smell, a supertype and its subtypes conceptually share an IS-A relationship, but some methods defined in subtypes violate this relationship. For example, for a method defined by a supertype, its overridden method in the subtype could:

- throw an exception rejecting any calls to the method

- provide an empty (or NOP i.e., NO Operation) method

- provide a method definition that just prints "should not implement" message

- return an error value to the caller indicating that the method is unsupported

Please note that this above list is not exhaustive and is meant only to be indicative of examples of how subtype methods can reject a supertype method.

6.7.1 RATIONALE

A subtype can mutate behavior it inherits from its supertype. The mutation is harmless when the behavior is enhanced (i.e., specialized) while overriding the supertype methods. However, when the overriding method restricts, or cancels the behavior of the supertype method, the mutation is harmful [34]. Though the supertype and subtypes may conceptually share an IS-A relationship, the implementation of the subtype does not conform to the interface or implementation of the supertype, breaking the IS-A relationship. In such a case, when a supertype reference points to one of its subtype objects, it may result in defects because the subtype's behavior does not conform to the supertype's behavior. Thus, the subtype objects cannot be safely substituted in place of a supertype reference, thereby violating Liskov's Substitution Principle (LSP) [36] and the enabling technique "ensure substitutability." Since the subtype "rebels" against the behavior promised by the supertype, this smell is named Rebellious Hierarchy.

6.7.2 POTENTIAL CAUSES

Creating a hierarchy rooted in an existing concrete class
In real-world projects, as the design evolves, existing concrete classes often become the root for new hierarchies. In this context, it is important to perform periodic refactoring of the hierarchy to ensure that the types toward the root are generalized abstractions. In the absence of such refactoring, subtypes may be forced to reject irrelevant methods they inherit from their supertypes.

Creating "swiss-knife" types
When designers try to create a supertype that provides everything, specialized subtypes may be forced to reject some of the methods they inherit from the supertype.

6.7.3 EXAMPLES

Example 1
Consider the abstract class `java.lang.invoke.CallSite` from JDK which is shown in Figure 6.26. Here is the Javadoc comment that describes this class:

A CallSite is a holder for a variable MethodHandle, which is called its target. An invokedynamic instruction linked to a CallSite delegates all calls to the site's current target.

The abstract class `CallSite` is the base type for three concrete classes: `ConstantCallSite`, `MutableCallSite` and `VolatileCallSite`. `CallSite` class defines two methods with default implementation that are of interest to us: `getTarget()` and `setTarget()`.

A `ConstantCallSite` is a `CallSite` whose target is permanent, and can never be changed. However, its sibling classes `MutableCallSite` and `VolatileCallSite` have targets that are not permanent, i.e., their targets can be changed. For this reason, `ConstantCallSite` rejects `setTarget()`; any attempt to call `setTarget()` on a `ConstantCallSite` object will result in an `UnsupportedOperationException`. Hence, this hierarchy exhibits the Rebellious Hierarchy smell.

Example 2
Consider the `java.awt.Toolkit` which is the abstract superclass of all actual implementations of the Abstract Window Toolkit. The problem with the `Toolkit` class is

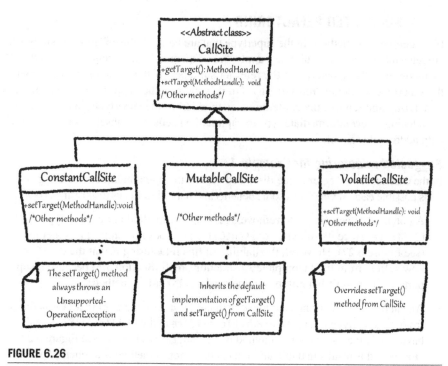

FIGURE 6.26

Hierarchy of java.lang.invoke.CallSite (Example 1).

that it contains methods that are not supported by all the classes extending it. An extreme case of Rebellious Hierarchy is seen in sun.awt.HeadlessToolkit class which extends Toolkit class. A toolkit may be created and used in an environment which supports display, keyboard, and mouse; otherwise, the toolkit is called a HeadlessToolkit. Most of the methods in HeadlessToolkit throw HeadlessException (which derives from UnsupportedOperationException)! For example, the definitions of methods such as createWindow(), getGlobalCursorManager(), and areExtraMouseButtonsEnabled() throw HeadlessException. Clearly, this hierarchy has Rebellious Hierarchy smell.

Example 3

Consider the well-known java.util.Iterator interface from Java 7. It declares three methods hasNext(), next() and remove(). Interestingly, remove() method can throw UnsupportedOperationException if the class implementing this interface does not support remove operation.

For example, consider the java.util.Scanner class that implements Iterator. This class implements remove() method by throwing UnsupportedOperationException. Since the Scanner class is meant to support tokenizing and should not support removal/mutation of underlying input source, the class overrides the remove() method by rejecting it. However, the fact that remove() method in the Iterator interface may be rejected by some of the subtypes indicates a Rebellious Hierarchy smell.

6.7.4 SUGGESTED REFACTORING

If the contentious methods in the supertype that are being "refused" in some subtypes are relevant only to some subtypes, apply "move method" refactoring and lower those methods from the supertype to the relevant subtypes. If the contentious methods in the supertype are being "refused" in *all* of its subtypes, then apply "remove method" refactoring and remove the contentious methods from the supertype. In some cases, introducing a new intermediate type to capture the needs of a subset of subtypes may help address this smell.

Suggested refactoring for Example 1

In the case of CallSite example discussed earlier, there are multiple refactoring solutions possible each of which has some benefits and liabilities. Let us discuss these below:

- A potential refactoring is to remove setTarget() method in the supertype (CallSite) since its subtype ConstantCallSite does not support this method (see Figure 6.27). However, the liability of this refactoring is that the CallSite now suffers from the Incomplete Abstraction smell (Section 3.3) because it supports getTarget() but not its symmetrical setTarget() method.

- An alternative refactoring is to move both getTarget() and setTarget() methods from the supertype CallSite to MutableCallSite and VolatileCallSite, and having only the getTarget() method in the ConstantCallSite (see Figure 6.28). However, this results in duplication: the getTarget() method is duplicated across the three subtypes and the setTarget() method is duplicated across Mutable-CallSite and VolatileCallSite sibling types (indicating an Unfactored Hierarchy smell). To address this duplication problem, if we factor out the getTarget() method in the superclass, it brings us back to the Incomplete Abstraction smell!

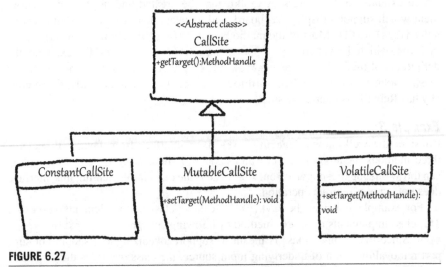

FIGURE 6.27

Suggested refactoring (Option-1) for CallSite hierarchy (Example 1).

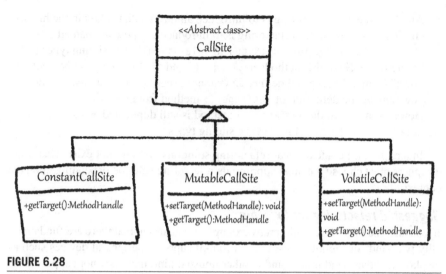

FIGURE 6.28

Suggested refactoring (Option-2) for CallSite hierarchy (Example 1).

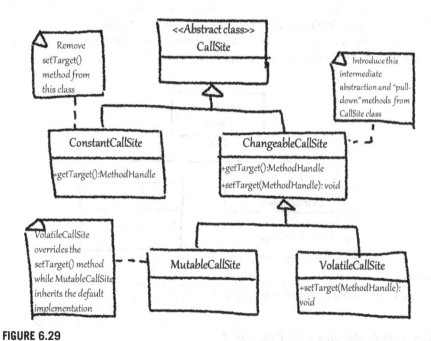

FIGURE 6.29

Suggested refactoring (Option 3) for CallSite hierarchy (Example 1).

- Another potential refactoring is to introduce an intermediate class in the hierarchy. The first step in this refactoring is to introduce a superclass named `Change-ableCallSite` for `MutableCallSite` and `VolatileCallSite` sibling types (see Figure 6.29). Next, the methods `getTarget()` and `setTarget()` can be "pulled-down" from `CallSite` and defined in `ChangeableCallSite`. Finally, we can now remove the definition of `setTarget()` method from `ConstantCallSite`. However, note that the `getTarget()` method is still duplicated across `Constant-CallSite` and `ChangeableCallSite` sibling types.

In a real-world context, ideal refactoring solutions often do not exist. Therefore, designers must choose the most appropriate refactoring solution depending upon the context.

Suggested refactoring for Example 2

If you analyze the `Toolkit` hierarchy example, you can see that there are fundamentally two kinds of toolkits—one kind of toolkit supports peripheral devices such as display, keyboard, and mouse and another unusual kind that does not support these devices. Hence the refactoring for the `Toolkit` hierarchy could be to declare a base class `Toolkit` that has methods unrelated to these devices. The `Toolkit` class could have two derived classes—`DefaultToolkit` that supports peripheral devices and `HeadlessToolkit` that does not support peripheral devices. The methods that relate to peripheral devices such as `createWindow()`, `getGlobalCursorManager()`, and `areExtraMouseButtonsEnabled()` could be provided only in the `DefaultToolkit` class (Figure 6.30). With this design, there will be no need for the `HeadlessToolkit` to reject any methods with `HeadlessException` since the supertype `Toolkit` would not have any methods that relate to peripheral devices.

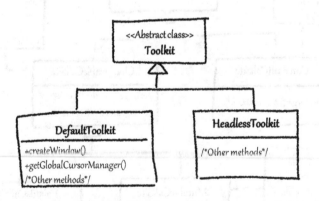

FIGURE 6.30

Suggested refactoring for Toolkit hierarchy (Example 2).

Suggested refactoring for Example 3

For the iterator example, one possible refactoring is to provide two iterators—one that is read-only and another that supports removal. For example, a new interface named

ReadOnlyIterator could be created which does not offer the remove() method in its interface. The existing Iterator type in JDK 7 supports removal during traversal, and could be left as it is. Thus, classes that do not want the underlying input source to be modified may choose to implement the ReadOnlyIterator interface instead of the Iterator interface.

An interesting question here is whether an iterator should support the remove method at all? The objective of an iterator is to facilitate sequential access to the elements of an underlying data structure [54]. Hence, it can be argued that the responsibility for mutating the underlying data structure (such as by adding or removing elements) should not really belong to the iterator.

6.7.5 IMPACTED QUALITY ATTRIBUTES

- **Understandability**—In the presence of this smell, clients may be surprised why subtype objects do not behave as intended and have to spend considerable time to understand that substitutability is broken. Moreover, in the future, clients have to keep in mind that when objects of subtypes are assigned to supertypes, all operations may not work. These factors impact the understandability of the hierarchy.

- **Changeability**—In the presence of this smell, clients cannot freely substitute supertype references with objects of subtypes. Thus, clients get coupled to concrete types in the hierarchy. This affects the changeability of the clients of the hierarchy.

- **Extensibility**—In a hierarchy, if subtypes are forced to reject methods declared in a supertype, it indicates a potential design mistake in the supertype. When a new subtype needs to be added to the hierarchy by extending this supertype, the subtype may also need to reject the method it inherits from the supertype. This increases the effort needed to extend the hierarchy thereby impacting its extensibility.

- **Reusability**—When a hierarchy with this smell is reused in a different context, the new clients may find it difficult to deal with the unexpected behavior of the rejected methods. This makes the hierarchy harder to reuse.

- **Reliability**—In the presence of this smell, attempts to call methods that are rejected by subtype objects using supertype references may result in exceptions being thrown or error codes being returned. If the client code does not handle the errors or exceptions, it may result in crashing the application thereby impacting the reliability of the design.

6.7.6 ALIASES

This smell is also known in literature as:

- "Refused bequest" [7,37]—This smell occurs when: (1) a class inherits from a parent, but just throws an exception instead of supporting a method (honest refusal); (2) a class inherits from a parent, but an inherited routine just doesn't work when called on the class (implicit refusal); (3) clients tend to access the class through a handle to the subclass, rather than a handle to the parent.

- "Refused parent bequest" [31]—This smell occurs when a subclass privately inherits interface methods or overrides them with empty methods.

- "Naughty children" [39]—This smell occurs when a subclass does not accept all the messages that the superclass accepts.

- "Premature interface abstraction" [20]—This smell occurs when a method is defined too high in the inheritance hierarchy and is consequently rejected by some of the concrete specializations.

6.7.7 PRACTICAL CONSIDERATIONS

Yet-to-be implemented functionality

Consider the class `javax.swing.text.rtf.RTFEditorKit` that provides support for RTF (Rich Text Format). This class and the `HTMLEditorKit` class both extend the `StyledEditorKit` (see Figure 6.31).

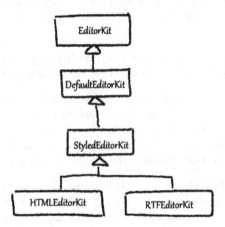

FIGURE 6.31

Inheritance hierarchy of RTFEditorKit.

In this hierarchy, the `write()` method in `RTFEditorKit` rejects the inherited `write` method by throwing an `IOException` as follows:

```
public void write(Writer out, Document doc, int pos, int len)
throws IOException, BadLocationException {
    throw new IOException("RTF is an 8-bit format");
}
```

Though this hierarchy exhibits Rebellious Hierarchy smell, an analysis of the RTFEditorKit documentation reveals an interesting insight:

> "This is the default implementation of RTF editing functionality. The RTF support was not written by the Swing team. In the future we hope to improve the support provided."

It is clear that the designers have chosen to reject the write() method because it is a work-in-progress or yet-to-be-implemented functionality.

Performance considerations

Sometimes, default implementation of classes may want to override methods with NOP methods for performance reasons. For example, consider the concrete class java.swing.JLabel which is used for displaying text, an image, or both. Its subclasses DefaultListCellRenderer, DefaultTableCellRenderer, and DefaultTreeCell-Renderer override methods such as invalidate(), validate(), revalidate(), repaint(), isOpaque(), and firePropertyChange() with empty methods. Here is the relevant JavaDoc comment provided in the class DefaultListCellRenderer:

> *"Implementation Note: This class overrides invalidate, validate, revalidate, repaint, isOpaque, and firePropertyChange solely to improve performance. If not overridden, these frequently called methods would execute code paths that are unnecessary for the default list cell renderer. If you write your own renderer, take care to weigh the benefits and drawbacks of overriding these methods."*

From this documentation comment, it is clear that the designer has consciously chosen to override methods with empty body for performance reasons, and hence makes a compromise to live with Rebellious Hierarchy smell.

Avoiding complex design

Sometimes, designers make a conscious engineering decision to reject methods in a hierarchy to keep the overall design simple. For example, consider the classes such as UnmodifiableList and UnmodifiableMap in JDK 7. These classes reject the methods such as add(), set(), and remove() they inherit from their base classes by throwing UnsupportedOperationException. Obviously, this design violates LSP, and these classes are examples of Rebellious Hierarchy smell.

However, this design was the result of a conscious decision made by the designers of JDK to avoid explosion in the number of classes and interfaces in JDK. For more details, refer to the "Java Collections API Design FAQ" [40]. This is again an example where a smell is intentionally introduced to achieve a bigger purpose in the overall design.

CASE STUDY

One of the implementation variants of the Composite design pattern [54] presents an interesting case of Rebellious Hierarchy. The Composite pattern uses a tree structure of objects to help represent part-whole hierarchies. The core idea behind the Composite pattern is to allow client code to treat both individual leaf nodes and composite nodes (containing a collection of lead nodes) uniformly. In other words, it should be transparent to the client code whether it is dealing with a leaf node or a composite node. Figure 6.32 shows the solution structure for the Composite pattern.

The Component class is an abstract class that provides a common interface to the client code. One of the methods in this class is addComponent(). Clearly, this method will be meaningful only in the case of a composite (which has children) and not in the case of individual leaf nodes. A designer would therefore, be tempted into rejecting this method in the Leaf classes, thus introducing a Rebellious Hierarchy.

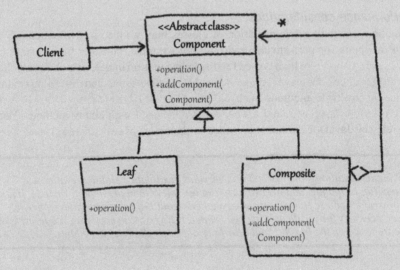

FIGURE 6.32

Composite design pattern structure.

An alternative solution is to remove the addComponent() method from the Component class and instead have it defined only in the Composite class. This looks like a cleaner design without a Rebellious Hierarchy, except that the core objective of the pattern is compromised. Specifically, the client code will now have to check (using type checks) whether a particular node is a composite before executing the addComponent() method. This results in a loss of transparency from the client code perspective.

A third solution exists—provide a default implementation of the addComponent() method in the Component class which does nothing. This avoids the need to reject this method in the Leaf classes. Further, since the method is defined in the base class Component, it is transparent to the client code whether it is dealing with a Leaf or a Composite class. However, if this method gets called on a Leaf class at runtime (due to a bug in the code), just having this method do nothing may not be enough to catch the bug. In some cases, it could even lead to unexpected behavior.

In summary, all three solutions have some benefits and liabilities, and the choice of the most appropriate solution will depend on the context. Thus, it is quite possible that a designer may consciously choose to introduce a Rebellious Hierarchy in order to achieve transparency and avoid runtime defects.

6.8 BROKEN HIERARCHY

This smell arises when a supertype and its subtype conceptually do *not* share an "IS-A" relationship resulting in broken substitutability. There are three forms of this smell:

- Form 1—The methods in the supertype are still applicable or relevant in the subtype (though the supertype and subtype do not share an IS-A relationship).

- Form 2—The interface (i.e., public methods) of the subtypes includes (by inheritance) the supertype methods that are not relevant or acceptable for the subtypes (note that there is no IS-A relationship); however, the subtypes do not reject those irrelevant or unacceptable methods that are inherited from the supertype.

- Form 3—The subtype implementation explicitly rejects irrelevant or unacceptable methods that are inherited from the supertype.

An extreme form of this smell occurs when the inheritance relationship between the supertype and its subtype is "inverted." In other words, the subtype is the generalization of the supertype instead of the other way around.

6.8.1 RATIONALE

A cardinal object-oriented principle is the "principle of substitutability" [36], which states that it should be possible for the supertype references to point to objects of subtypes without altering the desired behavior of the program. In other words, subtype and supertype should conceptually share an IS-A relationship. When the supertype and its subtypes do not share an IS-A relationship, it violates the "principle of substitutability" and the enabling technique "ensure substitutability." In such a case, when clients attempt to assign objects of subtype to supertype references, they are exposed to undesirable or unexpected behavior. Since the IS-A relationship is "broken," this smell is named Broken Hierarchy.

It should be noted that when the supertype and its subtype conceptually *share* an IS-A relationship but the subtype does *not* support operations inherited from its supertype, the resulting smell is Rebellious Hierarchy (Section 6.7).

6.8.2 POTENTIAL CAUSES

Inheritance for implementation reuse
The most common cause of this smell is the use of inheritance for implementation reuse i.e., the subtype inherits from the supertype for reusing the supertype's functionality without sharing a true IS-A relationship with the supertype.

Incorrect application of inheritance
Sometimes, an inexperienced designer may mistakenly invert the inheritance relationship between types. The case of `Manager` and `IndividualContributor` discussed in Example 5 illustrates such a case. The inverted inheritance relationship leads to a Broken Hierarchy.

6.8.3 EXAMPLES

Example 1

Consider the class `javax.print.attribute.standard.JobStateReasons` from JDK 7 (refer Figure 6.33). This class *extends* `HashSet`!

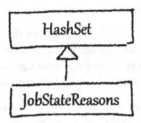

FIGURE 6.33

Partial inheritance hierarchy of JobStateReasons (Example 1).

Let us go through the Javadoc documentation for this class:

> *"JobStateReasons is a printing attribute class, a set of enumeration values, that provides additional information about the job's current state, i.e., information that augments the value of the job's JobState attribute... Class JobStateReasons inherits its implementation from class java.util.HashSet."*

Based on the first two lines of the above description the state the purpose behind the class `JobStateReasons`, it is difficult to understand why this class should be a subtype of `HashSet`. It is only when we read the last line "it inherits its implementation from `HashSet`" can we infer that the class `JobStateReasons` is made a subtype of `HashSet` just to reuse `HashSet`'s implementation. This argument is strengthened if we consider the documentation of the constructor of `JobStateReasons`:

```
/**
* Construct a new, empty job state reasons attribute;
* the underlying hash set has the default initial capacity
* and load factor.
*/
public JobStateReasons() {
    super();
}
```

From the above documentation comment, it is clear that this class extends `Hash-Set` for the purpose of implementation reuse. The methods from `HashSet` are still relevant or applicable for the `JobStateReasons` class though the supertype and subtype do not conceptually share an IS-A relationship. This example is an illustration of the first form of the Broken Hierarchy smell.

Example 2

Consider the relationship between `java.util.Stack` and `java.util.Vector` in JDK 7 [61]. According to the JavaDoc comments in JDK, the `Stack` class represents a last-in-first-out (LIFO) stack of objects, and the `Vector` class implements a growable array of objects. A `Stack` is definitely not a `Vector`, and hence this inheritance relationship is an example of Broken Hierarchy (see Figure 6.34). Because of this design mistake, it is possible to insert or remove elements from the middle of a `Stack` (since `Vector` allows such methods and `Stack` inherits them), which is obviously not desirable!

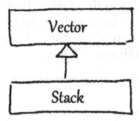

FIGURE 6.34

Partial inheritance hierarchy of Stack class (Example 2).

This example is an illustration of the second form of the Broken Hierarchy smell in which the subtype inherits the supertype methods (though they are not relevant or acceptable) and does not reject them.

Example 3

Consider the example of `Properties` class in JDK. `Properties` class supports property files that store configurable parameters for an application. The keys and the corresponding values in the property files are strictly of type `String`. The class `Properties` does not allow non-string values.

So, for implementation, the `Properties` class could have *used* a `Hashtable` internally via delegation [61]. However, as indicated in Figure 6.35 `java.util.Prop-erties` *extends* `java.util.Hashtable<Object, Object>`! This leads to undesirable behavior, as this JavaDoc description for `Properties` class warns the user of this class:

> *Because Properties inherits from Hashtable, the put and putAll methods can be applied to a Properties object. Their use is strongly discouraged as they allow the caller to insert entries whose keys or values are not Strings. The setProperty method should be used instead. If the store or save method is called on a "compromised" Properties object that contains a non-String key or value, the call will fail. Similarly, the call to the propertyNames or list method will fail if it is called on a "compromised" Properties object that contains a non-String key.*

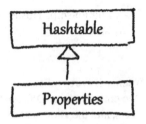

FIGURE 6.35

Partial inheritance hierarchy of Properties class (Example 3).

Properties class abstracts a persistent stream of property values, such as property files. Hence, Properties does not share an IS-A relationship with Hashtable and this inheritance results in a Broken Hierarchy smell. Further, the Properties class does not explicitly reject any of the Hashtable methods, so, this is an example of the second form of Broken Hierarchy smell.

CASE STUDY

One of the participants in the Smells Forum shared a very interesting reason behind the occurrence of Broken Hierarchy. He was involved in a software development project that developed custom GUI controls. In this project, the module that implemented Grid related functionality had a Cell class. This Cell class had a concrete subclass viz. BorderCell. When the participant first joined the project, he assumed that the BorderCell represents a specialized cell with a border and hence the IS-A relationship between the BorderCell and Cell was valid.

However, one day, during the course of the project, he was working with BorderCell and decided to substitute a reference to Cell with BorderCell. It is at this point that he recognized that the IS-A relationship between the two classes was not really valid. When he explored the source code of the two classes, he realized that the BorderCell class was in fact a collection of cells. He concluded that there were two relationships between the Cell and BorderCell classes—one, an inheritance relationship, and the other a composition!

If BorderCell was merely a collection of Cells and not a specialized version of Cell, the IS-A relationship between BorderCell and Cell was not really valid. Hence, this was a clear case of Broken Hierarchy. The developer realized that this smell had not been caught so far in spite of the usual design reviews because of the misleading name!

Example 4

Consider the example of java.util.Date and two of its derived classes java.sql.Date and java.sql.Time (see Figure 6.36). The class java.util.Date supports the functionality of date with methods such as getDate(), setDate(), getYear(), and setYear(). The problem is that it also supports time related functionality with methods such as getTime(), setTime(), getHours(), and setHours().

The java.sql package provides a set of abstractions for supporting SQL (Structured Query Language) related functionality in the Java library. The types java.sql.Date and java.sql.Time are programming abstractions for SQL's DATE and TIME values, respectively. The two subtypes java.sql.Date and java.sql.Time try to reuse the functionality provided by java.util.Date through inheritance. But the

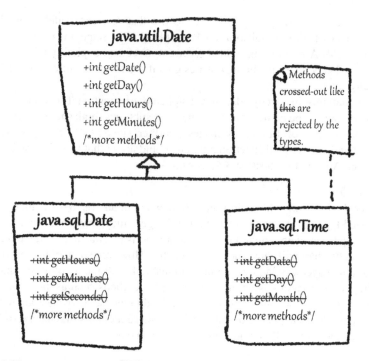

FIGURE 6.36

Partial hierarchy of java.util.Date class (Example 4).

problem is that `java.sql.Date` does not support time related functionality and `java.sql.Time` does not support date related functionality. For this reason, `java.sql.Date` rejects all the time related methods such as `getTime()` and `setTime()` that are inherited from the supertype. Similarly, `java.sql.Time` rejects all the date related methods such as `getDate()` and `setDate()` that are inherited from the supertype.

Consider the following simple code segment (which will throw an `IllegalArgumentException` when executed):

```
// create a Date object with default today's date
java.util.Date date = new java.util.Date();
int dateValue = date.getDate(); // okay
// now, create Time object with 10 hours,
// 10, minutes, and 10 seconds
// note that this Time object does not
// have any date associated with it
date = new java.sql.Time(10, 10, 10);
dateValue = date.getDate(); // throws IllegalArgumentException.
```

Now, given reference variables (such as `date`), the programmer should know whether the variable points to the supertype object (in this case `java.util.Date`) or subtype object (say `java.sql.Time`) to use that reference safely. Clearly, this design violates Liskov's Substitution Principle (LSP). Since `java.sql.Time` does not share an IS-A relationship with `java.util.Date` and explicitly rejects some of the inherited superclass methods, this design suffers from the third form of Broken Hierarchy smell.

Note that this hierarchy also has Duplicate Abstraction (Section 3.7) smell because the supertype name is same as one of its subtypes (both share the same name "`Date`" but are part of different packages). Further, since `java.util.Date` supports both date and time related functionality, one could argue that this class suffers from Multifaced Abstraction (Section 3.4) as well.

Example 5

Consider the hierarchy shown in Figure 6.37 wherein an `Employee` is modeled as a specialized type of `Manager` [18]. A novice designer may create such an inheritance relationship because an individual contributor reports to a manager and the organization hierarchy chart will show such a relationship. However, some of the responsibilities that a manager would have are not applicable for all the employees, and hence the inheritance hierarchy is wrong. For example, methods such as `getReportees()` and `conductPerformanceEvaluation()` provided in the `Manager` class are not applicable to employees who are not managers. So, these methods may be overridden to throw exceptions or NOP methods in the `Employee` class.

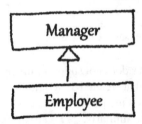

FIGURE 6.37

An example of inverted hierarchy (Example 5).

This is a case of Broken Hierarchy because the IS-A relationship is broken—an individual contributor IS-NOT-A manager. In fact, this is an example of an inverted hierarchy since the inheritance relationship between employee and manager is inverted.

6.8.4 SUGGESTED REFACTORING

A typical refactoring for Broken Hierarchy is to apply "replace inheritance with delegation" refactoring [7]. In some contexts, the smell may indicate the need to introduce relevant patterns such as "composite pattern" [54] for refactoring. In the case of an inverted inheritance relationship, consider reversing the inheritance relationship or introducing a common supertype depending on the context.

Suggested Refactoring for Examples 1–4

In Examples 1–4, it is clear that an IS-A relationship does not truly exist between the supertypes and subtypes. It appears that inheritance has been used in the design to leverage functionality offered by an abstraction, when using an association relationship between the participating types would have served the purpose. The recommended refactoring, therefore, is to apply "replace inheritance with delegation" refactoring [7]. In other words, the IS-A relationship should be replaced with a HAS-A relationship. Figure 6.38 shows how the `Stack-Vector` example described above can be suitably refactored using this technique. In the resulting design, instead of inheriting from a `Vector`, a `Stack` internally creates an instanceof a `Vector` and uses it.

FIGURE 6.38

Stack is refactored to use a Vector instead of inheriting from it (Example 2).

Suggested Refactoring for Example 5

For the "inverted hierarchy" smell, an obvious potential refactoring is to invert the relationship between the supertype and subtype. For the example we are discussing, a `Manager` IS-A `Employee`. Hence, one possible refactoring (also mentioned in Jones [18]) is to invert the inheritance relationship (see Figure 6.39).

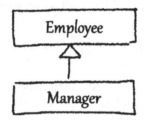

FIGURE 6.39

Suggested refactoring for inverted hierarchy (Example 5).

6.8.5 IMPACTED QUALITY ATTRIBUTES

- **Understandability**—When an inheritance relationship is forced upon types that do not conceptually share an IS-A relationship, the resulting design is confusing to the users. Hence, this smell impacts understandability of the hierarchy.

- **Reusability, Changeability,** and **Extensibility**—When a supertype and its subtype do not share an IS-A relationship, clients cannot write code in terms of a supertype reference and substitute the supertype reference with objects of desired subtypes as needed. This makes it difficult to use the hierarchy in a new context and to incorporate changes or enhancements to the hierarchy without impacting the client code. Hence, this broken substitutability impacts reusability, changeability, and extensibility of the hierarchy.

- **Reliability**—When clients aren't aware that the supertype and subtype don't share an IS-A relationship, and attempt to assign objects of subtype to supertype references, they are exposed to undesirable or unexpected behavior. For instance, the client code may receive an exception when invoking a method that is rejected by the subtype. If the client code does not handle the resulting exceptions or errors properly, it may manifest as runtime problems. This affects the reliability of the design.

6.8.6 ALIASES

This smell is also known in literature as:

- "Inappropriate use of inheritance" [65]—This smell occurs when subclassing is used in situations where the concepts do not share an IS-A relationship.

- "Containment by inheritance" [20]—This smell occurs when class inherits from another class, but the inheritance relation does not represent a valid specialization.

- "Mistaken aggregates" [18]—This smell occurs when the concepts of class inheritance and object composition are mixed up.

- "Misapplying IS A" [18]—This smell occurs when an attribute of an abstraction is mistakenly assumed to be its base type.

- "Improper inheritance" [70]—This smell occurs when inheritance was used instead of instantiating a class.

- "Inverse abstraction hierarchies" [70]—This smell occurs when a subclass is more abstract than a superclass.

- "Subclasses do not redefine methods" [35]—This smell occurs when subclasses do not redefine the methods of their superclass; this indicates that we are facing pure implementation inheritance.

- "Subclass inheriting inappropriate operations from superclass" [18]—This smell occurs when inheritance is used where message forwarding would be more appropriate.

6.8.7 PRACTICAL CONSIDERATIONS

"Class Adapter" pattern

Sometimes an abstraction offers an interface that is incompatible with the interface expected by a client. The Adapter pattern can be used to address this incompatibility of interfaces [54]. There are two variants of the Adapter pattern. The Class Adapter pattern (see Figure 6.40) relies on inheritance to adapt the Adaptee's interface (i.e., SpecificRequest) to Target which is the interface expected by the Client.

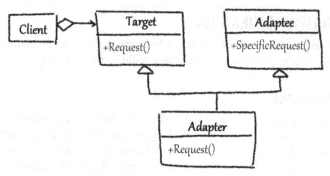

FIGURE 6.40

Structure of Class Adapter pattern.

However, we have observed in practice that the `Adaptee` and `Adapter` often do not follow an IS-A relationship and thus exhibit a Broken Hierarchy.

An alternative to the Class Adapter pattern is to use the Object Adapter pattern (see Figure 6.41). The Object Adapter pattern relies on delegation to adapt the `Adaptee`'s interface (i.e., `SpecificRequest`) to `Target`. This variant avoids the smell of Broken Hierarchy that may creep between the `Adaptee` and `Adapter`.

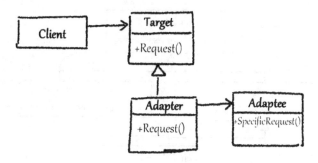

FIGURE 6.41

Structure of the Object Adapter pattern.

However, there are situations when Class Adapter may be preferred over Object Adapter pattern. One such situation is when you want to override some of `Adaptee`'s behavior. If Object Adapter were to be used, it is harder to override `Adaptee`'s behavior because it will require subclassing the `Adaptee` and making the `Adapter` refer to the subclass instead of `Adaptee`. However, if a Class Adapter were to be used, the `Adapter` can be used to override some of `Adaptee`'s behavior since `Adapter` is a subclass of `Adaptee`. Another advantage of Class Adapter over Object Adapter is that a Class Adapter introduces only one object compared to the Object Adapter which introduces two objects. Further, no pointer indirection is required in the Class Adapter pattern to get to the `Adaptee`.

In summary, there are situations where a designer or architect may consciously choose to use a Class Adapter pattern for the overall benefits it brings to the design even though this choice may introduce a Broken Hierarchy smell in the process.

6.9 MULTIPATH HIERARCHY

This smell arises when a subtype inherits both directly as well as indirectly from a supertype leading to unnecessary inheritance paths in the hierarchy.

6.9.1 RATIONALE

A hierarchical organization of types helps designers to better comprehend and understand the relationship between the types. However, when there are unnecessary paths in an inheritance hierarchy (i.e., there is a violation of the enabling technique "avoid redundant paths"), it clutters the hierarchy making it difficult to understand the relationship between the types. Such unnecessary paths can sometimes lead to runtime problems as well. Since a subtype inherits a supertype from one or more unnecessary paths, this smell is named Multipath Hierarchy.

MULTIPATH HIERARCHY VERSUS DIAMOND HIERARCHY

Please note that Multipath Hierarchy is different from the case where a subtype inherits a supertype *indirectly* from more than one path (via multiple interface inheritance in Java, for example). Consider a diamond hierarchy shown in Figure 6.42.

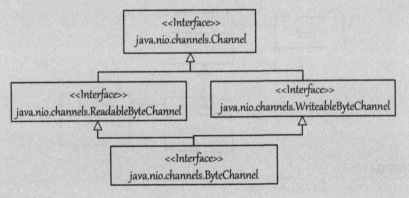

FIGURE 6.42

Diamond hierarchy between Channel and ByteChannel in JDK.

In this figure, the `ByteChannel` interface inherits the `Channel` supertype via two intermediate types namely `ReadableByteChannel` and `WritableByteChannel`. In other words, two inheritance paths exist from `ByteChannel` to `Channel`—one through `ReadableByteChannel` and another through `WritableByteChannel`. Neither path in this hierarchy is unnecessary or redundant. In fact, removing one of the paths will change the semantics of the `ByteChannel` interface. However, in case of Multipath Hierarchy, there exists at least one unnecessary path and removing it would not change the semantics.

6.9.2 **POTENTIAL CAUSES**

Overlooking existing inheritance paths

The most common cause of this smell is when designers often overlook existing inheritance paths while defining a type and unnecessarily inherit a supertype again. The possibility of this mistake is accentuated in inheritance hierarchies that are deep.

6.9.3 **EXAMPLE**

Figure 6.43 illustrates the inheritance hierarchy of `java.util.concurrent.Concur-rentLinkedQueue` which implements the `java.util.Queue` interface. Further, this class extends `java.util.AbstractQueue` class which already implements the `java.util.Queue` interface. Thus, `ConcurrentLinkedQueue` redundantly implements the `Queue` interface. Since an inheritance path (i.e., `ConcurrentLinkedQueue` implementing `Queue`) is redundant, this hierarchy suffers from Multipath Hierarchy smell.

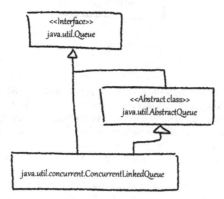

FIGURE 6.43

Redundant path between Queue and ConcurrentLinkedQueue in JDK.

CASE STUDY

Software for industrial systems often create complex objects. Initialization of such complex objects typically involve a sequence of steps, including "pre-initialization" and "post-initialization".
A pre-initialization step, for instance, could create some temporary data structures that are used in the actual initialization step. A post-initialization step, for instance, could clear these temporary data structures and also register with a broker or a class manager that the class has finished initialization and is ready for further processing.

Since these pre- and post-initialization steps are crucial, it is important that software developers do not forget to write an implementation for these steps. To address this, a common practice is to create an interface which encapsulates these steps and which must be realized by a class. If software developers fail to realize this interface, an error is thrown.

Continued

CASE STUDY—cont'd

In this context, we discuss the case of an application that supports the creation of visually-pleasing user interfaces using the concept of gadgets. Figure 6.44 shows a fragment of the application design wherein a `TextGadget` class extends its parent class `GadgetBase` and realizes an `ISupportInitialize` interface. This interface contains two methods "`preInitialize()`" and "`postInitialize()`" that must be defined by the `TextGadget` class.

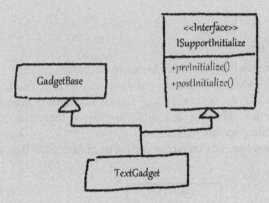

FIGURE 6.44

TextGadget class hierarchy.

This looks great so far. But, let's say over time you have multiple gadgets such as `GraphicGadget`, `NumericGadget`, etc. and the team realizes that the implementation for these `preInitialize()` and `postInitialize()` methods does not change across gadgets. So, the team decides that instead of each gadget separately deriving from the `ISupportInitialize` interface, it would be better for the base class `GadgetBase` itself to realize the `ISupportInitialize` interface and provide the default implementation. This is illustrated in Figure 6.45.

What is interesting to note here that the refactoring to optimize the above design has two steps that MUST both be completed to be considered a correct refactoring. The first is to add a realization relation between the `GadgetBase` and `ISupportInitialize`. The second is to remove the realization relation between ALL the gadget classes and the `ISupportInitialize` interface. If the first step is executed properly and the second step is not executed for all gadgets, then a Multipath Hierarchy as shown in the figure below will be seen (Figure 6.46).

The obvious question is why the second step in the optimization process would not be completely executed. Our experience shows that when software developers work on refactorings/optimizations, they may sometimes overlook to make the desired change across ALL instances—in this case, across ALL derived gadget classes of the base class. To address this kind of a problem, it is important that refactoring be properly thought out and a detailed review needs to be conducted to ensure that the complete refactoring has been performed.

It is also possible that a developer may be on leave and when he returns, he may not know that this optimization has been done, and when he creates a new gadget he uses the old paradigm of inheriting from the interface. To prevent the occurrence of this problem, it is important that design changes be communicated in an effective manner to the rest of the team. It is also important that design and coding practices followed in a project are maintained in a document and adhered to by everyone.

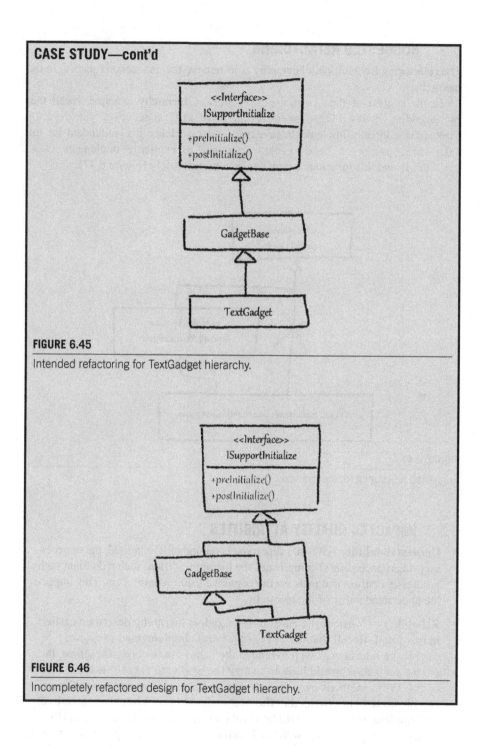

CASE STUDY—cont'd

FIGURE 6.45

Intended refactoring for TextGadget hierarchy.

FIGURE 6.46

Incompletely refactored design for TextGadget hierarchy.

6.9.4 SUGGESTED REFACTORING

The refactoring for Multipath Hierarchy is to remove the unnecessary path(s) in the hierarchy.

In the context of the `ConcurrentLinkedQueue` hierarchy example, recall that by extending `java.util.AbstractQueue`, `java.util.concurrent.Concurrent-LinkedQueue` already implements `java.util.Queue`. Hence it is redundant for the `java.util.concurrent.ConcurrentLinkedQueue` to explicitly implement `java.util.Queue` and this inheritance path can be removed safely (Figure 6.47).

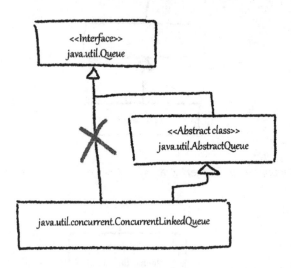

FIGURE 6.47

Suggested refactoring for the example.

6.9.5 IMPACTED QUALITY ATTRIBUTES

- **Understandability**—When a supertype is redundantly inherited, the unnecessary inheritance path(s) complicates the hierarchy. Often, such redundant paths needlessly confuse and increase the cognitive load on developers. This impacts the understandability of the hierarchy.

- **Reliability**—Consider the case study of gadget hierarchy described earlier in this smell. Recall that the `TextGadget` class implemented `ISupportInitialize` interface as well extended the `GadgetBase` class. Therefore, the `TextGadget` class would have to realize the `preInitialize()` and `postInitialize()` methods even though standardized implementations of these two methods were provided in the `GadgetBase` class. While these standardized implementations can still be invoked from the `TextGadget` class (for instance, using `super` keyword in Java), because the developer was not aware that the `GadgetBase` superclass provides the standardized definitions of these methods, he could end-up providing considerably different implementations (or no implementation!) of these two methods. Such accidental mistakes can lead to runtime problems. Hence, this smell can impact reliability.

6.9.6 ALIASES

This smell is also known in literature as:

- "Degenerate inheritance" [55,9]—This smell occurs when a subclass inherits directly and indirectly from a superclass.

- "Repeated inheritance" [42]—This smell occurs when a class inherits from the same ancestor more than once via different paths.

6.9.7 PRACTICAL CONSIDERATIONS

Introducing a redundant inheritance path for convenience

Sometimes designers intentionally introduce a redundant inheritance path for convenience as discussed in the anecdote below.

ANECDOTE

One of the participants at a software engineering conference shared this experience with the authors. He was involved in a Java project where there was a need to serialize objects. The easiest way was to use the `java.io.Serializable` interface; any class whose object needed to be serialized could be defined to implement the `java.io.Serializable` interface.

The correct approach would have been to identify one of the top nodes in the inheritance hierarchy to implement the `java.io.Serializable` interface. This would allow all derived classes to provide serialization capability. However, it was observed that the `java.io.Serializable` interface was being explicitly "implemented" by the lower rungs of the hierarchy as well. In other words, the hierarchy exhibited a Multipath Hierarchy smell.

A deeper investigation revealed that since the existing hierarchy was quite complex, developers found it difficult to trace the inheritance graph to find out whether a particular class in the lower rungs of the hierarchy was serializable or not. Such classes, were therefore, made to explicitly implement the `java.io.Serializable` interface so that a quick look at the class would indicate whether it was serializable or not. Thus, a Multipath Hierarchy smell was intentionally introduced in the design with convenience in mind.

The key take away from this experience is that it may be okay to make design decisions that lead to a smell in the design when the overall benefits of that design choice outweigh its liabilities.

6.10 CYCLIC HIERARCHY

This smell arises when a supertype in a hierarchy depends on any of its subtypes. This dependency could be in the following forms:

- a supertype contains an object of one of its subtypes

- a supertype refers to the type name of one of its subtypes

- a supertype accesses data members, or calls methods defined in one of its subtypes.

6.10.1 RATIONALE

The key benefit of a hierarchical organization stems from its ability to provide us with a means to address the complex relationship between types. Hence, it is critical to express these relationships in a simple logical fashion and maintain them consistently within the hierarchy. For example, it is intuitive to understand that a subtype depends on a supertype; however, when a supertype depends on its subtype(s) directly or indirectly, it is harder to understand the design. Hence, a reference from a supertype to any of its subtypes is undesirable. This violates the enabling technique "ensure proper ordering" and also violates the Acyclic Dependencies Principle.

When a supertype has a reference to its subtype, it introduces a "cycle" in the hierarchy, and hence this smell is named Cyclic Hierarchy.

An especially undesirable form of Cyclic Hierarchy arises when the constructor of a supertype makes active use of one of its subtypes. Since the subtype would not have been initialized when the supertype is being constructed, the code in the supertype could end up accessing the uninitialized parts of the subtype [43]. Thus, using a subtype during the initialization/construction of its supertype can result in subtle bugs.

6.10.2 POTENTIAL CAUSES

Improper assignment of responsibilities

The most common cause of Cyclic Hierarchy is improper assignment of responsibilities across types. For instance, if a responsibility that ideally should have belonged to a subtype is assigned to the supertype, the supertype will have a dependency on the subtype leading to a Cyclic Hierarchy.

Hard-to-visualize indirect dependencies

In complex software systems, designers usually find it difficult to mentally visualize dependency relationships between types. As a result, designers may inadvertently end up creating a long chain of indirect dependencies from supertypes to subtypes.

6.10.3 EXAMPLE

Consider the AbstractButton class that depend on its subtype JButton indirectly through the classes SwingUtilities and JRootPane (see Figure 6.48).

The class AbstractButton refers to SwingUtilities class for invoking the methods such as doesIconReferenceImage(). SwingUtilities—being a utility class—refers to many other classes; one such class is the JRootPane class which is referred in the getRootPane() method. In turn, JRootPane has numerous references to JButton, including a field of type JButton. These references complete the dependency cycle between AbstractButton and its subtype JButton, resulting in Cyclic Hierarchy smell.

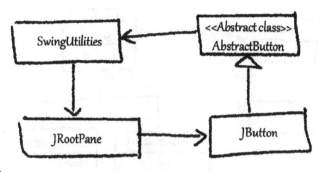

FIGURE 6.48

Cyclic Hierarchy smell between AbstractButton and JButton.

6.10.4 SUGGESTED REFACTORING

Consider the following approaches for refactoring Cyclic Hierarchy:

- If the reference from the supertype to its subtype(s) is unnecessary, remove that reference.

- If there is an extensive coupling between a supertype and its immediate subtype, consider merging them together.

- Depending on the context, consider applying refactoring such as "move method" or "extract class" to help break the cyclic dependency from the super- type to its subtype(s).

- Consider applying State or Strategy patterns if the supertype requires the ser- vices of one of its subtypes [27].

  - Introduce State pattern—Sometimes, a type wants to change its behavior when it's internal state changes. In that case, if that type directly refers to its subtypes that implement behavior for specific states, it results in a Cyclic Hierarchy. Instead, use the State pattern [54], i.e., make the original type assume the role of "Context" (see Figure 6.49). This Context *delegates* state-specific behavior to subtypes rooted in the State hierarchy.

  - Introduce Strategy pattern—Sometimes, a type wants to change its compu- tational algorithm depending on the runtime need. In such a case, if the type directly refers to its subtypes that implement different algorithms, it results in a Cyclic Hierarchy. Instead, use the Strategy pattern [54], i.e., make the original type assume the role of "Context" (see Figure 6.50). This Context *delegates* the computational algorithm to subtypes rooted in the Strategy hierarchy.

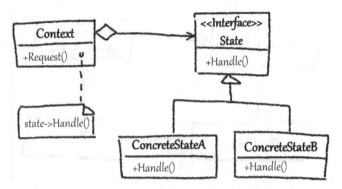

FIGURE 6.49

The structure of State design pattern.

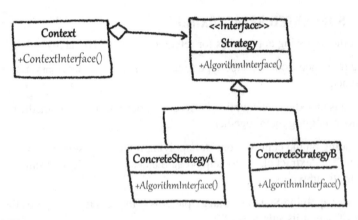

FIGURE 6.50

The structure of Strategy design pattern.

Suggested refactoring for the Example

In the case of the Cyclic Hierarchy between AbstractButton and JButton, there is an indirect dependency from AbstractButton to its subtype JButton. This indirect reference is through SwingUtilities class, which is an overloaded class with very high incoming and outgoing dependencies (i.e., high fan-in and fan-out). If we were to refactor this class for refactoring, we can improve the overall design on multiple fronts. Hence, a suggested refactoring is to break-up the SwingUtilities class. The method SwingUtilities.getRootPane() could be moved to a new class named ComponentUtilities (in addition, other methods related to Component class in SwingUtilities could be moved to this new class). Note that AbstractButton class does not call getRootPane(), so AbstractButton will not have any reference to ComponentUtilities class. So, with this refactoring one of the links in the reference chain from AbstractButton to its subtype JButton is broken, thus addressing the Cyclic Hierarchy smell (see Figure 6.51).

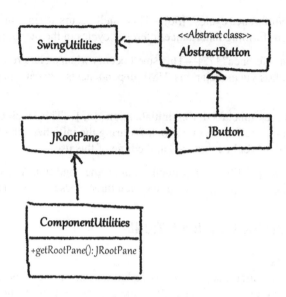

FIGURE 6.51

Refactoring for Cyclic Hierarchy smell between AbstractButton and JButton.

6.10.5 IMPACTED QUALITY ATTRIBUTES

- **Understandability**—In the presence of this smell, in order to understand the supertype, one has to understand the subtype as well. Moreover, the natural ordering of the dependencies in the inheritance hierarchy (i.e., only subtypes depend on the supertypes) is not followed. These factors affect understandability.

- **Changeability**, **Extensibility**, and **Reliability**—Modifications to or removal of subtypes may potentially affect supertypes, which may in turn affect other subtypes in the hierarchy. Such ripple effects often manifest as runtime problems. These factors affect the changeability, extensibility, and reliability of the hierarchy.

- **Reusability**—In this presence of this smell, a supertype cannot be used independent of its subtype. This impacts the reusability of the supertypes.

- **Testability**—The supertype cannot be tested independently of the subtype(s) it depends on, impacting its testability.

6.10.6 ALIASES

This smell is also known in literature as:

- "Knows of derived" [28]—This smell occurs when a superclass or interface has a compile dependency on one of its direct or indirect descendants.

- "Curious superclasses" [9]—This smell occurs when superclasses call or contain instances of their subclasses.

- "Inheritance/reference cycles" [56]—This smell occurs when a superclass refers to its children (forming inheritance/reference cycles in the hierarchy).

- "Descendant reference" [72]—This smell occurs when a class references a descendant class via associations, UML dependencies, attribute or parameter types.

- "Superclass uses subclass during initialization" [43]—This smell occurs when a class makes an active use of a subclass during the initialization of a class (the subclass will not yet be initialized at the time of this use).

- "Inheritance loops" [39]—This smell occurs if the condition A hasSuper C, B hasSuper A, C hasSuper B holds true (given three classes A, B, and C).

6.10.7 PRACTICAL CONSIDERATIONS

Stable subtypes

The main problem with the supertype having knowledge of one of its subtypes is that changes to subtypes can potentially affect the supertype. Hence, this design smell might be acceptable if it is known that the subtypes are not going to change in the future [56].

The Smell Ecosystem

7

Our study of design smells has revealed some interesting characteristics about them. If we were to consider the design as an ecosystem in which design decisions and smells coexist, we can see that smells both influence and are influenced by their ecosystem. Let us explore this further.

How does a smell manifest in design? A smell occurs as a result of a combination of one or more design decisions. In other words, the design ecosystem itself is responsible for the creation of the smell. The presence of the smell in turn impacts the ecosystem in several ways. First, it is likely that the presence of the smell triggers new design decisions that are needed to address the smell! Second, the smell can potentially influence or constrain future design decisions as a result of which one or more new smells may manifest in the ecosystem. Third, smells also tend to have an effect on other smells. For instance, some smells amplify the effects of other smells, or co-occur with or act as precursors to other smells. Clearly, smells share a rich relationship with the ecosystem in which they occur.

In this chapter, we discuss this *smell ecosystem*. We reflect upon the role of context in the identification and treatment of smells, and the interplay among smells.

7.1 THE ROLE OF CONTEXT

A software design can be described as a collection of design decisions. These design decisions include decisions about what classes should be included, how classes should behave, and how they should interact with each other. Each and every design decision is influenced by previously made design decisions, constraints on the design, and the requirements. In turn, every design decision also impacts the design; it can narrow down the set of future design decisions considerably or widen the scope of possible design decisions. In other words, each and every design decision impacts and even changes the context of the design.

Let us look at this from another perspective by considering an analogy from the medical domain. Most people who have taken medication for an illness would be familiar with the term "side effects." For instance, use of commonly available sleeping pills is usually accompanied with side effects such as headache, stomach pain, and constipation. Similarly, every design decision is accompanied by certain benefits and liabilities that it brings to the overall design. Sometimes, the benefits resulting from a design decision outweigh its liabilities, while at other times the liabilities outweigh the benefits. To understand this better, let us ask what would happen if we apply an identical design decision to two different pieces of design. Would the impact on both designs be identical? Most likely, no! The impact would be different. For instance, a design decision to include a new class in one design may help improve the quality of that design, but the same decision might adversely affect the quality of a different design to which it is applied.

Clearly, design decisions should be made with full awareness of the benefits and liabilities on the overall design to ensure the high quality of the overall design. However, in practice, software developers tend to have an eye only on the benefits and ignore the liabilities of their design decisions. This introduces smells in their design.

Does this mean that if a design decision imposes a liability, it should not be made? No. On the other hand, awareness of the liabilities of a design decision brings to the fore an analysis and evaluation of the ways in which those liabilities can be addressed or diluted by introducing new design decisions. This process ensures that as the design evolves, its quality remains high.

What does all this mean? The take-away from the above discussion is that context plays a key role in software design. Similar to how the context has a significant influence on what design decisions are adopted, the context also determines several considerations with respect to design smells. We can explore this further by asking the questions below.

Q1. Are there cases in which a designer could use a smell acceptably because it achieves a larger purpose in the overall design? The answer is a definite YES. In fact, we have tried and captured many such cases in our catalog in the subsection "Practical Considerations" for each smell.

Q2. Are there cases when the violated principle behind a smell actually depends upon the context? The answer again is a definite YES. For instance, consider the case of two Graphical User Interface (GUI) editors shown in Figures 7.1 and 7.2. While these editors are independent of each other, they have a lot of similarities in terms of layout and features. For the sake of the discussion here, assume that the underlying code that supports these editors is similar. In such a case, if a feature change is needed across all editors, it will have to be made across the corresponding business logic of multiple editors. Clearly, it would be quite difficult to maintain this code.

What is the smell that we are discussing here? Depending upon the "context," this can be viewed as one of the following smells:

- *Duplicate Abstraction smell*: It can be argued that the classes underlying the two editors (let us call them `DefinitionEditor` and `ObservationEditor`, respectively) suffer from the "Identical Implementation" form of Duplicate Abstraction. A refactoring suggestion here would be to take the common code and put it into a new class named `CommonEditor`, and have the `DefinitionEditor` and `ObservationEditor` reference it for the common features.

- *Unfactored Hierarchy smell*: If `DefinitionEditor` and `ObservationEditor` are already part of a hierarchy and derive from a common base class (let us call it `Editor`) that does not contain the common features across the two editors, then

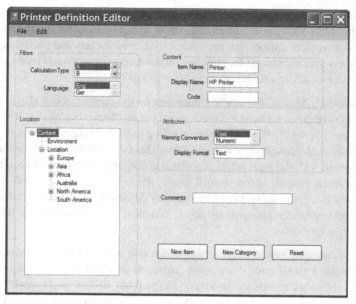

FIGURE 7.1

Printer Definition Editor user interface.

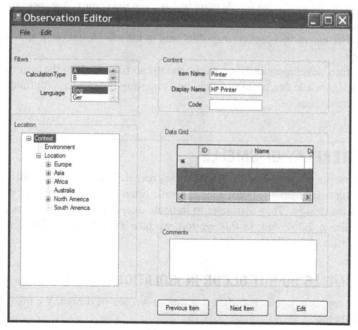

FIGURE 7.2

Observation Editor user interface.

it can be argued that an Unfactored Hierarchy smell is present in the design. A refactoring solution to address this smell would be to factor out the features common to these editors into the `CommonEditor` base class and encapsulate all the editor-specific unique features within the respective derived classes (i.e., `DefinitionEditor` and `ObservationEditor`) of `Editor`.

- *Unnecessary Abstraction smell*: Depending on the context, it can also be argued that there really is no need to create two separate classes (i.e., `DefinitionEditor` and `ObservationEditor`) corresponding to the two editors. Perhaps the design can contain only a single editor class that can be instantiated and configured with the right set of properties according to the specific requirements needed for an editor. In such a case, the `DefinitionEditor` and `ObservationEditor` classes become Unnecessary Abstractions and the refactoring solution to address this smell would be to remove these classes and instead have a single editor class.

As you can see, context plays an important role in determining if a design fragment exhibits a smell and, if so, what particular smell. The refactoring solution, similarly, not only depends on the identified smell but also on the context. It is quite possible that a refactoring unnecessarily complicates the design or even introduces another design smell if the refactoring does not consider the context. For instance, to refactor a smell, a designer may adopt a design pattern. However, if the forces behind the pattern do not match the forces that emerge from the context, the pattern may turn out to be a misfit for that context, and the liabilities of the pattern may outweigh its benefits. The use of this pattern may thus lead to the manifestation of new smells in the design.

Therefore, developers and designers need to carefully analyze the context and the overall design while determining smells and choosing the most appropriate refactoring to address them.

7.2 INTERPLAY OF SMELLS

Our experience with real-world projects has revealed that there is a strong interplay among design smells. For instance, smells often impact and interact with other smells in the design. They also tend to indicate deeper problems, such as architectural smells, in the design. In this section, we take a brief look at these interesting characteristics of smells.

7.2.1 SMELLS DO NOT OCCUR IN ISOLATION

Typically, multiple smells manifest together in a piece of design. We provide some examples below.

- Every experienced designer would have seen inheritance hierarchies that are "complex." Such complex hierarchies are often wide and deep making it quite difficult to understand. Further, they also also have redundant inheritance paths and cycles making it difficult to comprehend the dependencies between types within the hierarchy. Such complex hierarchies often exhibit the following smells: Deep Hierarchy, Wide Hierarchy, Multipath Hierarchy, and Cyclic Hierarchy.

- Consider the dependency graph for some of the types in java.util library in Figure 7.3. The figure shows three smells: Cyclic Hierarchy (Section 6.10), Cyclically-dependent Modularization (Section 5.3), and Hub-like Modularization (Section 5.4). Classes Calendar and Date have large number of incoming and outgoing dependencies and hence suffer from Hub-like Modularization smell. Further, there is a Cyclically-dependent Modularization smell between the TimeZone and Date classes. Finally, there is a Cyclic Hierarchy smell between Calendar and GregorianCalendar class.

- Consider a design with a large and complex central class that has multiple responsibilities and is strongly coupled to satellite classes that have only data members. This design is quite common in real-world industrial projects and has been described as "abusive centralization of control" by Trifu and Marinescu [29]. Such a design exhibits various smells including Multifaceted Abstraction (Section 3.4), Broken Modularization (Section 5.1), and Insufficient Modularization (Section 5.2).

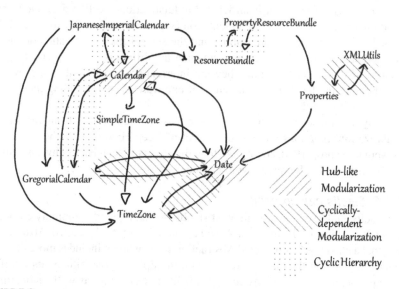

FIGURE 7.3

Smells found among some of the types in java.util library (not all dependencies shown).

While analyzing several such cases in real-world projects where multiple smells manifest together, we observed some interesting patterns emerging with respect to the interaction among smells. For instance, sometimes the effect of some smells is more pronounced in the presence of other smells, or sometimes smells co-occur or even act as precursors to other smells. We provide a brief overview of these types of interactions between smells in the following subsections.

7.2.1.1 Smells can amplify other smells

Design smells can amplify the effect of other smells. For instance, if there is a hierarchy suffering from a Deep Hierarchy smell, the presence of a supertype near the root that suffers from Insufficient Modularization can amplify the negative effects of the Deep Hierarchy smell. We will discuss how this occurs.

A subtype inherits methods from all its supertypes in a hierarchy and may override some of them. In a hierarchy suffering from Deep Hierarchy smell, overriding a method in the subtype toward the leaves poses the question: How do you know the semantics of the method that is to be overridden? One way is to look up the documentation comments for the method, but you will only get some information about its semantics and how to override it. Hence, you need to understand the method definitions all the way up to the type in which it originates. It is difficult to follow such a chain of overriding and the method definitions.

This problem is accentuated when a supertype near the root suffers from Insufficient Modularization. Consider the `javax.swing.ColorChooserDialog` hierarchy shown in Figure 7.4, which suffers from Deep Hierarchy. It should be noted that the `java.awt.Component` class is near the root of this hierarchy. Recall that this `Component` class suffers from Insufficient Modularization (Section 5.2) due to both bloated interface and bloated implementation (see Example 2 in Section 5.2). It has 332 methods, of which 259 are public, and the sum of the Cyclomatic complexity of its methods is 1143. One can only imagine the difficulty in comprehending the semantics of these methods, how they are interrelated, and how they are overridden in the multiple levels in the hierarchy if one were to try overriding them in the `ColorChooserDialog`!

Clearly, the presence of this `Component` class (which suffers from Insufficient Modularization) *amplifies* the negative effect of Deep Hierarchy. If the `Component` class were to be properly decomposed, then the effect of Deep Hierarchy smell in the `ColorChooserDialog` hierarchy would reduce.

7.2.1.2 Smells can co-occur

Some smells tend to co-occur with other smells. An example of commonly co-occurring smells is that of Insufficient Modularization with Multifaceted Abstraction. Recall that a class has Multifaceted Abstraction smell when it includes more than one responsibility. When the class is loaded with multiple responsibilities, its interface size, implementation complexity (or both) is likely to be high as well (indicating it has Insufficient Modularization). Hence, typically a class with Multifaceted Abstraction is likely to suffer from Insufficient Modularization as well.

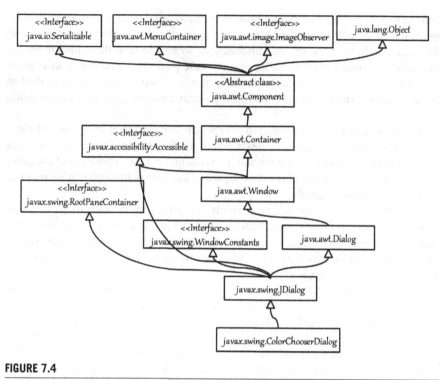

FIGURE 7.4

The ColorChooserDialog hierarchy.

The opposite is also true! A class with Insufficient Modularization is also likely to suffer from Multifaceted Abstraction. Due to this strong correlation between Insufficient Modularization and Multifaceted Abstraction, we term them *co-occurring* smells.

In fact, in practice, it is much easier to detect a class with Insufficient Modularization (using a static analysis tool) than to find one with Multifaceted Abstraction. The fact that they often co-occur can be leveraged to reduce the effort required in identifying each separately. This in turn reduces the time and effort required to improve the quality of the design.

It should be pointed out that once you commence the task of finding smells, you are likely to find quite a few smells hiding in your design. However, just because all these smells happen to be present in your design, it does not mean that they are co-occurring because they may not have a correlation.

7.2.1.3 Smells act as precursors to other smells

Depending on the design context, smells can often act as precursors to other smells. For instance, we have come across many cases in our experience where the presence of a Broken Modularization smell in a design has caused a Deficient Encapsulation smell! Recall that Broken Modularization arises when members that ideally belong to a single abstraction are instead split and spread across multiple abstractions. Often in such a case, methods from these other abstractions need access to the data members of the original abstraction. To enable this, these data members that ideally should have private access are made publicly accessible, thus causing a Deficient Encapsulation smell. Similarly, it is not hard to imagine that a Broken Modularization smell can also lead to the occurrence of a Leaky Encapsulation smell.

We have seen that this relationship between Broken Modularization and Deficient Encapsulation occurs in contexts where the Broken Modularization involves the separation of the data members and methods, and not the separation of methods. In other words, the context of the design plays a key role in determining such causal relationships between smells.

Since the design context can vary widely, a precise identification of the different kinds of such causal relationships between smells would require extensive treatment, and is the subject of a different book altogether. We, however, encourage our readers to explore the smells in their designs and to learn from the different smell interactions that emerge from their exploration.

It is important also to add a note about addressing smells that have causal relationships. In cases where such causal relationships between smells manifest, when the root smell is addressed via proper refactoring, the smells that are caused due to the root smell also disappear along with it. However, the root smell is often not directly visible; in such a case, one has to start with a visible smell and slowly unravel the underlying smells one by one until the root smell is discovered.

7.2.2 SMELLS CAN INDICATE DEEPER PROBLEMS

An interesting aspect of smells is that often when you examine them, you may find a deeper underlying problem in the design. When we were looking for Cyclically-dependent Modularization smell in `java.awt` package, we found several cases of cyclic dependencies between classes. When we analyzed these cycles, we found that many of the cycles spanned across subpackages, indicating an architectural-level smell (see Figure 7.5). Addressing this architectural smell would likely require performing a large-scale refactoring to remove the cyclic dependencies between packages.

Other examples of possible deeper problems underlying the smells described in this book include:

- If you find Broken Hierarchy smell often in your designs, it could be indicative of the larger problem of using inheritance extensively for implementation reuse.

- If you find numerous classes with Imperative Abstraction smell, it may indicate the problem of "functional decomposition" (using procedural design in an object-oriented language).

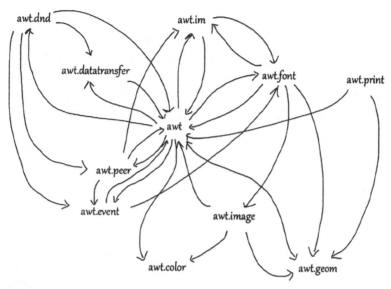

FIGURE 7.5

Cyclically-dependent Modularization smell at package-level in java.awt.

ANECDOTE

One of the authors was involved in the development of a software system that was structured using a layered architectural style. There were three layers: presentation layer, business layer, and data layer. The prescribed architecture clearly enunciated that the layering rules should not be violated; i.e., the layer on top should depend on the layers below but not vice versa. For instance, the presentation layer could use the services of the business and data layer; however, the data layer should not invoke the services of the business layer or presentation layer.

While analyzing the software, he found a cyclic dependency between the classes in the data layer and the presentation layer. When he explored further, he found that there were numerous references from the data layer to the presentation layer! Clearly, this meant that the actual architecture was violating the layering rules. This violation of layering is a well-known architectural smell. In this case, investigating the Cyclically-dependent Modularization smell led to the detection of an underlying architectural smell.

Resolving such deeper problems may yield a great benefit to the overall design. Hence, we recommend strongly that you not stop with just finding smells in your design; instead, you should use the discovered smells to unravel deeper problems in your design.

Repaying Technical Debt in Practice

In the earlier chapters, we discussed design smells and explained how they contribute to technical debt by impacting the design quality. We also looked at a number of refactoring techniques that help repay the accumulated technical debt. However, in practice, refactoring is not an easy or simple task. There are a number of challenges that have to be overcome while refactoring in a real-world context. In this chapter, we leverage our experience to provide practical guidelines to address these challenges.

Refactoring is a vast area and includes a wide array of topics. Bearing in mind that this book is about design smells, in this chapter, we focus specifically on refactoring for design smells as a way to repay technical debt. We center our discussion along three dimensions: tools, processes, and people (Figure 8.1). We begin with an overview of the different kinds of tools that help detect, analyze, and address smells. Since an important consideration in real-world projects is getting buy-in from the management for refactoring, we next outline a few practices that can be adopted in a real-world setting to ensure backing from the management. We also present a structured process to guide effective refactoring in practice. Ultimately, the key to developing high-quality software is to have a team of competent and committed software engineers. Hence, we conclude this chapter with a brief discussion on some effective ways of building such a team.

8.1 THE TOOLS

There are various kinds of tools available to help you identify design smells and candidates for refactoring, quantify their significance, visualize the accumulated technical debt, and perform refactoring to repay debt. Specifically, we will discuss the following kinds of tools in this section:

- Comprehension tools

- Critique tools, code clone detectors, and metric tools

- Technical debt quantification and visualization tools

- Refactoring tools

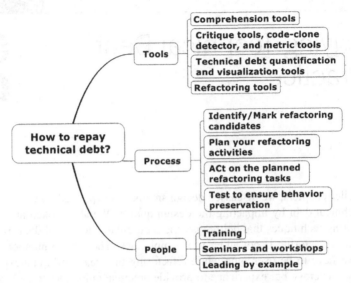

FIGURE 8.1

Key aspects for repaying technical debt.

In this section, we provide only a general description of these tools. Please check Appendix B for a detailed listing of commercial and open source tools.

8.1.1 COMPREHENSION TOOLS

An important prerequisite for proposing and making proper changes in the code base of any real-world software system is to understand the internal structure of the code. Large software systems (the ones that span millions of lines of code) are difficult to comprehend due to their size and complexity. To address this, you can employ comprehension tools to understand the internal structure of the code (through visual aids such as control structure visualization, data flow analysis, call-sequence analysis, and inheritance graph).

8.1.2 CRITIQUE TOOLS, CODE CLONE DETECTORS, AND METRIC TOOLS

Critique tools analyze the software and report problems in the form of violations of predefined rules. Depending on the granularity of the smells they report, they can be classified as:

- **Architectural critique tools** that report architectural violations

- **Design critique tools** that report design smells

- **Code analysis tools** that identify potential bugs (aka "bug patterns") at source code level

The presence of code clones indicate the possibility of smells such as Duplicate Abstraction and Unfactored Hierarchy. It is, therefore, important to detect code clones so that they can be addressed. In this context, code clone detectors can be used to analyze source code and identify code clones.

Metric tools analyze the code or design and report the results in the form of numeric values. These results then have to be analyzed to garner insights on design quality. Let us consider the example of Weighted Methods per Class (WMC), an object-oriented metric, which is a summation of Cyclomatic complexity of the methods in that class. By looking at the average values for WMC, a designer can get an idea of the level of complexity of the classes in his design. Further, by checking the reported WMC value against a fixed threshold value (say 50), he can detect instances of Insufficient Modularization smell (Section 5.2).

8.1.3 TECHNICAL DEBT QUANTIFICATION AND VISUALIZATION TOOLS

Given the significance of technical debt, it is important to be able to measure it. A prerequisite for measuring something is to be able to quantify it. In this context, technical debt is very difficult to quantify accurately. There are two main reasons for this. First, there is no clear consensus on the factors that contribute to technical debt. Second, there is no standard way to measure these factors. It is pertinent to note that there are some recent attempts that try to quantify technical debt; however, these approaches consider only a few factors which limits the usefulness of these approaches.

8.1.4 REFACTORING TOOLS

Broadly, refactoring tools can be classified into the following two categories:

- **Tools that detect refactoring candidates**—These tools analyze the source code and identify not only the entity or entities that need to be refactored but also the potential refactoring steps that can be applied. However, note that these tools are still in a nascent phase of development.

- **Tools that perform a refactoring**—these tools can be employed to perform the required refactoring in the source code once the refactoring candidates have been identified. There are a few popular IDEs (Integrated Development Environments) that provide some automated support for refactoring; however, their support is limited to executing simple refactoring steps.

8.1.5 APPLYING TOOLS IN PRACTICE

It is important to consider the following practical aspects while using these tools in real-world projects.

- Violations or suggestions generated by critique and refactoring identification tools should be treated only as indications. These must be carefully analyzed manually by looking at the context (recall the importance of context that we discussed in the previous chapter) to eliminate false positives.

- As of this writing, refactoring tools are still maturing. For instance, there are IDEs that support carrying out refactoring tasks such as "extract class" refactoring, but they do not execute the task flawlessly i.e., they require moving of methods manually and leave broken code throughout the code base. Further, existing refactoring tools do not support refactoring complex smells such as Hub-like Modularization (Section 5.4) automatically. Hence, in practice, you may need to carry out refactoring tasks manually without any tool support.

- Selection of tools should be carefully performed depending on the project needs and organizational context. For instance, one of the authors of this book purchased a UML analysis tool to detect smells. However, this tool did not work with the UML diagrams that were created using Rational Rose and Enterprise Architect tools due to XMI (XML Metadata Interchange) compatibility issues. Hence, it is important to evaluate a commercial tool before purchasing it.

8.2 THE PROCESS

In this section, we discuss how refactoring should be systematically approached in a real-world setting. There are many challenges in taking up refactoring to repay technical debt in large-scale industrial software projects (especially the ones in maintenance phase with the team distributed globally). We first outline a few of these challenges and list a few best practices that could be useful to get buy-in for refactoring from concerned stakeholders. Next, we present a process model for systematic refactoring in a real-world context. We conclude with a few practical suggestions for effective refactoring.

8.2.1 CHALLENGES IN REFACTORING

There are many challenges you may come across when you plan to take up refactoring tasks in real-world projects. Some important ones are:

- **Lack of infrastructure and tools**: It is hard to ensure that the behavior of the software is unchanged post-refactoring when unit tests are missing. However, unit tests cannot be written before making the code/design testable. This leads to a "chicken-and-egg" problem for taking up refactoring tasks (especially in the context of legacy projects, which usually lack unit tests and require refactoring as well). In addition, many projects do not have access to automated analysis tools that identify smells or quantify technical debt. Lack of sufficient infrastructure and tool support makes project teams hesitant to take up refactoring tasks.

- **Fear of breaking working code**: The fear of breaking working code is the major obstacle in taking up refactoring tasks. Many developers and managers believe in "if it ain't broke, don't fix it" (and by "broke" they mean defects that can be found in the software using testing or reported by customers). Some team members even fuel fears in other team members by arguing that refactoring can break the working software and make it even worse. In cases where it is hard to comprehend the software code base (for instance, in the case of a complex legacy software where the team may have no access to the original developers of the software), the fear is even more pronounced. This fear of breaking code is a legitimate one because even small changes can often break working software thus impacting customers who are using the software. Further, it is often hard to find the root cause of regressions in large code bases.

- **Focus on feature-completion**: Many project managers are often focused on feature-completion and neglect design quality. They don't appreciate the role of refactoring in creating high-quality designs, and consider refactoring as "needless rework." In fact, many managers have an unrealistic expectation that designers should "get the design right the first time" irrespective of project considerations like changing requirements.

- **Mental blocks**: When a team inherits a legacy code base with massive technical debt, some team members (including the manager) may not want to notice or acknowledge the "elephant in the room" (which in this case is the massive technical debt). Or, some team members have a "get-the-work-done-no-matter-what" mindset and lack quality-orientation. Such team members tend to discourage any attempts at refactoring. There are many such mental blocks one needs to be aware of when proposing refactoring tasks in a project.

8.2.2 GETTING BUY-IN FOR REFACTORING

Getting buy-in from project stakeholders is important for repaying technical debt. In fact, the word "technical debt" was coined by Ward Cunningham to convey the extent of the deterioration of the software structure in the form of a metaphor so that managers from non-technical backgrounds can easily relate to the problem.

Below, we outline some approaches that we have found to be effective in getting a buy-in from stakeholders for repaying technical debt:

- **Quantify and visualize debt**: The first step toward getting a buy-in is to show the current state of quality to the stakeholders. This can be achieved in many ways:

  - Quantifying technical debt and putting a monetary value to the debt (though the current tool support is limited) is one of the important ways to show the extent of debt to the stakeholders (see Section 8.1.3).

  - Using various metrics is an alternative way to quantify the quality of a software system. Showing key metric values can attract focus on aspects that need immediate attention. For instance, while consulting in a project, one of the authors showed that 40% of the code was duplicated in the analyzed code base (against 3% of duplicate code threshold prescribed in their organization's process and quality guidelines). The project management could not ignore these numbers and had to urgently formulate an action plan to address it.

- Presenting numerical values (such as metrics) in a graphical form is an effective approach to visually demonstrate the debt to stakeholders, especially those who do not have a technical background in software development.

- Demonstrating quality-violation trend, i.e., how quality-violations have changed over time for the software could prove an eye-opener for the stakeholders. In one of the projects, an architect known to the authors used a bar chart to plot the measure of total Cyclomatic complexity/LOC (Lines of Code) of the software across its releases and demonstrated deterioration of the quality by showing how the bars grew bigger over time. The graphs drew the stakeholders' attention and subsequently mitigation steps were taken up to address the problem of growing complexity in the code base.

- **Demonstrate the viability of refactoring**: Once stakeholders understand the need for refactoring, the next task is to show them that refactoring is feasible despite the existing challenges that confront a development team. Here is a list of practical guidelines that could help in this context:

  - Plan a refactoring activity on a smaller scale. Take baby steps: for example, only refactor one smell at a time.

  - Quantify design quality before and after the refactoring so that a subsequent comparison of design quality highlights the positive impact of refactoring. For instance, select a set of metrics that you measure periodically and create a visualization showing the trend of quality violation (or selected metrics) over a few builds. If you can showcase successful refactoring at a smaller scale, you can gain the trust of the stakeholders making it easier to get their buy-in for refactoring at a larger scale.

8.2.3 "IMPACT" - A REFACTORING PROCESS MODEL

We have come across a number of cases in industrial projects where refactoring is performed in an ad hoc fashion, resulting in numerous problems. It is, therefore, important to follow a structured approach while refactoring. In this section, we describe a process model called "IMPACT" that provides guidance for systematic refactoring in practice. IMPACT is comprised of the following four fundamental steps that are executed in order:

1. <u>I</u>dentify/<u>M</u>ark refactoring candidates
2. <u>P</u>lan your refactoring activities
3. <u>AC</u>t on the planned refactoring tasks
4. <u>T</u>est to ensure behavior preservation

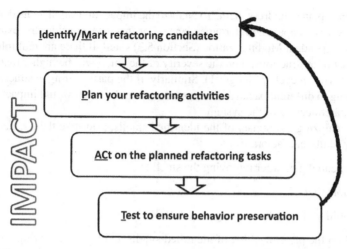

FIGURE 8.2

IMPACT refactoring process model.

These steps are described in the following sub-sections and illustrated in Figure 8.2. Note that these steps are performed in an iterative loop for the following reasons:

- While executing Steps 3 and 4, often previously-hidden refactoring candidates may become visible. This will require revisiting Step 1 to update and possibly re-prioritize the list of refactoring candidates.

- In a real-world context, often project conditions are in a state of flux, i.e., requirements may be added, changed, or even removed, or priorities in the project may change. Thus, Step 2 may need to be revisited to update the refactoring plan (during the refactoring process) to reflect changing project considerations.

8.2.3.1 Identify/mark refactoring candidates

The first step in the refactoring process is to analyze the code base and identify refactoring candidates. Projects can carry out manual code/design reviews and employ automated code/design analysis tools to find smells and determine candidates for refactoring (See Section 8.1 on refactoring tools). In large code bases, executing analysis tools is a faster and less effort-intensive way to find refactoring candidates as compared to performing a manual review. However, manual reviews are more effective and less error-prone since they can consider and exploit domain knowledge, the context of the design, and design expertise more effectively. In our experience, combining manual analysis with tool analysis is a practical and effective way to identify refactoring candidates in industrial projects [4].

8.2.3.2 Plan your refactoring activities

Once you identify smells using design analyzers, clone analyzers, metric threshold violations, or manual reviews, it is important to analyze their impact, prioritize them, and prepare a plan to address them. To analyze the impact of a smell, consider factors such as severity, scope, and interdependence. For instance, consider the example of Cyclically-dependent Modularization (Section 5.3) smell. If there are multiple cycles among a set of abstractions, then the severity of the smell will be higher than that of a unit cycle (i.e., a cycle of length 1). Similarly, if the participating abstractions in a cycle belong to different packages/namespaces, then the smell would impact a wider scope i.e., architecture of the system.

After analyzing the impact of the identified smells, prioritize them based on the following additional factors:

- The potential gain after removing the smell

- Available time

- Availability of tests for the target module(s).

Based on the prioritized list of identified smells and their refactoring, an execution plan for the refactoring can be appropriately formulated.

8.2.3.3 Act on the planned refactoring tasks

Team members can take up planned refactoring tasks and execute them by carrying out the refactoring in the code. In this process, they can also use any automated refactoring support provided by IDEs to carry out the refactoring tasks.

8.2.3.4 Test to ensure behavior preservation

This is an important step in the refactoring process. Each refactoring activity should be followed by automated regression tests to ensure that the behavior post-refactoring is unchanged.

Often, automated tests may not be available for an entity that needs to be refactored. In such scenarios, refactoring presents an opportunity to create automated tests. A recommended practice for such cases is to first write tests for the entity that needs to be refactored, then refactor the entity, and finally test it to verify the behavior.

Our experience shows that in addition to executing various tests, manual code and design reviews are necessary to ensure that refactoring has been correctly and completely performed (see anecdote below). Hence, we recommend complementing regression tests with manual reviews after refactoring.

ANECDOTE

One of the participants in the Smells Forum shared this experience. His team was working on a large multithreaded application. The architect of the team identified a method in a critical component of that application that needed to be refactored. One of the developers took up that task and extracted methods from that large and complex method to simplify it. All the tests passed for this refactoring, and these changes became a part of the next release.

A few months later, a high-priority defect was received from a customer who was using that application. The reported problem was that the application crashed unexpectedly when run continuously for a few days. When the team analyzed the problem, they found that the application

> **ANECDOTE—cont'd**
>
> kept creating threads without terminating some of them; eventually, the application crashed because new threads could not be spawned.
>
> A root cause analysis of this problem pointed to the refactoring that the developer had performed. While refactoring the large and complex method, he had accidentally broken the logic that involved thread termination. Since multithreading is non-deterministic, this problem was not discovered while testing. Eventually, the thread termination problem was fixed and a patch was delivered to the customer.
>
> The key take-away from this experience is that post-refactoring, testing alone is not sufficient to ensure the correctness of the behavior. Manual code and design reviews are needed to ensure that the behavior is preserved, especially when refactoring critical or multithreaded components.

8.2.4 BEST PRACTICES FOR REFACTORING TO REPAY TECHNICAL DEBT

In the real world, the business objectives of a project are typically given a higher priority over its quality goals. As a designer or architect, it is important to ensure you are meeting both objectives. We outline a few best practices that we have found useful to help you take care of the quality goals of your project while honoring its business goals:

- Often, you may realize that a part of the design needs to be refactored; however, there are more urgent tasks that need your attention. In such a case, make a note of the pending refactoring task in a TO-Refactor list (similar to a TO-DO list that people maintain for their day-to-day tasks) so that you do not lose sight of the refactoring that needs to be taken up (or assigned) in the future.

- A "Big-bang" refactoring approach does not work well in practice due to various reasons (e.g., tight schedule and continuous integration and release). Therefore, in real world projects, it is wise to refactor small portions of the code base at a time. Additionally, automate tests and run them after every refactoring to ensure that everything still works as intended.

- Since tests are essential to ensure that refactoring does not change the intended behavior of the system, it is important to ensure that unit tests have been created and are maintained. The absence of unit tests is a powerful deterrent for refactoring. Therefore, if unit tests are missing, break the chicken-and-egg problem (discussed earlier in Section 8.2.1) by iterating between creating unit-tests and performing relevant refactoring.

- Allocate sufficient buffer time to address refactoring tasks in your TO-Refactor list (along with corresponding tasks such as updating design documents.)

- In a real-world project with a short time to market, it is not always feasible to allocate a dedicated time for refactoring. This requires a smart approach to refactoring, and you should try and club refactoring with bug-fixes. In particular, when a bug is assigned to you, first fix the bug and then use the opportunity to refactor relevant parts within the code that was touched during the bug fix. This is in line with the philosophy "check-in code better than what you checked-out."

- Allocate dedicated time after each major release for refactoring tasks to keep technical debt under control before commencing development on the next major release.

8.3 THE PEOPLE

People are the real heart and soul of a software project. It is not surprising to note that a software reflects the quality and commitment of the software development team. It is, therefore, important to educate the team about why refactoring is important and raise awareness about repaying technical debt. In this context, we have found the following approaches to be most effective:

8.3.1 TRAINING

Fred Brooks, in his book "Mythical Man Month," suggests the use of short courses to help train potential practitioners for future assignments [6]. Our experience supports this—in fact, the feedback for employees who have undergone software design training sessions conducted by us suggests that focused workshops can significantly raise their awareness of good design practices. We therefore believe that short and focused (preferably hands-on) training sessions on design principles, design smells, and refactoring can help sensitize developers to good design practices.

8.3.2 SEMINARS AND WORKSHOPS

In our experience, seminars by eminent thought leaders on repaying technical debt and refactoring tend to generate interest and excitement in development teams. Further, internal refactoring workshops provide a platform for project teams to share their real-world experiences and lessons learned.

8.3.3 LEADING BY EXAMPLE

While training sessions and seminars can certainly help increase awareness, what we have found to be most effective in fostering a culture of refactoring is when a role-model, mentor, or team-lead sets an example for the rest of the team by adopting these practices himself. Very often, we have come across instances where a team-lead or architect "preaches" about the importance of following good design practices but fails to demonstrate it in action in his own work. This ends-up demoralizing the team. In conclusion, leading by example is the best way to foster excellence and create a culture of quality in the organization.

Software Design Principles

The Oxford English Dictionary defines "principle" as "a fundamental truth or proposition that serves as the foundation for a system of belief or behavior or for a chain of reasoning." Software design principles lay down fundamental guidelines for designers and developers to effectively build, understand, and maintain a software system.

A number of design principles have been documented in literature. This appendix only lists the principles that have been mentioned in this book for your quick reference.

A.1 ABSTRACTION

The principle of abstraction advocates the simplification of entities through reduction and generalization: reduction is by elimination of unnecessary details and generalization is by identification and specification of common and important characteristics [2].

A.2 ACYCLIC DEPENDENCIES PRINCIPLE

Acyclic dependencies principle (ADP) says that "The dependencies between packages must not form cycles" [10]. ADP mainly targets package relationships and thus the general tendency is to consider its applicability at the architecture level only. However, cyclic dependencies are undesirable at the class level as well. Dependency cycles impose a constraint: Entities that are part of a cycle need to be used, tested, developed, and understood together. In case of cyclic dependencies, changes in one class/package (say A) may lead to changes in other classes/packages in the cycle (say B). However, because of the cyclic nature, changes in B can have ripple effects on the class/package where the change originated (i.e., A). Large and indirect cyclic dependencies are usually difficult to detect in complex software systems and are a common source of subtle bugs. To summarize, avoid introducing direct/indirect cycles between classes/packages.

A.3 DON'T REPEAT YOURSELF PRINCIPLE

The DRY principle states that "Every piece of knowledge must have a single, unambiguous, authoritative representation within a system" [11]. The principle advocates "single source of truth" philosophy and is broadly applicable to all software artifacts including documents, architecture and design, test code, and source code. In the context of our discussion of detailed design, duplication in design entities and code could manifest in the form of duplicated type names and duplicated implementation.

213

Intentional or inadvertent duplication is a common source of subtle defects. Therefore, duplication in any form should be avoided in software systems.

A.4 ENCAPSULATION

The principle of encapsulation advocates separation of concerns and information hiding through techniques such as hiding implementation details of abstractions and hiding variations.

A.5 INFORMATION HIDING PRINCIPLE

The information hiding principle advocates identifying difficult or likely-to-change design decisions, and creating appropriate modules or types to hide such decisions from other modules or types [41]. This design approach helps to protect other parts of the program from extensive modification if the design decision is changed. In this book, we also refer to the principle of information hiding to mean that the public interface of an abstraction should expose the "what" aspects of the abstraction and not the "how" aspects.

Adherence to this principle makes the clients of the abstraction less vulnerable to change when implementation details of the abstraction are modified, thereby improving the changeability and extensibility of the software design.

A.6 KEEP IT SIMPLE SILLY

The keep it simple silly (KISS) principle states that simplicity should be a key goal while designing a software system by avoiding the introduction of unnecessary complexity. In this book, we refer to the KISS principle as stated by Tony Hoare [12]: "… there are two ways of constructing a software design: *One way is to make it so simple that there are obviously no deficiencies* and the other way is to make it so complicated that there are no obvious deficiencies."

A.7 LISKOV'S SUBSTITUTION PRINCIPLE

The formal definition of Liskov's substitution principle (LSP) [36] is: "…What is wanted here is something like the following substitution property: If for each object o1 of type S there is an object o2 of type T such that for all programs P defined in terms of T, the behavior of P is unchanged when o1 is substituted for o2 then S is a subtype of T." An informal description of LSP [14] is: "derived classes must be usable through the base class interface without the need for the user to know the difference." In other words, all subtypes must provide the behavior at least promised by the supertype and an instance of a subtype should be replaceable wherever a reference of its supertype is used.

A.8 HIERARCHY

The principle of hierarchy advocates the creation of a hierarchical organization of abstractions using techniques such as classification, generalization, substitutability, and ordering.

A.9 MODULARIZATION

The principle of modularization advocates the creation of cohesive and loosely coupled abstractions through techniques such as localization and decomposition.

A.10 OPEN/CLOSE PRINCIPLE

The Open/Close principle states that a "module should be open for extension but closed for modification". In particular, a module should be able to support new requirements without its code being modified. According to Bertrand Meyer [24], once the implementation of a type is complete, the type could only be modified to fix bugs; any new requirement that needs to be supported has to be achieved by extending the class without modifying the code within that class.

A.11 SINGLE RESPONSIBILITY PRINCIPLE

According to Robert C. Martin [15], "There should never be more than one reason for a class to change." Each responsibility is an axis of change, thus each change should impact a single responsibility. When a class has multiple responsibilities, it takes more time and effort to understand each responsibility, how they relate to each other in the abstraction, etc. This impacts understandability negatively. Further, it is difficult to figure out what members should be modified to support a change or enhancement. Further, a modification to a member may impact unrelated responsibilities within the same class. This makes maintenance of the class difficult.

A.12 VARIATION ENCAPSULATION PRINCIPLE

The variation encapsulation principle advocates a form of information hiding and suggests encapsulating the concept that varies [54]. This design principle is reflected in a number of design patterns including Strategy, Bridge, and Observer.

Tools for Repaying Technical Debt

As discussed in Chapter 8, software tools play a critical role in the process of repaying technical debt. In this appendix, we provide a nonexhaustive list of commonly available tools—along with their categories, supported languages, license, and Web site link—that can help in the process of repaying technical debt.

Tool Name	Category							Supported Languages	License	Web site/Author
	Comprehension	Critique	Code Clone Detector	Metric	TD Quantification and Visualization	Refactoring (Candidate Identification)	Refactoring (Execution)			
ArgoUML		Y						UML	Free	http://argouml.tigris.org/
Axivion Bauhaus Suite	Y	Y	Y	Y				C/C++, Java, C#, and many others	Commercial (free license available for academic users)	http://www.axivion.com/products.html
Clone Doctor			Y					C++, Java, C#, and many others	Commercial	http://www.semdesigns.com/Products/Clone/
Coverity		Y						C/C++, Java, C#	Commercial	http://www.coverity.com/
CppDepend	Y	Y		Y				C++	Commercial	http://www.cppdepend.com/
Eclipse							Y	Java	Free	https://www.eclipse.org/
FxCop		Y						C#	Free	http://msdn.microsoft.com/en-us/library/bb4294 76(v=vs.80).aspx

Tool						Language	License	URL
Imagix 4D	Y				Y	C/C++, Java	Commercial	http://www.imagix.com/index.html
Infusion		Y			Y	C/C++, Java	Commercial	http://www.intooitus.com/products/infusion
iPlasma		Y			Y	C/C++, Java	Free	http://loose.upt.ro/reengineering/research/iplasma
JArchitect	Y	Y			Y	Java	Commercial	http://www.jarchitect.com/
Jdeodorant		Y				Java	Free	http://www.jdeodorant.com/
Jdepend			Y		Y	Java	Free	http://clarkware.com/software/JDepend.html
McCabe IQ	Y	Y		Y	Y	C/C++, C#, Java, and many more	Commercial	http://www.mccabe.com/iq.htm
MOOSE tool suite	Y	Y	Y		Y	C/C++, Java, and other languages	Free	http://www.moosetechnology.org/
NDepend	Y	Y			Y	C#	Commercial	http://www.ndepend.com/Default.aspx

(Continued)

Tool Name	Category							Supported Languages	License	Web site/Author
	Comprehension	Critique	Code Clone Detector	Metric	TD Quantification and Visualization	Refactoring (Candidate Identification)	Refactoring (Execution)			
PC-lint		Y						C/C++	Commercial	http://www.gimpel.com/html/pcl.htm
PMD		Y						Java, JavaScript	Free	http://pmd.sourceforge.net/
PMD-CPD			Y					C++, Java, C#, and many others	Free	http://pmd.sourceforge.net/
ReSharper		Y					Y	C#	Commercial	http://www.jetbrains.com/resharper/
RSM Metrics				Y				C/C++, Java, C#, and many others	Commercial	http://msquaredtechnologies.com/
Scout						Y		C#	Not released publicly	Tushar Sharma

Tool						UML	Languages	License	URL
SDMetrics			Y				UML	Commercial	http://www.sdmetrics.com/
Simian		Y					C++, Java, C#, and many others	Commercial	http://www.harukizaemon.com/simian/
Sissy	Y						C++, Java, and Delphi	Free	http://www.softpedia.com/get/Programming/Other-Programming-Files/SISSy.shtml
Sonargraph	Y	Y	Y	Y				Commercial	http://www.hello2morrow.com/products/sonargraph
SonarQube		Y		Y			C++, Java, C#, and many others	Free	http://www.sonarqube.org/
Sotoarc	Y		Y		Y	Y	C/C++, Java, C#, and many others	Commercial	http://www.hello2morrow.com/products/sotoarc
Sotograph	Y	Y	Y				C++, Java, C#	Commercial	https://www.hello2morrow.com/products/sotograph

(Continued)

Tool Name	Category							Supported Languages	License	Web site/Author
	Compre-hension	Critique	Code Clone Detector	Metric	TD Quanti-fication and Visual-ization	Refac-toring (Candidate Identifi-cation)	Refac-toring (Execu-tion)			
Source-Monitor				Y				C++, Java, C#, and many others	Free	http://www.campwoodsw.com/sourcemonitor.html
STAN4j		Y		Y				Java	Com-mercial	http://stan4j.com/
Struc-ture101	Y	Y						Java, C#	Com-mercial	http://structure101.com/
Under-stand	Y			Y				C++, Java, C#, and many others	Com-mercial	http://www.scitools.com/
Visual Studio (Archi-tecture Explorer)	Y			Y			Y	.NET	Com-mercial	http://www.visualstudio.com/

Notations for Figures

We have used UML-*like* class diagrams throughout the book. In this appendix, we succinctly describe the notations we have used in this book for such class diagrams with the help of a figure (refer Figure C.1).

With respect to the Figure C.1, following notations are used in this book:

- A rectangle represents an entity such as an interface, an abstract class, a concrete class, or an enumeration. Some of the rectangles may have three partitions:

  - The first partition shows the name of the type. If the type is an interface or abstract class, then keywords "≪interface≫" or "≪abstract‑class≫" appear before the name of the type.

  - The second partition lists the used data members along with the access specifier as shown in `Image` class, i.e., "`-imageType: ImageType.`" The "–" and "+" symbol prefixes denote private and public members, respectively.

  - The third partition lists all the supported methods of the type along with parameters and access specifier; for instance, the `Image` class supports a

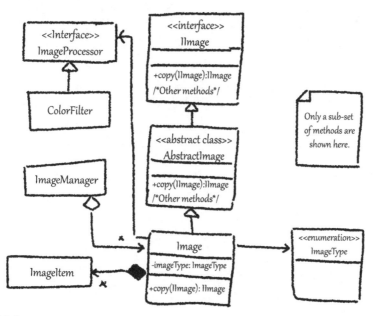

FIGURE C.1

An example to illustrate notations used in this book for UML-like class diagrams.

public method `copy()` that accepts an input parameter of type `Image` and returns an `Image` instance, which is shown by "+copy(IImage): IImage."

- A solid line with a hollow triangle at one end denotes an inheritance relationship between two types; for instance, in this figure, `Image` extends `AbstractImage`.

- A solid directed arrow denotes an association between two types. In this figure, an `Image` has a reference to `ImageProcessor`.

- A line with a filled diamond at one end and an arrow at the other end shows a composition relationship. In this figure, `Image` is composed of `ImageItem` objects. The symbol * near the arrow shows multiplicity, i.e., `Image` contains zero or more `ImageItem` objects.

- A line with a hollow diamond at one end and an arrow at the other end shows an aggregation relationship. In this figure, `ImageManager` is an aggregation of `Image` objects.

- The keyword "≪enumeration≫" along with the name of the type represents an enumeration type; in this figure `ImageType` is an enumeration type.

- A "dog-eared" rectangle is used for conveying a note or comment to the reader (such as the note shown toward the right top corner of this figure).

Suggested Reading

This book covered structural design smells and their corresponding refactoring suggestions. Software design is a vast topic, and you may be interested in learning more about some of the relevant topics discussed in this book. In this appendix, we list some of the essential books to read on the related topics.

D.1 ESSENTIALS

- *Object-Oriented Analysis and Design with Applications*, Grady Booch, Robert A. Maksimchuk, Michael W. Engle, Bobbi J. Young, Jim Conallen, Kelli A. Houston, 3rd Edition, Addison-Wesley Professional, 2007

- *Object-Oriented Software Construction*, Bertrand Meyer, 2nd Edition, Prentice Hall, 1997

- *Fundamentals of Object-Oriented Design in UML*, Meilir Page-Jones, Addison-Wesley Professional, 1999

- *Designing Object-Oriented Software*, Rebecca Wirfs-Brock, Brian Wilkerson, and Lauren Wiener, Prentice Hall, 1990

- *Agile Software Development, Principles, Patterns, and Practices*, Robert C. Martin, Prentice Hall, 2002

D.2 REFACTORING AND REENGINEERING

- *Refactoring: Improving the Design of Existing Code*, Martin Fowler, Kent Beck, John Brant, William Opdyke, Don Roberts, Addison-Wesley Professional, 1999

- *Object-Oriented Reengineering Patterns*, Serge Demeyer, Stéphane Ducasse, Oscar Nierstrasz, Morgan-Kaufmann, 2002

- *Working Effectively with Legacy Code*, Michael Feathers, Prentice Hall, 2004

- *Refactoring to Patterns*, Joshua Kerievsky, Addison-Wesley Professional, 2004

- *Object-oriented Metrics in Practice*: Using Software Metrics to Characterize, Evaluate, and Improve the Design of Object-Oriented Systems, Michele Lanza, Radu Marinescu, Springer, 2006

- *Refactoring in Large Software Projects: Performing Complex Restructurings Successfully*, Martin Lippert, Stephen Roock, John Wiley & Sons, 2006

D.3 PATTERNS AND ANTI-PATTERNS

- *Design Patterns: Elements of Reusable Object-Oriented Software*, Erich Gamma, Richard Helm, Ralph Johnson, John Vlissides, Addison-Wesley Professional, 1994

- *Pattern-Oriented Software Architecture Volume 1: A System of Patterns*, Frank Buschmann, Regine Meunier, Hans Rohnert, Peter Sommerlad, Michael Stal, John Wiley & Sons, 1996

- *AntiPatterns: Refactoring Software, Architectures, and Projects in Crisis*, William J. Brown, Raphael C. Malveau, Hays W. McCormick, Thomas J. Mowbray, John Wiley & Sons, 1998

D.4 TECHNICAL DEBT

- *Managing Software Debt: Building for Inevitable Change*, Chris Sterling, Addison-Wesley Professional, 2010

Bibliography

[1] Lehman MM. Laws of software evolution revisited. In: 5th European workshop on software process technology; 1996.

[2] Tsui F, Gharaat A, Duggins S, Jung E. Measuring levels of abstraction in software development. In: International conference on software engineering and knowledge engineering; 2011. p. 466–9.

[3] Jones C. Software quality in 2012: a survey of the state of the art, Available online at: http://sqgne.org/presentations/2012-13/Jones-Sep-2012.pdf.

[4] Samarthyam G, Suryanarayana G, Sharma T, Gupta S. MIDAS: a design quality assessment method for industrial software. In: International conference on software engineering, software engineering in practice track; 2013.

[5] Samarthyam G, Sharma T, Suryanarayana G. Towards a principle-based classification of structural design smells. J Object Technol 2013.

[6] Brooks Jr FP. The mythical man-month. Anniversary ed. Boston, MA, USA: Addison-Wesley Longman Publishing Co., Inc.; 1995.

[7] Fowler M. Refactoring: improving the design of existing code. Boston, MA, USA: Addison-Wesley Longman Publishing Co., Inc.; 1999.

[8] Demeyer S, Ducasse S, Nierstrasz O. Object-oriented reengineering patterns. Morgan Kaufmann; 2002.

[9] Beyer D, Lewerentz C. Crocopat: efficient pattern analysis in object-oriented programs. In: Proceedings of the 11th IEEE international workshop on program comprehension, IWPC'03, Washington, DC, USA; 2003. p. 294.

[10] Martin RC. Design principles and practices. Object Mentor; 2000. Available online at: http://www.objectmentor.com/resources/articles/Principles_and_Patterns.pdf.

[11] Hunt A, Thomas D. The pragmatic programmer. Addison Wesley; 2000.

[12] Hoare T. The emperor's old clothes. In: The ACM turing award lecture; 1980.

[13] Opdyke WF. Refactoring object-oriented frameworks [Ph.D. thesis]. University of Illinois at Urbana-Champaign; 1992.

[14] Liskov B. Data abstraction and hierarchy. SIGPLAN Not January 1987;23:17–34.

[15] Martin RC. Single responsibility principle. Object Mentor; 2000. Available from: http://www.objectmentor.com/resources/articles/srp.pdf.

[16] Roy CK, Cordy JR. A survey on software clone detection research. Technical Report 2007-541. Canada: Queen's University; 2007.

[17] Evans E. Domain-driven design: tackling complexity in the heart of software. Addison Wesley; 2003.

[18] Page-Jones M. Fundamentals of object-oriented design in UML. Addison-Wesley Professional; 1999.

[19] Buschmann F, Henney K, Schmidt DC. Pattern-oriented software architecture: a pattern language for distributed computing, vol. 4. John Wiley & Sons; 2007.

[20] Trifu A. Towards automated restructuring of object oriented systems [Ph.D. thesis]. Universität Karlsruhe (TH), Fakultät fér Informatik; 2008.

[21] Lanza M, Marinescu R. Object-oriented metrics in practice: using software metrics to characterize, evaluate, and improve the design of object-oriented systems. Springer; 2006.

[22] Schader M, Korthaus A. The unified modeling language: technical aspects and applications. Physica; 1998.

[23] Shalloway A, Trott JR. Design patterns explained: a new perspective on object-oriented design. Addison-Wesley; 2004.

[24] Meyer B. Object-oriented software construction. 2nd ed. Prentice Hall PTR; 2000.

[25] Ratzinger J, Fischer M, Gall H. Improving evolvability through refactoring. In: Proceedings of the 2005 international workshop on mining software repositories, MSR '05, New York, NY, USA; 2005. p. 1–5.

[26] Van Emden E, Moonen L. Java quality assurance by detecting code smells. In: Proceedings of the ninth working conference on reverse engineering (WCRE'02), Washington, DC, USA; 2002. p. 97.

[27] Garzas J, Piattini M. A catalog of design rules for OO micro-architecture. In: Garzas J, Piattini M, editors. Object-oriented design knowledge: principles, heuristics and best practices. Hershey: IGI Global; 2007. p. 307–47.

[28] Structural Investigation of Software Systems (SISSy) Tool. Available at: http://sissy.fzi.de/SISSy/CMS/index.html.

[29] Trifu A, Marinescu R. Diagnosing design problems in object oriented systems. In: Proceedings of the 12th working conference on reverse engineering, Washington, DC, USA; 2005. p. 155–64.

[30] Trifu A. Automated strategy based restructuring of object oriented code. In: Proceedings of the 7th German workshop on software-reengineering (WSR); 2005.

[31] Dudziak T, Wloka J. Tool-supported discovery and refactoring of structural weaknesses in code [Master's thesis]. Faculty of Computer Science, Technische Universität Berlin; February 2002.

[32] Linnaeus C. Systema naturae. B. De Graaf; 1735.

[33] Bass L, Clements P, Kazman R. Software architecture in practice. 3rd ed. Addison-Wesley; 2012.

[34] Hitz M, Montazeri B. Measuring product attributes of object-oriented systems. In: Proceedings of the 5th European software engineering conference. London, UK: Springer-Verlag; 1995. p. 124–36.

[35] Lippert M, Roock S. Refactoring in large software projects: performing complex restructurings successfully. John Wiley and Sons; 2006.

[36] Liskov BH, Wing JM. A behavioral notion of subtyping. ACM Trans Program Lang Syst November 1994;16:1811–41.

[37] Wake WC. Refactoring workbook. Boston, MA, USA: Addison-Wesley Longman Publishing Co., Inc.; 2003.

[38] Becker P. Common design mistakes – part II. C/C++ Users J February, 2000.

[39] Binder RV. Testing object-oriented systems: models, patterns, and tools. Boston, MA, USA: Addison-Wesley Longman Publishing Co., Inc.; 1999.

[40] Java Collections API Design FAQ. Available at: http://docs.oracle.com/javase/8/docs/technotes/guides/collections/designfaq.html.

[41] Parnas DL. On the criteria to be used in decomposing systems into modules. Commun ACM December 1972;15:1053–8.

[42] Meyer B. Touch of class: learning to program well with objects and contracts. Springer; 2009.

[43] Findbugs Tool for Java. Available at: http://findbugs.sourceforge.net/.

[44] Cunningham W. The WyCash portfolio management system. In: Addendum to the proceedings on object-oriented programming systems, languages, and applications. OOPSLA '92; 1992.

[45] Highsmith J. Zen and the art of software quality. In: Agile2009 conference; 2009.

[46] Kelion L. Why banks are likely to face more software glitches in 2013. Available at: http://www.bbc.co.uk/news/technology-21280943.

[47] Booch G, Maksimchuk R, Engle M, Young B, Conallen J, Houston K. Object-oriented analysis and design with applications. 3rd ed. Addison-Wesley Professional; 2007.

[48] Tsui F, Gharaat A, Duggins S, Jung E. Measuring levels of abstraction in software development. SEKE 2011:466–9.

[49] Bloch J. How to design a good API and why it matters. In: Companion to the 21st ACM SIGPLAN symposium on object-oriented programming systems, languages, and applications (OOPSLA '06); 2006.

[50] Kerievsky J. Refactoring to patterns. Pearson Higher Education; 2004.

[51] Llano MT, Pooley R. UML specification and correction of object-oriented anti-patterns. In: Proceedings of the 2009 fourth international conference on software engineering advances, ICSEA '09, Washington, DC, USA; 2009. p. 39–44.

[52] Rumbaugh J, Blaha M, Premerlani W, Eddy F, Lorensen W. Object-oriented modeling and design. Upper Saddle River, NJ, USA: Prentice-Hall, Inc.; 1991.

[53] Succi G, Marchesi M. Extreme programming examined. Pearson Education; 2001.

[54] Gamma E, Helm R, Johnson R, Vlissides J. Design patterns: elements of reusable object-oriented software. Addison-Wesley Longman Publishing Co.; 1995.

[55] Sonargraph-quality: A tool for assessing and monitoring technical quality. Available at: https://www.hello2morrow.com/products/sonargraph/quality.

[56] Sefika M, Sane A, Campbell RH. Monitoring compliance of a software system with its high-level design models. In: Proceedings of the 18th international conference on software engineering, ICSE '96, Washington, DC, USA; 1996. p. 387–96.

[57] Choinzon M, Ueda Y. Detecting defects in object oriented designs using design metrics. In: Proceeding of the 2006 conference on knowledge-based software engineering, Amsterdam, The Netherlands; 2006. p. 61–72.

[58] Moha N. DECOR: Détection et Correction des Défauts Dans les Systémes Orientés Objet [Ph.D. thesis]. Université de Montréal et Université de Lille; August 2008.

[59] Semmle Code Tool. Available at: http://semmle.com/semmlecode/; 2012.

[60] Johnson P, Rees C. Reusability through fine-grain inheritance. Softw Pract Exp December 1992;22:1049–68.

[61] Bloch J. Effective Java. 2nd ed. Addison-Wesley; 2008.

[62] Khomh F, Di Penta M, Guehéneuc Y-G, Antoniol G. An exploratory study of the impact of anti-patterns on software changeability. Technical report EPM-RT-2009-02. Iecole Polytechnique de Montreal; April 2009.

[63] Simon F, Seng O, Mohaupt T. Code quality management: Technische Qualität industrieller Softwaresysteme Transparent und Vergleichbar Gemacht. dpunkt-Verlag; 2006.

[64] Ford N. The productive programmer. O'Reilly; 2008.

[65] Budd T. An introduction to object-oriented programming. 3rd ed. Addison Wesley; 2001.

[66] Meyer B. The many faces of inheritance: a taxonomy of taxonomy. Computer May 1996;29(5):105–8.

[67] Ingalls DHH. Design principles behind smalltalk. BYTE Mag August 1981.

[68] Biehl M. APL – a language for automated anti-pattern analysis of OO-software. CS 846: Source Transformation Systems, Project Report. University of Waterloo; 2006.

[69] Arévalo G. High-level views in object-oriented systems using formal concept analysis [Ph.D. thesis]. The University of Bern; 2004.

[70] Miller BK. Object-oriented architecture measures. In: Proceedings of the thirty-second annual Hawaii international conference on system sciences, vol. 8. HICSS '99; 1999. p. 8069.

[71] Page-Jones M. The practical guide to structured systems design. 2nd ed. Prentice Hall; 1988.

[72] SDMetrics. A UML design quality metrics tool; 2012. Available at: http://www.sdmetric s.com.

[73] Marquardt K. Dependency structures – architectural diagnoses and therapies. In: Proc. of EuroPLoP; 2001.

[74] Stal M. Software architecture refactoring. Tutorial. In: The international conference on object oriented programming, systems, languages and applications (OOPSLA); 2007.

[75] Hannemann J, Kiczales G. Design pattern implementation in Java and AspectJ. In: Proceedings of the 17th ACM SIGPLAN conference on object-oriented programming, systems, languages, and applications, OOPSLA '02, New York, NY, USA; 2002. p. 161–73.

[76] InFusion Hydrogen. Design flaw detection tool; 2012. Available at: http://www.intooitus .com/products/infusion.

[77] Structural Analysis for Java Tool (Stan4J). Available at: http://stan4j.com/.

[78] Gil JY, Maman I. Micro patterns in Java code. SIGPLAN Not October 2005;40:97–116.

[79] Martin RC. Agile software development, principles, patterns, and practices. Addison-Wesley; 2003.

[80] Bouwers E, Visser J, Lilienthal C, Deursen A. A cognitive model for software architecture complexity. In: Proceedings of the IEEE 18th international conference on program comprehension (ICPC '10), IEEE computer society, Washington, DC, USA; 2010. p. 152–5.

[81] Buschmann F, Henney K, Schmidt. Pattern oriented software architecture: on patterns and pattern languages, vol. 5. Wiley; 2007.

[82] Yu L, Schach SR, Chen K. Maintaining Linux: The Role of current. In: Proceedings of the Fourth International Symposium on Empirical Software Engineering, Noosa Heads, Queensland, Australia; November 2005. p. 44–52.

[83] Riel AJ. Object-Oriented Design Heuristics. Addison-Wesley Professional, 1996.

[84] Fowler M. Patterns of Enterprise Application Architecture. Addison-Wesley Professional; 2002.

Index

Note: Page numbers followed by "b", "f" and "t" indicate boxes, figures and tables respectively.

Printed in the United States
By Bookmasters